THE
OTHER CUSTERS

TOM, BOSTON, NEVIN, AND MAGGIE IN THE SHADOW OF GEORGE ARMSTRONG CUSTER

BILL YENNE

Skyhorse Publishing

Copyright © 2018 by Bill Yenne
Foreword © 2018 by George Armstrong Custer IV

Skyhorse Publishing books may be purchased in bulk at special discounts for sales promotion, corporate gifts, fund-raising, or educational purposes. Special editions can also be created to specifications. For details, contact the Special Sales Department, Skyhorse Publishing, 307 West 36th Street, 11th Floor, New York, NY 10018 or info@skyhorsepublishing.com.

Skyhorse® and Skyhorse Publishing® are registered trademarks of Skyhorse Publishing, Inc.®, a Delaware corporation.

Visit our website at www.skyhorsepublishing.com.

10 9 8 7 6 5 4 3 2 1

Library of Congress Cataloging-in-Publication Data is available on file.

Cover design by Rain Saukas
Cover photo credit: Top, left, and center photos courtesy of Little Bighorn Notional Monument. Right photo courtesy of Monroe News

ISBN: 978-1-510-73034-2
Ebook ISBN: 978-1-510-73035-9

Printed in the United States of America

THE CUSTER SIBLINGS WERE:

George Armstrong Custer (1839–1876)
Nevin Johnson Custer (1842–1915)
Thomas Ward Custer (1845–1876)
Boston Custer (1848–1876)
Margaret Emma Custer Calhoun (1852–1910)

Three of the four Custer boys died violently on the same day in the most cele-brated battle within the United States since the Civil War. Margaret's husband died there as well.

The younger Custer boys were known among the immediate family by the single-syllable nicknames "Nev," "Tom," and "Bos." Margaret was known universally as "Maggie," and is known as such herein. Likewise we use the nickname "Tom" for "Thomas."

George Armstrong Custer was rarely referred to as "George." Within the family, he was formally known as "Armstrong," though when he was a young child he pronounced his name as "Autie," and by this name he was most commonly referred by the family and by his wife and friends. Taking the liberty of familiarity, we follow suit herein. His single-syllable nick-name, occasionally seen in family correspondence, was "Aut." During his life, and in the years after his death, his wife and family routinely referred to him in the third person as "the General," a reference to the brevet rank of major general that he held for three years during the Civil War.

CONTENTS

ACKNOWLEDGMENTS

In the preparation of this book, I am indebted to many people who helped supply information, who answered questions, and who aided me in sorting out details. Special thanks are due to George Armstrong Custer IV, who helped with much information about his family; to Cindy Hagen at the Little Bighorn Battlefield National Monument, who gave me access to many historical photographs; to my wife, Carol, who is a brilliant genealogist; and to Charmaine Wawrzyniec at the Monroe County Library in Michigan, who generously shared countless items from their immense collection of Custer family material, and who devoted a great deal of time to answering so many of my questions.

The vital statistics herein are from state and county records, the US Census, military records, and the indispensable early twentieth-century work of family genealogist Milo Custer (1879–1952). Other sources, including books and periodicals, are cited in the text and detailed in the bibliography.

FOREWORD

The Custer Family

My grandfather, Brice Calhoun William Custer, was the first family member to enlist in the service since the Little Big Horn. My dad would occasionally tell me stories about his father's career. Amongst Dad's papers one day, I found a short biography he documented about his father, Brice. Describing his military service, a few paragraphs caught my eye. He would write:

Shortly after World War I started, farm boys were given their high school diplomas and told to go help their fathers get the crops in. Instead, Brice went to Detroit to enlist in the Navy at age 16. He advised them he was 18. However the physical showed he had an enlarged thyroid, common in Michigan prior to iodized salt. Disappointed, he went home, pondering his fate, and went to Toledo to try again. He artfully explained that they must have made a mistake in Detroit. His feet didn't look flat to him. Toledo agreed and he was in.

His service was not uneventful. He survived the great flu epidemic during boot camp. Assigned to the black gang (coal fired boilers) of a ship going up and down Chesapeake Bay, he was caught up in a riot following the killing of a Marine guard in Newport News. Shot in the leg, he survived a bedside court of inquiry. In the meantime he was quartered next to the detention barracks for underage sailors and Elizabeth Custer (the General's widow), incensed that he was in the Navy, paid the Secretary of the Navy a personal visit demanding that he at least transfer Brice to the Marine Corps. All this illustrious service came to a merciful ending by release from active duty in 1919 and honorable discharge from the Navy Reserve in 1921.

I was always amazed that it appears she was less concerned about the wound and more concerned that my grandfather had entered the Navy! But worry not. He would enlist again (the Army of course) in 1922, and served a long and distinguished career.

Almost a hundred years ago, in February of 1924, a letter arrived at the door of my grandparents, Brice and Lenore Custer of Monroe, Michigan. It was addressed to them from Elizabeth Custer. She related:

My dear Brice and Lenore;

I am so pleased that you have named your little son for your Uncle Autie. That there should be two named for him in Monroe (the town I love best in the world) makes me happy. And the beautiful statue will make your little son so much better acquainted with his uncle than any picture.

Affectionately,
Aunt Elizabeth

The first namesake she refers to would have been Nevin Custer's first son, who would pass away five years later at the age of sixty-five. The second was my father, Colonel George Armstrong Custer III. This letter would become his prized possession and his bridge to the past, a bridge he happily crossed over many times in his life. As his father before him, he became a career military man; both men reached the rank of colonel and both became decorated combat vets, culminated by their both receiving the Silver Star. And both, as well as my uncles Colonel Charles Custer and Major Brice Custer, all Monroe boys, were staunch defenders of the Custer name.

I fondly remember a day in Monroe, over thirty-five years ago, when my father was talking to my wife and I about deceased family members while visiting the Custer burial plot. In my amazement, he could methodically identify our family members buried there and tell a story about each one, some of whom he never met, and most of whom I still have a difficult time keeping straight.

He would like to tell the story of Boston Custer and Autie Reed, both of whom perished at the Little Big Horn. In 1877 the Army would not pay for the removal and shipment of their remains to Monroe, as they were civilians. In fact the Army would not even pay for the removal and reburial of the officers initially. The Custer family received gracious help from the Calhoun family, who retrieved the bodies in the middle of hostile territory and then shipped them to Monroe on their own dime. The Reeds and Custers then started the Custer/Reed plot at Woodland cemetery in Monroe, where today over twenty-seven family members rest in peace. My father and mother were the last Custers to have been buried there.

Duty, Honor, Country. These were serious business for generations of Custers. In 1971, my father was outraged at the prospect of losing the family name at the Custer Battlefield, and publicly protested its proposed name change to Little Big Horn National Monument, an obvious appeasement to the politically correct crowd. But it wore on him. And in May of that year, tragedy struck my dad. My Uncle Brice would reflect: ". . . he delivered the principle speech at the dedication of the Vietnam Veterans Memorial in Monroe and his words were very much appreciated by, and helpful to, the Vietnam vets in attendance. In my view, he also died with his boots on. A few hours later and still in his uniform, his heart gave out and he was suddenly gone."

My father, as those before him, was a patriot, and possibly surpassed only by Libbie in an aggressive effort to portray the General in a positive light. But there were many others as well, and this defensive effort has become an unusual glue that has bonded generations together. But most importantly, the Custer family of the General's generation, the ones that knew him best, who either defended him loudly or subtly, did so because they knew the man, and not the legend he would become. It is this generation that is the focus of this book.

Nevin Custer was the General's brother and my great-great-grandfather. Family legend has it that he too was invited along to participate in the Little Big Horn campaign, as were his other brothers. But he was the only one to survive. Not due to combat, but rather due to being sidelined at the last minute by an asthma attack. He begrudgingly had to decline. He never left Monroe.

Nevin was as quiet and unassuming as the General was outgoing. One was a quiet farmer on the banks of the River Raisin, the other a flamboyant cavalryman riding to the sounds of the guns. But they were brothers nonetheless, who shared a most precious gift, a quiet brotherly love that bound them. Maria Custer, Nevin's mother, could not have heard more tragic news than when she heard of her son's deaths. Armstrong (Autie), Tom, and Boston. And her grandson and son-in-law, Autie Reed and James Calhoun.

One cannot imagine the depths of her shock and despair. If there was any solace, it was in remembering their young and energetic lives, and the great care they had for each other. Remembering their days growing up on the farm in Ohio, the pranks they would play on their father Emanuel, and maybe even Autie's struggles at West Point followed by his rebound to national prominence, had to give her darkest moments some semblance of hope. In some ways she never recovered.

The same could be said of course of all the Custer clan, including Libbie. My grandfather, Colonel Brice C.W. Custer, was lucky enough to have spent some time with her over the years despite their difference in age of sixty years. In his writings, he would fondly reminisce about those visits. His first memory was when he was quite young, and listened in as Libbie and his grandfather Nevin met at the Custer farm in 1909. They were there to discuss with Mr. Potter, the sculptor of the equestrian statue of General Custer in Monroe, the details of how Custer's horse should look like. The monument would be dedicated the following year.

And one of his fondest memories was a long afternoon spent with Libbie in her New York apartment in 1926, when he and Lenore listened to her many tales about visits with General's Sherman and Sheridan, her complete disgust with President Grant, hard campaigning in the West, or the last time she would see her husband before he rode off on his last campaign. Of note also was Grandpa's recalling; "She also told us that the General was most concerned about the rumors that he was very reckless in the Civil War in charging the enemy without apparent tactical planning, and said he told her that he never went into a battle without first reviewing all he had learned about tactics, and the strategy of the Confederate commanders, many of whom had been West Point classmates of his before they resigned to join the Confederacy."

I'm sure Lenore would starkly remember Libbie's story regarding the wives at Fort Lincoln, Dakota Territory, when they learned the fate of their husbands who would not return from the bluffs above the Little Big Horn River. "The ladies gathered together and sang 'Nearer my God to Thee.'" Finally, Brice would write: "Lenore and I met her for the last time when we honeymooned in New York. She entertained us at the then famous Delmonico's restaurant. Aunt Elizabeth died on Army Day, April 4,1933, and was given military burial at West Point, and buried next to the General." She was ninety-one years old.

Bill Yenne, while using the story of General Custer's life as a foundation, has beautifully blended in the stories of the forgotten Custers, and in doing so has better told the story of a close knit and loving family. In his tale, he reveals more about the Custer family and the relationships within, and conversely more about how the family dynamic impacted the General's life. The result is a more human Custer, and for that, I am grateful. His experience in writing both fiction and nonfiction books over his career has produced a nice combination of easy to read but well-researched prose. I hope you enjoy Mr. Yenne's work within these pages.

May 2018
George Armstrong Custer IV

INTRODUCTION

"Twasn't more than yesterday, was it, that George and Tom and Boston and me were all down on the old farm near New Rumley, Ohio, going to school in the district school house, with the pine slabs for seats and old Foster layin' for us up in front with the birch?"

Nevin Custer recalled his brothers and their boyhood schoolmaster, William Foster, as he sat on the front porch of his white farmhouse overlooking the historic River Raisin, north of downtown Monroe, Michigan, on a warm spring day in 1910.

As he sat with an unnamed journalist for an interview that was to be syndicated across the country, they could look up at a picture of Nevin's older brother in an impressive gilt frame that hung above old farmer's cherrywood desk. The inscription read: "General George A. Custer. Died at the Little Big Horn, June 25, 1876."

More has been written about that battle than about any battle to have occurred within North America since the Civil War. Perhaps more has been written about Nevin's brother George than about any American soldier whose career centered on the half century between the Civil War and World War I. Controversial both in life and in death, he is the inescapable central figure of the drama of the Little Bighorn. Once lionized as a hero, he was in a later era demonized as a villain—both times mainly by people with little understanding of the drama that took place there and throughout his career in the American West.

It can be said that the Little Bighorn achieved its place of prominence among the great battles of American history because Custer himself was already a war hero and a favorite of the Eastern media. An aggressive, skilled cavalry commander, George had performed admirably in a number of Civil War campaigns, and especially at Gettysburg. He had charisma, and a great deal of newspaper ink was devoted to him during and after the Civil War.

The Battle of the Little Bighorn has been deemed one of the crossroads of American history, and George's name is still a household word. Yet many people do not realize that he was not the only Custer to die at the Little Bighorn that day.

On that hill overlooking the Little Bighorn River in southeastern Montana lie the markers of not just one, nor two, but three Custer brothers who died here on June 25, 1876. So too lies the marker for the husband of their young sister, Margaret, as does that of their young nephew, Henry Armstrong "Autie" Reed. Of the four brothers who grew up on the old farm near New Rumley, Ohio, and who felt the sting of William Foster's birch, only Nevin Custer survived this crossroads of American history.

A few years ago, I stood alone atop that hill at the climax of a hot June day watching the sun set over the shoulders of the distant Bighorn Mountains. My only company was the crisp, melodic call of a Western Meadowlark and the cluster of tombstone-like markers which have stood here for more than a century.

As the glow of the sun faded from the markers, I was thinking not of George Armstrong Custer, but beyond his media-gilded patina, to the *other* Custers. Bookshelves groan under the weight of books about George and about the battle that took place here—but what about the *others*?

I looked at Tom Custer's marker and recalled that he had outperformed his brother when it came to military decorations. He was awarded not one, but *two* Medals of Honor for two separate actions during April 1865. I found Boston Custer's marker and wondered what about *him*? What about young, impulsive Maggie? She yearned so much to be part of the Western drama of her older brothers that she literally *married into* their colorful regiment so that she could live that life and share those adventures. Her husband's marker resides near here. It is a five-minute hike to the place where Jim Calhoun fell and where Maggie's dreams of that life and those adventures died.

Among the literature weighing heavy upon those bookshelves, only scant mention is made of the *other* Custers. In some cases, there is just a passing reference in a sentence or two, and in others, even less.

In the pages of this book, the other Custers are brought to the forefront—not just the siblings, but their parents, their ancestors, and their descendants. This is *their story*.

In this book, George remains, but as a supporting character in a narrative that focuses upon other lives, and other journeys along the roads that converged for three brothers on that hill overlooking the Little Bighorn on that hot and fateful June day. But this is *also* the story of the roads that took Nevin, Maggie, and those around them, into the decades beyond.

CHAPTER 1
FAMILY ROOTS

IN AMERICA'S CENTENNIAL year, Monroe, in southeast Michigan, was the archetype of the small and reasonably prosperous city in the American Heartland. In July of 1876, in Monroe and across all of the states of the nation, the red, white, and blue bunting had hung on homes and businesses, and the flags flew in celebration of Independence Day. This celebration was made most poignant by the fact that only about a dozen years before, men by the tens of thousands had shed their blood and their lives for the preservation of the union made independent by the Declaration of Independence that was signed exactly one hundred years before. The Civil War, and indeed the preservation of that union, was still fresh in the memories of the people who had put up the bunting and brought out the flags on the eve of July 4, 1876.

Every town had its own hero, greater or lesser in the overall scheme of the victory, a hero to his locale whose heroism in the minds of his neighbors had not dimmed. In Monroe, the most celebrated of such local heroes was a man who had become a national hero at Gettysburg. Promoted to the rank of brevet major general by the age of twenty-six, George Armstrong Custer led the Michigan Cavalry Brigade in a heroic action that defeated an effort by J.E.B. Stuart's Confederate cavalry to outflank the Union lines at Gettysburg.

Monroe had become the nexus of the Custer family. Three generations now lived here. It had become their hometown. Among those who celebrated the dashing Boy General, and this celebration was virtually unanimous in Monroe, there were none more ardent than Nevin Johnson Custer, George's brother, younger by three years, and the father of all his nieces and nephews. Nevin had grown up idolizing George, and hanging on all the words written in the newspapers about his Civil War exploits. Nevin had even named his firstborn son after brother George.

Nevin had celebrated the centennial not knowing that all three of his brothers, George, Tom, and Boston, had died on a distant Montana hillside overlooking the Little Bighorn River nine days earlier. For him that week, in blissful ignorance, it was business as usual. The news had not reached the Associated Press wire until July 5, and was not published in the newspapers east of the Mississippi until the day after that.

"I remember I had been down in Ohio to see about some land and was driving back to Monroe," Nevin recalled of the day that he learned the news. "I pulled into Hastings, Ohio, for the night, and when the mail came in there was the news of the battle. I didn't believe it at first, but I drove on home 120 miles as fast as the team could travel and there I found Monroe all draped in mourning."

By the time that he got home, the whole town was in mourning for the boy general who was their beloved hero. Black bunting had replaced the red, white, and blue. It was a turning point in his life. As he watched Monroe turn out to commemorate his brother—indeed *all three* of his brothers were mentioned in the tributes—Nevin was taken aback and driven to tears by an emptiness that we can all imagine, but which is just the same, unimaginable. As he listened to the eulogies, spoken by men with voices far more eloquent than his own, it only served to underscore that emptiness, and the chill-to-the spine void that came with knowing that they had all left him, and that they now belonged not to him or his family, or even to Monroe, but to the whole nation, and to the ages.

Nevin's path to Monroe that day, as well as all the roads and byways taken by the Custer family through the preceding decades, had forked from the road which had brought the Custer family to America from Europe more than two centuries before. No history of the Custer siblings who are the subject of this book can be complete without a sketch of the paths taken by the Custer ancestors, and how these had led the family to the upper Midwest when it was still the American frontier.

The family originated within that complicated patchwork of dozens of small duchies west of the Rhine River that were once part of the Holy Roman Empire, later of the Prussian and German empires, and which are now part of Germany and the Netherlands (see the map on page 295).

Paulus Van Haren Küster was the first ancestor to bring his family across the Atlantic. The patriarch of the Custers in America, he was a true son of that maze of Rhenish principalities, having a German father, Arnold Küster, and a Dutch mother, Catharina Van Haren. Paulus was born in 1644 in the small town of Kalderich, later known as Kaldenkirchen. The woman who would become Paulus's wife and the matriarch of American Custers was Gertrude Streypers Doors, sometimes called Gietgen (Dutch for Margaret). She and Paulus were married at the Evangelical Church in Kalderich in 1668.

In his 1912 family genealogy *The Custer Families*, Milo Custer writes that the family name, spelled Coster or Koster before being Anglicized, means "sacristan," meaning one who is in charge of the equipment and supplies in the sacristy of a Roman Catholic church. Indeed, there was a Pieter Koster who was the sacristan of a Catholic church in Oost Zaandam in the Netherlands in the early sixteenth century. He was a contemporary of Martin Luther and of many other former Catholic clerics who departed the Roman church during the Reformation to found or to join new denominations. In Pieter's case, he gravitated toward the teachings of Menno

Simons, another former priest, whose followers came to be known as Mennonites.

The Mennonites, like the other new denominations, faced severe religious persecution in the sixteenth and seventeenth centuries. This would eventually lead Paulus Küster and his family to the New World. Mennonite pastor Franz Daniel Pastorius crossed the Atlantic in 1683 with 13 families. Here, he was welcomed by Quaker leader William Penn, who had founded his Province of Pennsylvania in 1681. Pastorius acquired 15,000 acres northwest of Philadelphia from Penn, where he founded the city of Germantown. The following year, twenty-eight additional Mennonite families arrived in Germantown, and among these families was that of Paulus and Gertrude Küster and their children. In Germantown, Paulus Küster resumed his trade as stonemason, later served as a Corporation of Germantown committeeman. In 1706, he was appointed overseer of the fences, presumably made of stone, in Germantown. Both Paulus and Gertrude died in 1707.

Of the children of Paulus and Gertrude, Milo Custer's 1912 genealogy and many other genealogical sources list Arnold, Hermanus, Johannes, and Eliza (sometimes anglicized as Elizabeth) who also made the journey to America. At least two more children, Eva and Margaret, were born after the family arrived in Pennsylvania.

As is detailed in Appendix 1, the Custers who are the subject of this book descend from Arnold Arndt Doors Küster, the eldest son. He was married twice, both times to women who were immigrants from Kalderich, and certainly from families well known to the Küsters. In 1699, after his first wife died, Arnold married nineteen-year-old Elizabeth Rebecca Sellen. It was their sons, George and Nicholas, who anglicized the family name from "Küster" to "Custer." Arnold's son, Nicholas Custer, the third in the American lineage of our subjects, married Susanna Margaretta Sprogel Hoppe (whose surname is occasionally listed as "Hoppin") in about

1732. Nicholas died in 1784, six days after turning seventy-eight, and Susanna died three years later at the age of seventy-three.

In the late nineteenth century, after the notoriety of the Custer family was assured by the Little Bighorn, erroneous accounts of the family tree entered the discourse of popular culture. These yarns are worth mentioning, not because of their possible veracity, but because of those who believed them, and how widely they were believed.

One long circulated myth that still haunts various genealogy blogs and online chatrooms, holds that the Custers who are our subject were somehow related to George Washington. As Milo Custer wrote in 1912, Paul Custer, the son of Hermanus Küster, "married Sarah Martha Ball, daughter of John Ball of Virginia about the year 1730. She was, it is said, a sister of Joseph Ball, maternal grandfather of President George Washington." Milo went on to confirm that this "persistent tradition, old and often repeated, is erroneous and incorrect."

In fact, the Joseph Ball who was Washington's grandfather was born in 1649 and died in 1711. According to Washington biographer Douglas Southall Freeman and Ball biographer Earl Heck, John Ball did have a son named Joseph, but no daughter named Sarah or Martha.

Margaret Kinsey, in her 1981 book *Ball Cousins*, confirms that *a* Sarah Martha Ball, born in 1722, did marry Paul Custer in 1740. In any case, this would place the Ball connection on the lineage leading from Hermanus to Milo, *not* on that leading from Arnold Arndt Doors Küster to our subjects.

Another popular myth tells the story of the family having originated in the Orkney Islands off northern Scotland. This theory was apparently first suggested to George Armstrong Custer in April 1876 as he was passing through New York City on his return to Dakota Territory after testifying before Congress in Washington.

"I received a letter [presumably in care of his New York publisher] from a gentleman at Kirkwall, in the Orkneys, of the name of Custer," he told his wife in a letter. "He traces our relationship to the family, back to 1647, and gives the several changes the name has undergone, Cursetter, Cursider, Cusiter, Custer, all belonging to the same parish. He writes 'I have been established in business here for thirty-three years. I have noted your name, conspicuous as a General, and occasionally as author, and from descriptions of you I am convinced we are of the same stock.'"

Tongue in cheek, Custer added, "Tell Maggie that when I come into my Orkney inheritance . . ." allowing the phrase to trail off with the implication that he did not take the man from Kirkwall seriously.

This would hardly be worth recalling here if it did not crop up again much later. In 1950, the playwright Marguerite Merington published *The Custer Story*, an annotated compendium of correspondence between George Armstrong Custer and his wife. In it, Merington stated unambiguously that "the Custers were of English origin, descended from the Custers of the Orkney Islands. In the words of a pamphlet circulated in the family, they were 'agriculturists, working for themselves, not for wage; strong, healthy, industrious, living to a great age on their own farms, law-abiding and religious.'"

This fallacy could easily be discounted but for the fact that Merington was the closest confidant of Elizabeth Bacon "Libbie" Custer in her later years—and Libbie, the wife of George Armstrong Custer, had evolved as the defacto family scribe. As Merington wrote in the foreword to her book, "For some decades, ending only with her death in 1933, I was her nearest friend." It is improbable that Libbie believed the story, but Merington's stating it so emphatically is illustrative of the mythic dimensions of the whole Custer narrative.

Another alternative fiction of Custer origins gained traction in the chronicles of popular culture through Frederick Whittaker's *A Complete Life of General George A. Custer*, which was rushed into publication at the end of 1876, only six months after the Little Bighorn. The publishers, Sheldon & Company of New York City, had published George's *My Life on the Plains*, and were anticipating another book from him. When he died, they contracted with Whittaker, well-known in pulp magazine circles, to quickly pen a substitute. The fable as purveyed by Whittaker, concerns George's great grandfather, Emanuel Custer, born on July 29, 1754, during the first year of the French and Indian War. He was the son of Nicholas Custer and great grandson of Paulus Van Haren Küster. As told by Whittaker, Emanuel Custer was not born in Philadelphia, but rather he was a Hessian mercenary imported by the British during the Revolutionary War.

Whittaker wrote that Emanuel "was one of those same Hessian officers over whom the colonists wasted so many curses in the Revolutionary war, and who were yet so innocent of harm and such patient, faithful soldiers. After British General John Burgoyne's surrender in 1778, many of the paroled Hessians seized the opportunity to settle in the country they came to conquer."

A further reference to Emanuel having been a Hessian appeared in *Historical Collections of Ohio: An Encyclopedia of the State* by Henry Howe, which appeared in several editions between 1847 and 1907. Howe apparently interviewed a man named John Giles, who was married to a cousin of Emanuel's grandson, so somehow the Hessian story, like the Orkney story, had taken root like an insidious weed.

In fact, Emanuel Custer *was* a soldier in the Revolutionary War, but on the side of the colonists. Indeed, he was the first in his Custer line to serve in the armed forces of the United States. According to the files of the Military Accounts (Militia) held at Pennsylvania Historical and Museum Commission Division of Public Records, Emanuel enlisted to fight in the Revolutionary War and served as "a Private, in Fifth Class" in the 8th Company of the 6th Battalion of the Philadelphia County Militia under Captain

Arnold Francis. United States War Department records show that Emanuel, now a sergeant, was later on the muster roll of the 5th Battalion of the Philadelphia County Militia.

Around this time, he married Anna Maria Fedele (sometimes spelled phonetically as Fadley). As Whittaker colorfully described it, Emanuel was "captivated by the bright eyes of a frontier damsel, and captivated her in turn with his flaxen hair and sturdy Saxon figure."

In the wake of this mutual captivation, Emanuel and Anna Maria had five children, Emanuel, John, Susannah, Jacob, and Charlotte, born between 1782 and 1796. They then began the Custer family's migration away from Germantown, moving first to Cambria County, Pennsylvania, 250 miles westward, and next to Howard County, Maryland, in about 1790. Maria died in the town of Jessup (then spelled Jessups) in Howard County in 1799 at the age of forty, but Emanuel lived on until 1854, when he died at the age of one hundred. He had outlived his wife, as well as surviving three of his children.

John Fedele Custer, born to Emanuel and Anna Maria, was the grandfather of the subjects of this book. He was born on February 16, 1782, in Cambria County Pennsylvania, and married Catherine (sometimes written as Katherine) Valentine, who was also born in 1782. Six of their seven children, Ann, Emanuel Henry, Mary, George Washington, James, and Alexander, were born between 1804 and 1819 in Cresaptown in Allegheny County in western Maryland. Ellen was born in 1825 in Clarksburg, Virginia (West Virginia after 1863). Of them, Emanuel Henry Custer, born on December 10, 1806, was to be the father of George, Nevin, Tom, Boston, and Margaret.

Grandfather John Fedele Custer passed away on December 16, 1830, in Cresaptown, about 100 miles to the south of his birthplace. However, it is routinely overlooked in Custer biographies that grandmother Catherine Valentine Custer lived until August 8, 1877, fourteen months *after* the Battle of the Little Bighorn.

CHAPTER 2

GROWING UP IN THE DINING FORK

WHEN HE WAS twenty-four, Emanuel Henry Custer moved west to Ohio, and into a region that was then widely known as "the Dining Fork." It took its name from the Dining Fork Valley, so called because it was shaped like the table implement. The stream in that valley, occasionally called by the same name, is officially Conotton Creek, a tributary of the Tuscarawas River.

The Dining Fork encompassed the southern part of Carroll County and the northern part of Harrison County, and it was in the town of New Rumley in the latter county that Emanuel Henry Custer settled. The town had come into being in 1813, a decade after Ohio achieved statehood, platted by none other than Jacob Fedele Custer, the younger brother of John Fedele Custer, and Emanuel's uncle. Jacob and others considered its proximity to a main road between the Ohio cities of New Philadelphia and Steubenville to be an important civic consideration in its placement. Jacob would become so prominent in village life that he would be referred with the honorary title "squire," denoting a distinguished citizen of the community.

A post office, usually the measure of a town's viability, was established in New Rumley in 1820, but it was closed in 2013, and mail is now directed to Jewett, 3 miles to the south. Today, both towns are unincorporated communities.

In New Rumley, Emanuel joined his uncle, Squire Jacob Custer, in the blacksmith business. This was a trade that was certainly valuable near a well-traveled road through farm country where wagons needed maintenance and repairs, and horses always needed shoeing. The village blacksmith also became a justice of the peace in about 1830 and served in that post for a dozen years.

It was in the Dining Fork that Emanuel met Matilda Viers, the daughter of Brice Viers, a previous justice of the peace. They were married in 1828 at the Ridge Presbyterian Church in New Rumley with Reverend John Rea officiating. Of their four children, the oldest, Hannah, died in 1835 at the age of four, and John A. Custer died in 1836 at the age of three. Brice William Custer and Henry C. Custer were born in 1831 and 1833, respectively. Brice married Mariah Stockton in Harrison County, Ohio, in 1857, but they later moved south to Franklin County where Brice served as county sheriff between 1887 and 1891. Henry C. Custer, meanwhile, moved north from Ohio to Osceola County, Michigan, more than 200 miles north of Monroe.

Maria Ward, who was to be Emanuel's second wife and the mother of our subjects, was born on May 31, 1807, in Burgettstown, Pennsylvania, a town that was informally known as "West Boston" after its founder, Boston Burgett. As we see in Appendix 2, Maria was the daughter of James Grier Ward and Catherine Rogers Ward, both Pennsylvania-born grandchildren of immigrants, and who themselves felt the urge to continue the westward trek that landed them and their four children in New Rumley in 1816.

Harrison County records reveal that shortly after arriving in New Rumley, James purchased some property in the Western Liberties district northwest of the center of New Rumley, where he built a log home and where he operated a tavern until his death in 1824. Charles Wallace has stated that James Ward was "not a particularly successful businessman," leaving his family with "a pile of debts." Furthermore, county court records indicate multiple charges of assault being lodged against Ward for attacking his neighbors.

Maria Ward wed her first husband, merchant Israel Reed Kirkpatrick, age thirty-two, in New Rumley in 1823 when she was sixteen. In 1830, Israel purchased the tavern previously operated by James Ward, and later by Maria's older brother. They also moved into the house in Western Liberties that Maria's father had built. The children of Israel and Maria who lived to adulthood included David, born in 1823, and Lydia Ann, born in 1825.

When both Matilda Viers Custer and Israel Kirkpatrick died within the space of four months in 1835, Emanuel and Maria were left as widower and widow, he with two children aged four and two, she with two children aged twelve and ten. They entered quickly into what would be a brief courtship, neither waiting the traditional year before becoming engaged.

They were married on February 23, 1836, in New Rumley, and moved into the house in Western Liberties. Five months later, three-year-old John A. Custer, Emanuel and Matilda's youngest son, died in the home where the six sons of Emanuel and Maria would later be born.

As seen in Appendix 5, which lists all of the children of Emanuel and Maria, their first two, James and Samuel, born in 1836 and 1838, respectively, each died at about the age of one year, with young James passing away on Christmas Eve in 1837. After the tragedy of losing three young boys in the space of less than three years, and one at Christmastime, things changed in 1839.

Their third son was born on December 5, 1839, and they named him George Armstrong Custer. There were several Georges in the Custer lineage and Maria's great grandfather on her mother's side was James Armstrong from County Fermanaugh. Indeed, George was called by his middle name, and his family nickname, "Autie," came about because, as a small child, he had difficulty pronouncing "Armstrong."

In this book, I have adopted the family convention of referring to him as "Autie," rather than as "George."

It was also in 1839 that Emanuel was elected as justice of the peace, having run as a Democrat, a party affiliation to which he was staunchly devoted. Meanwhile, he became a founding member of the New Rumley Methodist Church. The Custers had long since left their Mennonite roots behind. Uncle Jacob Custer still lived in New Rumley after helping found it twenty-six years earlier, and was now a practicing Lutheran.

Emanuel and Maria's second surviving son was born on July 29, 1842, and christened Nevin Johnson Custer, names that apparently had no recent precedents in the families on either side. By Nevin's later recollection, he was named "after a Presbyterian man who said he'd educate me into the clergy." Apparently this man faded from the scene fairly quickly as Nevin was never educated for the clergy.

The third son, born on March 15, 1845, was named Thomas Ward Custer, his first name common in both Maria's Rogers and Ward lines, and his middle name being her maiden surname. In fact, she had an uncle named Thomas Ward.

By all accounts, the older Kirkpatrick children, in their teens when Autie, Nevin, and Tom were born, got along well with the new additions. Lydia Ann, who went by her middle name as "Ann," was extremely fond of the younger Custer boys, especially Autie. His letters to her typically began with the salutation, "My Dear Sister." Charles Wallace observed that "outsiders knew no difference between full and half brothers, and they themselves resented the question."

Among the three eldest boys, Autie and Tom are recalled as having been outgoing to the point of rambunctiousness, while Nevin, by all accounts, was described as introverted and sickly. Their cousin, Mary Custer, quoted by L. Milton Ronsheim, writing in Ohio's *Cadiz Republican* newspaper in

1929, commented that Autie "would show what a good horseman he was by riding standing up on the horse and running it around in a circle in the barnyard. Although much younger, cousin Tom was quite an adventurous boy and also enjoyed riding and in a way imitating his older brother Armstrong. Nevin was of a more quiet nature and, as I now recollect, did not indulge so much in the adventurous play of his older brothers."

Even though he was older than Tom, Nevin was smaller, and was easily mistaken for having been younger.

Stephen Ambrose, the late twentieth-century historian points out their father was "a practical joker and so were his children—George worst of all." He might also have added that Tom was a close second. He looked up to his big brother, endeavoring hard to mimic him, and later trying his best to outdo Autie in both pranks and feats of physical prowess. Nevin looked up to them both, but apparently idolized Autie.

Their father was also a member of the local militia troop which was officially know as the New Rumley Guards, and unofficially—and apparently with tongue-in-cheek irony—as the "New Rumley Invincibles."

Though Emanuel never actually saw combat, he was fascinated with uniforms and things military. As he much later reminisced to his daughter-in-law, Autie's wife Libbie, "As a boy I was greatly stirred by a character, a veteran of the Revolution, also of the War of 1812, who used to come around piping war tunes on a fife. A Democrat, he professed himself. And then I made up my mind that if that was the side a man could come out on, after two wars, that would be the side for me." Emanuel had cast his first vote in a presidential election in 1832, the year that Democrat Andrew Jackson won reelection, taking the state of Ohio in the process. Thereafter, Ohio disappointed Emanuel, going for the Whigs in the next three elections.

Apparently, for all their uniforms, muskets, and drilling, the New Rumley Invincibles were mainly a social club whose musters provided an opportunity for local men to enjoy some camaraderie and to get together for a few drinks. It also afforded an opportunity for the young sons of militiamen to spend time in the proximity of muskets, sabers, and uniforms. Indeed, when he was a toddler, young Autie's mother made him a little uniform, and he learned to do the manual of arms with his toy musket. As such, he was probably a popular addition at militia musters.

There is a tale originally related by Elizabeth Bacon Custer, Autie's future wife, in her memoir *Tenting on the Plains* that finds its way into most Custer biographies because it establishes his military inclination. The incident occurred in around 1845 at the time of the lead-up to the Mexican War when George was five or six. There was much talk about the issues of the day, and Autie was certainly aware.

"Almost the first little speech he learned was a line he picked up from a declamation one of his brothers was committing to memory as a school task," she wrote. "His father was proud, as well as surprised to hear the little Armstrong lisp out one day, waving his tiny arm in the air, 'My voice is for war.'"

The declamation appears in Volume IV of the *Southern Literary Messenger* of 1838, attributed to the Cherokee leader Tuskenehaw whose families were embarking upon the Trail of Tears. This version had often been quoted in recent tellings of the story, but the phrase was probably committed to memory as a school task in the 1840s as quoted from Congressman John G. Jackson of Virginia in his famous March 30, 1812, memo to President James Madison on the eve of the War of 1812.

Needless to say, had Tom been conversant in 1845, rather than a babe in arms, he would have seconded his brother in eagerness for cannonballs to fly.

The fourth son, Boston Custer, was born on October 31, 1848. It has been suggested that his mother named him after her Pennsylvania birthplace, the town sometimes called "West Boston."

Six months later, in April 1849, Emanuel Custer left the blacksmith business, and sold the house in Western Liberties to a man named William Welling. He purchased eighty acres of farmland in North Township,

3 miles northeast of New Rumley, and moved his family to a place that is still referred to locally at the "Custer Homestead." Not the only such place in Ohio, it once shared this description with a farm near Tontogany where the Custers lived in the late 1850s that is described in Chapter Three.

It is unclear whether the move was precipitated by a change in Emanuel's relationship with his uncle, Squire Jacob Custer, with whom he had been in business in the blacksmith shop, or if he was just fulfilling a dream to own land. Jacob, who would live until 1862, turned fifty-nine in 1849, and it is conceivable that he was no longer involved in the shop himself.

Emanuel and Maria's youngest child and only daughter, Margaret Emma Custer—known within the family as Maggie—was late in joining the already established family. She was born at the family homestead on January 5, 1852. By this time, Emanuel Custer was forty-five years old, Maria was forty-four, and eldest son Autie was almost ready for secondary school. Though they were in the middle of their lives at the time their children were still in their childhood years, both Emanuel and Maria would both outlive their three sons who were to die at the Little Bighorn.

By the time that Maggie was born, the three older Custer boys were attending classes in the one-room district schoolhouse, known as Creal's School, in New Rumley. Recollections of their school days in Henry Howe's 1896 *Historical Collections of Ohio*, describe Tom as a "born leader" and Autie as "an apt scholar, a leader among boys, mischievous and full of practical jokes; withal very plucky."

Joseph T. Harrison, who in 1927 penned *The Story of the Dining Fork*, attended classes in the same school room and wrote that Tom and Nevin "were big boys when I was a little boy at the Creal School." Of Boston Custer, who was closer to his own age, Harrison wrote that he "was frequently the envy of other boys of his age in his ability to stand on his head or execute a handspring."

Harrison goes on to say that Tom Custer "easily comes to my mind as the leading spirit among them, for he always had a kind word for the little boy, and it is a pleasure to remember him. He was the adventurer who climbed the trees in the late autumn season in the Creal orchard and shook off the apples for us. He also took care of the small boy in the toboggan slides in the lane to the south of the schoolhouse. His device was a long board, of tolerable width, which turned up slightly at the front end, and with him at the head to steer; the other boys sat behind him in the order of their sizes, and at the extreme rear end sat the smallest of the boys. The grade was steep enough to cause the board with its freight to go down the hill with great velocity, but as the mid-roadway was lower than the sides, there was no way for it to get off the track, but it frequently caused a 'spill' at the foot of the hill. Such exercise was pretty hard on clothing, and Tom kept within his desk an old pair of trousers, which he pulled on over his others for such sport."

Harrison supposes that "if baseball had been known then, as it is now, Tom would have been a leader in that game as he was in the old game of 'town-ball.' His feats as a batter, frequently drove the ball clear off the only level ground there was to play upon, and it would be occasionally found at the foot of the hill or in the woods."

Most accounts, including Harrison's, reveal Nevin Custer as just the opposite of Autie and Tom, and as a boy who had difficulty keeping up. Harrison recalled that Nevin "had difficulty in making the signs on the blackboard, used in Apothecaries weight, to the satisfaction of William Foster, teacher, and he was called upon frequently to describe what he meant by the rude figures which he drew, some of which looked like pictures of bugs."

The teacher is referred to in Nevin's later recollections as "Old Foster," though he may well have been still in his twenties. He would have had his hands full, with the ages of his students spanning several years. When Tom was in the first grade, Nevin was in fourth and Autie was among Foster's oldest group. Perhaps out of necessity, Foster was a strict disciplinarian.

Nevin would later describe the school as having "pine slabs for seats and old Foster layin' for us up in front with the birch [switch]."

"Lawsey, how that man could whip!" Nevin recalled in a rambling syndicated interview he gave shortly before he died. "But George never got licked, somehow. It was always some of the rest of us. Maybe that was because George kept his geography on top of his paper backed novels. He used to read 'em all the time in school, but Foster never caught him, for he was bright as a dollar and never missed a recitation. Foster'd come along and pat George on the head, and then yank up the rest of us, and make us stand on our toes on one crack and our fingers touching another while he lashed us over the backs."

In his description of Foster's program of castigation, Nevin provides an insight into the early lives and habits of the Custer boys.

"I got it for whispering about a spelling lesson; and Tom, he was always getting licked," Nevin explained. "Tom chewed tobacco, same as most of the boys did, but of course 'twasn't allowed in school. However, Tom couldn't let it alone, so he bored a hole in the school room floor with an auger to give him a place to spit. He tried to keep it covered with his foot, but of course after a while Foster found it and Tom got licked. No teachers like them nowadays [in 1910]."

Was Foster a cruel man beyond the limits necessary for maintaining discipline? Nevin suggested as much when he commented that "it was unusual for the schoolmaster to treat the pupils at every holiday vacation, but old Foster wouldn't treat, so we locked him out of the schoolhouse and when he tried to come in through the window we kept him out with the coal shovel that we heated in the stove. I guess we all got licked for that."

Joseph Harrison recalled the same incident differently when he wrote that "in those days it was the custom to 'bar the teacher out' at the holiday season if he did not treat the scholars. On one of these occasions, Tom Custer called the scholars together when the teacher was not present, and commenced preparations for the ceremony. The first thing was to secure the door from the inside so that it could not be opened from the outside. To accomplish this the long bench seat was lifted so that the upper end fell below the cross piece at the top of the door, and at the lower end it was held from being pushed down by the poker, which had been heated in the old cannon stove, and burned through the floor.

"As a preliminary to all this, he had asked the small boys to sit still in their places at the side of the room, with the promise that if they did so, they would all get candy. Then when all the windows had been fastened, but one on the lower and highest part of the house, Tom got out first and helped the small scholars down to the ground. No key could then open that door, and the teacher had to capitulate before he could resume teaching."

When not in school, the older boys, especially Maria's son David Kirkpatrick, as well as Autie, had also helped out at Emanuel's blacksmith shop, and they all worked on the farm. It was here, in the course of working around horses, that Autie and Tom first developed their skills in riding and horsemanship.

"Father was pretty strict: stricter than most fathers nowadays are," Nevin recalled. "Everybody had his work cut out an' he had to do it without whimpering and do it promptly; sort of religious duty . . . I remember George hated to get his clothes smelly; and he and I made a dicker so that I did all the work at the barns, while he split the wood and carried it in. I hated splitting wood . . . it was all done with a wedge in those days."

For Maria, it seems that the years at North Township were ones that would leave fond memories. In the late 1850s, when Autie had waxed nostalgically about their homelife in a letter to his mother, Maria had written back that "when you speak about your boyhood home in your dear letter I had to weep for joy that the recollection was sweet in your memory. Many a time I have thought there was things my children needed it caused me tears. Yet I consoled myself that I had done my best in making home comfortable. My darling boy, it was not for myself. I was not fortunate enough to have wealth to make home beautiful, always my desire. So I tried to fill the empty spaces with little acts of kindness. Even when there was a meal admired by my children it was my greatest pleasure to get it for them. I have no doubt I have said some things to you and my other children that was not always pleasant, but I have no regrets about that. You, my son, have more than compensated your mother for all she has done for you. It is sweet to toil for those we love."

Even as Maria was raising the children of her second family, her older son and daughter by her first marriage had grown up and had begun their adult lives. David Kirkpatrick, her eldest, was still in the household of Emanuel and Maria in the 1850 Census, but in April 1851, he married Cynthia Jane Patton of Rumley Township.

Maria's daughter, Lydia Ann, had married David Reed in 1846 when the three oldest Custer boys were small, and had moved north to Monroe, Michigan. David and Ann had four children who were roughly the same ages as Boston and Maggie, her youngest Custer step-siblings, and with whom they spent a great deal of time after the Custers moved to Monroe. For more details about the Kirkpatrick/Reed family tree, see Appendix 4.

The oldest of the Reed children, Marie, was born in 1848, two months before Boston Custer. The second, Lilla Belle Reed, was born in 1854 when Maggie was only two, but passed away in 1858, a month short of her fourth birthday. Emma Reed was born in 1856, and Harry Armstrong "Autie" Reed was born in 1858.

CHAPTER 3
MOVING ON

IN 1852, THE year that Maggie was born, Autie had turned thirteen and had outgrown the confines of William Foster's one-room schoolhouse in New Rumley. He was ready for high school. It was typical then, as it is typical now throughout the United States, for elementary school students in multiple rural communities to attend high school at a central location in a larger town. In this case, it was Cadiz High School in Cadiz, the Harrison County seat, 11 miles south of New Rumley.

However, it was decided that Autie should go north to Monroe, Michigan, where he would move in with his half-sister, Lydia Ann Reed and her husband, David. Here, he would enroll in Professor Alfred Stebbins' Boys' and Young Men's Academy, a new and potentially prestigious institution that had just opened. While so many accounts tell of Autie as a hooligan, it is also true that he had an inclination toward academics. Nevin recalled that his older brother was "always studying."

John McClelland Bulkley wrote in his *History of Monroe County, Michigan*, published in 1913, that the Boys' and Young Men's Academy was "the most creditable and important of any of the educational institutions of Monroe in the earlier years," adding ambiguously that it was "organized in 1851 or 1852."

Bulkley goes on to say that Stebbins, "an accomplished instructor from the eastern states, was engaged as principal with a corps of teachers." The school's own advertising described it as a place where the boys "could enjoy all the comforts and privileges of home, and at the same time be fitted for any of the colleges and universities of the United States." Students were enrolled from Chicago, Buffalo, and Detroit, as well as from Monroe.

It was not Autie's first extended stay in Monroe. He is recalled as having spent time with his half-sister and her husband while he was growing up, and, although Autie seemed to be a favorite of Ann's, it is probable that Nevin and Tom spent some of their early years on long visits as well.

It was in about 1854, while he was in Monroe to attend the "Stebbins Academy," that George Armstrong Custer first crossed paths with the girl who later became his wife. Though their first encounter was as brief as the fleeting of an eye, Elizabeth Clift Bacon would go on to be an integral part of the lives not only of Autie, but of the entire Custer family. She is especially important in our recollection of the Custers because in addition to her voluminous later writings about her husband, she also recorded a great many anecdotes about other members of the Custer family.

Known to her own family, to the Custers, and to posterity as "Libbie," she was born on April 8, 1842, the daughter and second of the four children of Judge Daniel Stanton Bacon and his wife Eleanor Sofia Page Bacon. The judge and his wife were pillars of the Monroe community. They lived in a big, rambling, two-story house on a corner lot at Monroe and Second Streets that was surrounded by a white picket fence. But there was sadness in the big house. By 1849, the judge and Eleanor had lost three young children, Eddie, Harriet, and Sophia, to illness. When Libbie turned seven, she was an only child.

The Bacons knew the Reeds, and Libbie, who was twelve years old by 1854, was well aware of the "Custer boy" who was boarding with them, and she took an interest in him. In the famous story, recounted by all of the George Armstrong Custer biographers, and by Nevin Custer in his 1910 récollections, the capricious girl was leaning on the picket fence or hanging on the gate, or in some way lying in wait for him as he passed en route to or from school.

"Hello, you Custer boy!" Libbie shouted before dashing inside her house, leaving him to contemplate his first encounter with the "Bacon girl."

It would be nearly a decade before they met again to begin their courtship, by which time Judge Bacon had become a widower and had remarried.

"Mother is sleeping her last great sleep from which she will never wake up, no never," wrote Libbie two weeks after losing her mother on August 12, 1854. "God only knows what anguish filled my heart." Her father married Rhoda Pitts Wells five years later.

As pretentious as its advertising made it seem, the Stebbins Academy lasted only until 1855, and after it had closed, George Armstrong Custer returned to New Rumley. By now, Tom was a precocious ten and Nevin was thirteen, the same age that Autie had been when he went away. Boston had just started at Creal's School, and had only just begun to feel the sting of Foster's birch switch.

Maggie, still a small child of three, had seen little of Autie during her short life, and she would grow up without the same sibling connection with him that her other brothers shared.

In 1855, Autie, as is typical of young men of that age, began casting about for whatever would come next in his life. He had no practical skills, nor had he been exposed to a trade other than blacksmithing, and his father had sold the shop when he was but ten so his experience was limited. Nevin was being groomed for the family farm, so that door was closed, but aside from a love of horsemanship, Autie had no interest in farming.

Having long since discovered that he had an aptitude for academics, Autie decided that he would become a teacher. Ironically, the kid who had once been the sharpest thorn in Old Foster's side now decided to *become* him.

At the time, becoming an elementary school teacher in Ohio required little more than demonstrating literacy and passing a written examination. However, passing that exam required preparation, and schools were being formed to provide such training. "Normal schools," as those institutions were then known, would become "teachers' colleges" later in the nineteenth century. They had only just begun to appear west of the Appalachians, and one opened in Harrison County in November 1855. Founded by pioneer educator Cyrus McNeely, the McNeely Normal School (later Hopedale Normal College) was located in Hopedale, just a dozen miles south of New Rumley, and operated until 1902.

George Armstrong Custer spent two four-month sessions at McNeely's, concluding at the end of July 1856. During that time, he apparently sat for several examinations because he was granted a series of teaching certificates in March, April, and June. The reason for seeking multiple certificates was that each was valid for just twelve months. He wanted to have one that was good for as long as possible, especially when he did not finally graduate until the summer.

He started his teaching career with District Five in Cadiz, taking over a schoolhouse filled with twenty-five students. Milton Ronsheim of the *Cadiz Republican* newspaper notes that on at least one occasion, his parents, with Maggie in tow, visited him at the schoolhouse. By the end of the year, however, he had transferred to Beech School in Athens Township. Part of the catalyst for the move had been a love affair. While he was in Cadiz, he boarded with the family of Alexander Holland, and he had fallen in love—in the head-over-heels way that eighteen-year-olds fall in love—with the landlord's daughter, Mary Jane "Molly" Holland. It was mutual. Because of Autie's drinking habits, her father disapproved, and encouraged the change of venue for his teaching career. Although—or perhaps because—Holland was anxious to be rid of the young man, he did him a favor.

Even before he graduated from McNeely's, George Custer was already thinking ahead to his *next* career. Since May 1856, he had been communicating with first-term Congressman John Armour Bingham—later the framer of the Fourteenth Amendment—about securing an appointment to the US Military Academy at West Point. By some accounts, Bingham—a Whig turned Republican—had turned Custer down at least twice, in part because Autie was tainted by his father's pedigree as a Democrat. Meanwhile, 1856 was a contentious presidential election year that brought Democrat James Buchanan to the White House. Indeed, it was also a bad year for Republicans in Ohio, as they lost nine Congressional seats to the Democrats.

However, it turned out that Holland knew Bingham and was a fellow Republican. After Bingham won reelection, Holland was able, as Charles Wallace suggests, undertaking some "quiet lobbying" to grease the skids for Autie.

"Bingham was a Republican and pap was a Democrat and we didn't think George would ever get anything," Nevin Custer recalled years later. "He did, though, after a while. Bingham appointed him in spite of politics—men was honester then than they are now [1910]."

In his *Reminiscences*, published many years after the young man achieved celebrity, Bingham spun the narrative a bit differently to make himself the protagonist. He wrote, "I had not been long in Congress when I received a letter, a real boy's letter, that captivated me. Packed among my papers I have it yet, but, written over forty years ago, I remember every word. Written in a boyish hand, but firmly, legibly, it told me that the writer—a 'Democrat boy,' that I might be under no misapprehension—wanted to be a soldier, wanted to go to West Point, and asked what steps he should take regarding it. Struck by its originality, its honesty, I replied at once."

Tom was jealous. In an 1865 letter to his friend, Joseph B. Campbell in Monroe, Michigan, which is preserved in the John S. Campbell Collection in Cadiz, he admitted that as he accompanied his brother to the train station, he was now thinking seriously of following in his footsteps.

Whatever the chain of events, as the bugle sounded to begin the academic year at West Point in July 1857, George Armstrong Custer was among the 125 plebes embarking on their five-year course of study as the Class of 1862.

By 1857, with his years at Creal's School about to close behind Tom, his parents were beginning to debate *his* future. His mother had it in her mind that he too should go on to the high school in Cadiz.

In the way that mothers often like to plan the lives of their children, she saw the high school as a stepping stone to Franklin College down at New Athens in southern Harrison County. In turn, she viewed Franklin, which had been founded in 1818 by the abolitionist Presbyterian Minister John Walker, as a stepping stone to a seminary. With one son bound for West Point and a military career, she had it in her mind that her second son should have a career as a member of the clergy. By now, the old idea to educate Nevin as a Presbyterian clergyman, which dated back to Nevin's birth, had been long forgotten. His academic ability, like his athletic prowess, seems not to have measured up those of Autie and Tom.

As Tom later told Joseph Campbell, his father put a stop to the track that would have led him to Franklin. Emanuel did not have faith in Tom as a good student, but mainly as a Democrat and a Methodist, he abhorred the idea of his son at a Presbyterian institution which he perceived as a detestable hotbed of Republicans and other forms of abolitionists. Thus it was that Tom Custer's educational career was nipped in the bud.

Marguerite Merington related a story of a conversation about a decade later when Libbie, by then his daughter-in-law, asked Emanuel whether it did not "shake your party faith that most of the clergy are Republicans?"

"Not a bit," he replied. "But it does shake my faith in their religion."

By that later time, there was a hint that he was having misgivings about having stymied Tom's career as a man of the cloth. In a letter to Libbie, he expressed concern about Tom's intemperance, and his succumbing to temptation. "Libbie, I want you to counsel Thomas," he asked. "I want my boys to be, foremost, soldiers of the Lord."

By the time that Autie had gone away and Emanuel had resolved that Tom was *not* going away, David Kirkpatrick, Emanuel's oldest stepson, had moved on. In October 1855, he purchased land near Tontogany, in Wood County, Ohio, about 200 road miles northwest of New Rumley and 50 miles south of Monroe.

His personal life is something of a mystery. David had married Cynthia Jane Patton in 1851 in Harrison County. Charles Wallace claims that she died around the time that David moved to Wood County. Other sources say that she lived until 1907, and the 1880 Census lists her as divorced and living with her brother in Ohio. Upon my inquiry, the Wood County District Public Library was able to offer no further clarification. In November 1857, in Wood County, David married seventeen-year-old Nancy J. Grundy (sometimes written as Gundy). Their oldest child, Emma, was born in 1860, and by the census of 1870, they had three sons, John, Thomas, and Myron. At least one of Nancy's cousins, or possibly her brother, would serve with Tom Custer in the Civil War.

The move by David is important to the story of our Custer family in that by 1860, Emanuel and Maria may have been convinced by him to relocate to Wood County from the Dining Fork. Despite this, David Kirkpatrick seems to have had very little contact with his mother and Emanuel. While Lydia Ann Kirkpatrick Reed was thoroughly involved with the Custer children throughout their lives, even to the extent of micromanaging their education, her older brother, seems generally to have made himself into a distant relative, not unlike Emanuel's older sons, Brice and Henry C. Custer.

In May 1860, Emanuel paid $481 (about $14,000 in current valuation) at a sheriff's sale for forty acres in Washington Township, near David's place. By the time the census takers came around that year, the whole family, less Autie, was living in Wood County. The following year, in March 1861, Emanuel paid $2,000 for an adjacent eighty. On this property, along the east bank of Tontogany Creek, a few miles upstream from the Maumee River and about a mile outside Tontogany, Emanuel built a house on the shoulder of a bluff. Though the Custers lived here for just a couple of years, the place would thereafter be known as the "General Custer Homestead." For many years a sign on the Tontogany Creek Bridge alluded to this claim, although George Armstrong Custer never lived there.

While researching this book, I came across an interesting story about this so-called "General Custer Homestead." This story is worth telling for it encompasses two fascinating detective stories while providing us a rare glimpse into the early and usually overlooked years of Maggie and Boston. On May 15, 1968, the *Sentinel Tribune*, published in Bowling Green, just 7 miles down State Route 46 from the Tontogany Creek Bridge, ran an article that opens a series of doors into the past. The piece was apparently based on an earlier article, because its first of several protagonists, Rosina William, had passed away in April 1960.

Intrigued by the sign on the Tontogany Creek Bridge, a *Sentinel Tribune* reporter stopped to visit the house, and was greeted by Mrs. Williams, who explained that she and her husband, Frank Martin Williams, who passed away in 1937, had owned the property for years. When queried about the "General Custer Homestead" story, she opened the second of the series of doors leading deeper into the past as she produced a yellowing scrap of newspaper. This clipping, undated and unattributed, which had probably appeared in the 1920s—and certainly before 1937—told of a previous reporter's having crossed the bridge and been intrigued by the sign.

"The situation was inviting," wrote the journalist from four decades before. "We crossed the bridge, wormed our way up the incline to a cluster of farm buildings and were greeted by the master and the owner of the house, who proved to be Frank Williams."

"Why do you say this is the General Custer home?" was the question asked.

"Because it's true," Williams replied. "We are not unused to visitors asking the same question as you have, but a few days ago among a party of people calling, was a fine old lady who said she once taught school in the district, lived with the Custers here, that she knew George Custer, later the general, and that a younger brother and sister of the famous soldier and Indian fighter, went to school to her."

Williams went on to say that "the fine old lady said that her name when she had taught school in Wood County was Lucy Hewlett." She declined to give her married name, but she *had* given Williams the address in Toledo where she lived with her married daughter, and her daughter's name.

Naturally, the 1920s journalist lost no time in dashing down Route 46 to Toledo, though he had the courtesy to call ahead before driving to the address on Scottwood Avenue.

"You can't imagine what a thrill it gave me when you asked over the phone for Lucy Hewlett," said the 86-year-old widow of George W. Carpenter as she came to the door. "It was like suddenly lifting the curtain of my girlhood, and myriads of scenes of my youth flashed by me with wonderful clearness like a moving panorama. I seemed to live years in a few seconds. It was a strange feeling."

Having gotten past the initial excitement, Lucy Hewlett Carpenter explained thats he had taught school in the Tontogany district for "two or three consecutive terms . . . Boston Custer and Margaret Custer, the youngest two children of the family, went to school to me."

Indeed, she had been to Boston and Maggie what William Foster had been to Autie, Nevin, and Tom at Creal's School back in Harrison County.

"As I remember, I had some 40 pupils," she continued, "and the school, house stood across the creek from the Custer home, near the old cemetery. Nevin Custer, older than the two children who attended school, was at home, but I do not remember much about Thomas Custer."

And well she would not, because by 1861, he was in the process of enlisting to fight in the Civil War.

She did, however, remember brother Autie as "a very attractive young man with light hair and rather thin features" who was "back and forth getting ready to enter the service," dating her recollections to 1861, when he briefly visited after graduating from West Point.

Of course, the name "General Custer Homestead," which references George is a misnomer, attached retrospectively in the years after he became an iconic figure. It was never his homestead, and the time he spent there is numbered in days, or at most weeks, when he was home on furlough during the first two winters of the war. Like the myriad of roadside hostelries up and down the Eastern Seaboard that once bragged "George Washington Slept Here," it was at best an exaggeration for effect, though it was guaranteed to lure the curious and grant a sense of importance to the property owner.

In fact, the house where Rosina Williams greeted the journalists was *not* home of Emanuel Custer, but rather a "new" house that had been built in 1892. Ironically, given the trade that Emanuel Custer had abandoned in order to become a farmer, Frank Williams had turned the old Custer house into a blacksmith shop!

The old home was finally torn down in 1970, because the then-owners, Laverdo and Rosemary Fox, had decided that it had become "too rickety and too dangerous for visitors, many of whom were boy scouts." An article in the August 24, 1976, issue of the *Sentinel Tribune* announced that Fox was selling off some of the fixtures that he had salvaged, including a chair rail, the back door, and a walnut staircase.

The Custers had climbed that Wood County stairway for less than three years. In 1863, Emanuel and Maria, along with Maggie and Boston, aged eleven and fifteen, moved north to Monroe, having been convinced by Lydia Ann Reed that the schools were better up there.

Perhaps the Custers entertained thoughts of returning to Wood County because Emanuel held on to the house and the 120 acres on Tontogany Creek until 1865. When it was sold to a man named John Tanke in August of that year, Emanuel was paid $5,000. Perhaps it was just wartime inflation, but he had doubled his money.

Neither Tom nor Nevin, aged eighteen and twenty-one, made the Monroe move in 1863, though Nevin would relocate there by 1871. Tom, inspired as always by brother George, had already followed his wanderlust into that bigger world beyond the counties of rural Ohio.

CHAPTER 4
GOING TO WAR

THE ISSUE OF slavery, the debate over the status—whether slave or free—of new states admitted to the Union, and the inexorable march toward the disaster of the Civil War all formed the disturbing backdrop of everything that happened to the Custer family through the 1850s.

This all seemed to reach a head in the election of 1860. Only just formed in 1854, the new Republican Party had quickly replaced the Whigs as the principal opposition to the Democratic Party—the party of Andrew Jackson and Emanuel Custer. Running strong on their anti-slavery platform, the upstart Republicans had taken control of the House of Representatives in the 1858 midterm election, much to the chagrin of the establishment Democrats.

In 1860, the Democrats were split into a Northern and Southern wing, with the latter leaning toward succession if they did not get their way. So disorganized were the Democrats that their first convention was adjourned in deadlock. After the second convention nominated Senator Stephen Douglas of Illinois for president, the Southern faction walked out and held a third convention, which nominated John Breckinridge of Kentucky, who was then the incumbent Vice President of the United States.

The Republicans nominated Abraham Lincoln, a former Illinois Congressman who had lost to Stephen Douglas in a bid for the US Senate in 1858.

When the dust settled on Wednesday, November 7, 1860, the morning after the most contentious election yet seen in the United States, Stephen Douglas was the biggest loser, having taken just one state, losing even to John Bell of the Constitutional Union Party, who won three. Breckinridge, as expected, won the South solidly, taking a swath of ten southern states plus Maryland. Lincoln did likewise in the North, taking a solid swath of sixteen states, plus California and Oregon, and beating Breckinridge 180 to 72 in the Electoral College.

It is not known which Democrat won favor with Emanuel Custer, but Lincoln won both Harrison County and Wood County, as well as the state of Ohio.

As promised, the southern states began steps toward secession. By March 1861, as Lincoln was being inaugurated and as Emanuel Custer was buying his eighty-acre parcel in Washington Township, seven southern states had left the Union to form a new country and the Confederate States of America was a month old. By April, eleven states had joined the Confederacy, the Provisional Forces of the Confederate States had captured Fort Sumter in Charleston Harbor, and the Civil War had begun.

At the US Military Academy, there was groundswell of urgency among the Corps of Cadets to put the walls of West Point behind them and join the fray. Cadets of all classes from southern states had already begun to drop out and go home to join the Confederate Army, and the remaining northern cadets were anxious to do the same with the United States Army. The remaining seniors, or First Classmen, even petitioned the War Department for early graduation.

George Armstrong Custer and the members of the Class of 1862 were anxious to apply the trade for which they were being educated. Under pressure from all sides, the Academy relented. The forty-five members of the Class of 1861 graduated on May 6, and the Class of 1862 became the Class of *June* 1861.

On June 24, Custer received his diploma and his commission as a second lieutenant in the US Army. Of the thirty-four men in the class, Custer observed in his *War Memoirs*, published in *Galaxy* magazine many years later, "Thirty-three graduated above me." Much has been made about him graduating last in his class, but to his credit, it should be added that fifty-five percent of those who started in 1857 had already flunked out, and of those who made it through to near the end, twenty-two resigned to go south without graduating.

On June 30, Custer and his classmates were relieved of duty at West Point and ordered to report to Washington, DC. Less than a month later, he would be riding with the 2nd Cavalry Regiment in the First Battle of Bull Run, the first major field battle of the Civil War.

Among young men is Ohio and across the country, both north and south, there was no less urgency to be part of the action than there was at West Point. Lines were forming at recruiting offices as the shells were still falling on Fort Sumter, though in some places the momentum was gradual.

"We didn't get the war spirit so fast, back on the farm, but it came, straight enough," Nevin Custer recalled.

One of the most colorful descriptions of this moment in the lives of the Custer family was in an essay about Tom that Libbie Custer penned in 1891 by for a thirtieth anniversary Civil War anthology compiled by wartime cavalry commander turned author Theophilus Rodenbough.

"The war-drum burst in upon this contented home, and scattered her dear ones far and near," Libbie wrote of the war's disruption of Maria Custer's home on Tontogany Creek. "Her heart had grieved enough over the departure of her ambitious eldest, Armstrong, who had implored his parents, four years before, to let him educate himself as a soldier at West Point. But after he had gone, she huddled the little curly-headed fellows that were left, more closely about her, and sang still, at her daily toil, for their comfort."

In the 1860s, the younger three of Maria's sons did not exactly meet the definition of "little curly-headed fellows," but Libbie was known to succumb to hyperbole. Nevin was only a month away from turning nineteen when Autie had been commissioned in June 1861, while Tom had recently turned sixteen, and Boston was four months shy of turning thirteen. "In 1861, peace departed from the hearth-stone," Libbie continued. "The two striplings [Nevin and Tom] began to beg to go to the war."

There are several variations on the enlistment narrative for the "striplings." In Libbie's account, Emanuel and Maria thought it sufficient that Autie alone should fight in the war, but Nevin and Tom exacted a promise from their parents that *one* of them could enlist. As the oldest brother still at home, certainly the burden would fall upon Nevin's shoulders to be the first to approach the recruiter. In 1910, Nevin recalled that "I enlisted. Yep, though I'd have to go along and fight with George, yuh know. Thought maybe we could fight together same as we'd hoed corn and picked berries together in the fields."

Citing family sources, Custer scholar Dr. Lawrence Frost wrote that Nevin was "rejected at the Cleveland recruiting office because of his chronic rheumatism." However, Custer biographer James Robbins writes that Nevin "joined up but was discharged for rheumatism."

In his 1890 book *History of Monroe County, Michigan*, Talcott Enoch Wing wrote tactfully that Nevin was "not judged robust enough to endure the fatigues of the camp."

Nevin himself remembered that "I went through all right till it came to the state camp at Columbus . . . and there I got thrown out for rheumatism." The 1910 interviewer wrote that Custer's voice "dropped to a disgusted drawl." Even after the passage of nearly half a century, he was embarrassed by having been rejected.

It has never been clear exactly what it was that ailed him, though rheumatism is widely mentioned, including in Nevin's own recollection. Libbie wrote simply that "although not an invalid, he was delicate." During the nineteenth century rheumatism was widely used as an umbrella term for numerous maladies, especially chronic joint pain, which were not fully understood at the time. Nevin had always been described as sickly and unable to keep up with the athletic exploits of Autie and Tom, but medical records are nonexistent. Whatever it was, being delicate did not preclude him from many decades of hard work on a series of farms.

"Mad?" Nevin asked rhetorically in recalling his reaction to being rebuffed. "Why, I was the maddest boy you ever saw in your life. I went back to the farm and Tom and Boston and I declared war against the whole United States, North, South, and in between. And then the next thing I knew, Tom came home and said he'd enlisted. He was almost seventeen then, which was under age. I laughed at him and told him I guessed he'd get as far as the state line maybe, but plagued if he didn't put it through, and off he marched with the 21st Ohio."

Indeed he did.

As Libbie recalled, Emanuel "had privately conferred with the local recruiting officer, and Tom was refused as under age."

However, undaunted, Tom tried again at Camp Vance, near Findlay, about 30 miles south of Tontogany. On September 2, 1861, having claimed to be eighteen, he was mustered into the 21st Regiment, Ohio Volunteer Infantry. As Libbie put it, "At sixteen he kissed the weeping mother and little sister Margaret, and was off to the wars."

He was not the only boy in America—North or South—to have aged a year or two that summer.

Tom Custer and a number of other Wood County men were assigned to the 21st's Company H, led initially by Captain Blackman, who was soon replaced by Captain Milo Caton. Also in the company was Christopher Grundy, who may have been a brother or cousin of Nancy Grundy, the wife of Tom's half brother, David Kirkpatrick. Grundy mustered in as a private on the same day as Tom, and would be promoted to sergeant in December 1863.

Another man who joined Company H on the same day as Tom was nineteen-year-old Liberty P. Warner, the son of Methodist Minister Henry Warner. Some of Liberty's Civil War–era correspondence with his parents, in which he mentions Tom Custer by name, is preserved in the collection of the Bowling Green State University Library in Bowling Green, Ohio.

The 21st Ohio had been activated just five months earlier on April 21, one of a host of Ohio regiments that were formed when the war began and President Lincoln called for 75,000 volunteers. As the units were filled with a sufficient number of young men to complete their rosters, more units were added. The 1st Ohio had been formed on April 17, three days after Fort Sumter fell. By the end of May, there were two dozen Ohio infantry regiments and several cavalry regiments. The 53rd Ohio was formed the day after Tom joined the 21st Ohio.

By coincidence, there was a man in the 21st Ohio who would later ride with Tom and Autie in the postwar 7th Cavalry, and who would be present at the Little Bighorn. Edward Settle Godfrey of Kalida, Ohio, was just seventeen when he lied about his age to join the 21st in April 1861. However, he mustered out in August after a three-month enlistment, a month before Tom joined, so they never crossed paths during the Civil War. Godfrey was admitted to West Point in 1863 and graduated in 1867.

As Captain Silas Canfield would later write in his definitive *History of the 21st Regiment, Ohio Volunteer Infantry in the War of Rebellion*, the regiment had been deactivated on August 10 after the men spent their three-month tour on the Ohio River warily watching Confederate troops on the Kentucky side.

The 21st Ohio, like many other regiments, had originally been activated on a three-month timetable under the prevailing theory that the war would be a brief one. After Bull Run in July 1861, however, it became clear that the Civil War would be anything but short.

When the regiment was reactivated in September, the term had increased from three months to three *years*. For the new batch of recruits, which now included Tom Custer, they would be in for a long haul within an organization which was developing a voracious appetite for new men.

"No medical examination was had to determine whether the men were sound or unsound," Canfield recalled of the urgency to enlist as many as possible. "If a man could use his arms and march well he passed. One man was about to be rejected on account of his teeth but on demonstrating his ability to tear a cartridge [using his teeth] he was retained."

When the 21st Ohio, commanded by Colonel Jesse S. Norton, was formally absorbed into the Regular US Army on September 19 at Camp Vance, Tom and the others were handed their blue uniforms. Several days later, they all boarded a train for Camp Dennison, outside Cincinnati. It was here that the men were issued their weapons and other gear.

In one of his letters home, Liberty Warner recalled that the train was traveling "at about the rate of 3 or 4 miles an hour, head car coming off the track 3 times. Some of the boys would go off and run along side of the train . . . On another track, changed engines and went like the wind. As we passed the citizen's towns everybody cheered and waved handkerchiefs. In some towns the Irish and Dutch wimmen would come out and fling their dirty dish soap, much to our amusement. When we arrived at Kenton we found a fine dinner spread out before us. We made no objection, so we filled our crops."

The role of the 21st Ohio in the overall Union strategy would be as one of the units that would march into Kentucky to counter moves being made by the Confederates there. The state, like the other "border" states, had declared itself neutral in the war, though there were strong factions supporting both the Union and Confederacy and pulling for the state to declare itself for one of the competing causes. Governor Beriah Magoffin had initially refused to furnish troops in response to Lincoln's call for volunteers. As the situation heated up, there were numerous small skirmishes,

and more than half of Kentucky's counties supported a shadow Confederate government. This was formed at a convention in October, and battle
lines were drawn.

On the second of October, Tom's regiment crossed the Ohio River and
marched 100 miles south into Kentucky, taking up a position at Nicholas-
ville, near Lexington. Here, they were assigned to a brigade being formed by
Major General William "Bull" Nelson, who now also had the 2nd, 33rd, and
59th Ohio Regiments under his command along with a battery of the 1st
Ohio Artillery. A Kentucky-born former US Navy officer, Nelson was a large
and imposing man whom Liberty Warner described as "a great fat fellow."

Canfield minced no words in his opinion of Nelson, describing him as
"haughty, dictational, overbearing and unfeeling toward his subordinates.
He would often give a harsh answer when a kind one would have answered
better . . . His manner to his inferiors in rank was what might have been
expected from a supercilious tyrannical master toward his slaves."

Nelson's combined force marched about 100 miles eastward toward the
valley of the Big Sandy River to confront the Confederate Army of Eastern
Kentucky. By now, 3,000 men this army had under Colonel John Stuart
Williams, had marched to the Big Sandy at Prestonsburg, Kentucky, and
were planning to continue westward into the state by way of Hazel Green.

"As I move along I find time to look about and see the country," Liberty
Warner wrote on October 18, giving his parents at home an idea of life on
the march with Tom Custer and the 21st Ohio. "I will tell you we are well
and harty [sic]. There has been no deaths, few accidents, and but little sickness. I am always well, can stand marching with any of them. We marched
15 or 16 miles day before yesterday. Some of the boys complained of sore
feet, my own being all right . . . We feed principally on sea-crackers hard
enough for sidewalk, at least they are hard. Plenty of side pork or beef
sometimes ham, plenty of coffy brown."

As Nelson's Big Sandy Expedition neared Hazel Green, about 80 road
miles east of Lexington, the 2nd Ohio had a brief skirmish with a

Confederate patrol, so Tom Custer and the men of the 21st made ready, sensing that their first contact with the enemy might be close. As Canfield recalled, "On the morning of the 23rd of October Colonel Norton ordered each Company commander to have his men carry their knapsacks and draw one thousand cartridges of the quartermaster but we entered Hazel Green in the evening without opposition. Here we were detained several days until supplies could be brought up."

Canfield also noted that while they were in Hazel Green, "the men were attacked with that scourge of camp life, diarrhea. Very few if any were exempt. All were complaining. The surgeon was overrun with patients and his medicine had little or no effect toward staying the plague."

On October 29, Liberty Warner wrote that he had been sick, but was well, adding that "we have just stopped a few days after a long march of seven days. We expect to go farther in a day or two . . . The officers and men think the war will be over by next spring, we'll be paid off and sent home. Some of the boys talk of getting home by Christmas, which I think is rather doubtful."

Indeed, the notion of being home for Christmas, which had been the consensus during the summer, had faded to wishful thinking by October.

The entire brigade moved out on the morning of November 1, marching toward the Big Sandy, which they planned to cross at Prestonsburg. As they began their march, they inquired locally about the distance and discovered that the people in the hills and hollars traveled so little, that none were sure how far it was to Prestonsburg. Canfield recalled that they encountered "one old gentleman whose hair was as white as the snow that covered the mountains in winter who lived in a cabin chucked against the foot of the mountain to get it out of the road."

When asked, he reckoned it was about 18 miles. In fact, it is about 44 road miles.

The 21st Ohio, with two other regiments in the vanguard of the brigade, reached the Big Sandy in a heavy downpour late in the afternoon of

November 6, arriving well ahead of their supply train. Despite the rain, Nelson ordered them to cross the river, and it was past midnight when they had finally made it, using a flatboat and a rope stretched across the river.

By the morning of November 8, it was raining hard and Tom Custer, Liberty Warner, and the men of the regiment were miserable. Beneath a heavy downpour, Nelson and his main column of 3,600 troops moved out in the direction of Pikeville, about 25 miles away. The objective was now to outflank elements of the Confederate Army of Eastern Kentucky.

Canfield recalled that early in the day, he was approached by a civilian who reported that "the rebels had fortified the side of Ivy Mountain four miles further on and intended to fight us there." The highest ground in the area, Ivy Mountain is a 1,000-foot hogback ridge about a half mile long that rises from the banks of the Big Sandy River. A reconnaissance team sent forward by Nelson observed that at the point where Gauley Creek flows off the mountain into the river, the enemy had burned the bridge across the creek and had constructed a stone barricade. Williams had positioned his men both on the side of the mountain and across the river to catch the Union troops in a crossfire.

Ivy Mountain was to be Tom Custer's first battle. Drawing his saber and leading from the front, Nelson used part of his force for a direct attack, while sending elements of the 21st Ohio Infantry up the mountain to outflank the enemy troops that were arrayed of the side. It was around 2:20 in the afternoon that Tom and his fellow solders reached the crest of Ivy Mountain and began rolling boulders down the hillside to scatter the Confederates.

Of the action of which Tom Custer was an integral part, Silas Canfield wrote that "the 21st without halting hastened up the end of the mountain approaching them on their right and rear . . . As soon as the 21st came in range it began firing into the enemy. The rebels fought us an hour and twenty minutes and then retreated precipitately down the end of the mountain and escaped."

Putting a positive spin on his defeat, Williams later asserted that Tom Custer and the others had merely routed an "unorganized and half-armed, barefooted squad that lacked everything, but the will to fight."

Though Ivy Mountain was an insignificant skirmish compared to what was to come, it made headlines in the North as a meaningful Union victory—and it had been Tom Custer's baptism of fire. He had experienced the thrill and terror of battle, emotions that would define much of the rest of his life.

Though the Confederate force withdrew, weather and road conditions compelled Nelson to halt his advance for the night. Casualty reports vary, but both sides apparently suffered losses in the low double digits. Two days later, as Nelson's brigade was closing in on Pikeville, they learned that Colonel Joshua Sill's 33rd Ohio Infantry, attacking from the north, had already secured the town.

Both sides expected that Nelson's brigade would pursue the enemy eastward as they retreated through Pound Gap into Virginia. However, this was not to be.

Apparently, the troops under Nelson's command conspired to sabotage any probability of their being ordered to undertake a November pursuit across the Appalachians. As Canfield later admitted, "Shortly after dark, the Surgeon of the 21st Ohio (and it was said the Surgeons of the other regiments did the same) came around and requested Company Commanders to report as many sick as possible. The reason for this was said to be General Nelson ordered the brigade to be in readiness to march the next morning at four o'clock, and the Surgeons reported the regiment not in condition to march to prevent it from going on a winter campaign into Virginia."

Indeed, given that many had not recovered from the dysentery that had dogged the troops since Hazel Green, such a campaign could have proven disastrous.

In the meantime, General Don Carlos Buell had succeeded William Tecumseh Sherman as commander of the Department of the

Ohio—which included Kentucky—and he ordered Nelson's brigade to withdraw into winter quarters to regroup.

The 21st Ohio reached Louisville on November 24. Many were still sick from dysentery, and there had been a widespread outbreak of measles on the return march. Canfield wrote that "the sanitary condition of the regiment at this time was bad . . . and the new cases of sickness that developed after arriving at Louisville had greatly diminished the number present for duty. I find no statistics by which to determine the strength of the regiment."

On top of this, they found themselves bivouacked with new, barely trained and very undisciplined recent recruits. Liberty Warner wrote that "it is a hard place here, for I suppose you know the scrapings of the world are collected here. I for one keep clear of it."

On December 18, the regiment went into winter quarters in Camp Jefferson at Bacon Creek (now Bonnieville), about 70 miles south of Louisville. Here, as Liberty Warner wrote to his brother on January 10, the Tontogany boys were bunking together and doing well.

Mentioning both Tom Custer and Christopher Grundy by name, he wrote that they had "received our new tents yesterday. They are well ditched around and we have plenty of straw inside. We have got a nice little stove that can afford to keep us warm. And we have plenty to eat. We draw rations of hard crackers, pickled pork, sugar, coffee, rice, salt, and occasionally potatoes, beans, vinegar, etc. When we were on the mountains we drew rations of milk when ever we come acrost any cows. We have not quite forgotten how to do it yet. I got a good dose of milk the last time I was on picket guard."

He added that "I do not know how long we shall stay here. It may be a good while."

It would be.

CHAPTER 5

TOM CUSTER'S LONG YEAR'S ROAD TO STONES RIVER

TOM CUSTER, LIBERTY Warner, Christopher Grundy, and the "Tontogany Boys" of Company H greeted the start of 1862 in winter quarters at Bacon Creek, Kentucky, where they languished for nearly three cold and damp months, waiting for the war to resume.

That depressing dampness and bone chilling coldness was an easy metaphor for the general mood within the United States and within the regiments and battalions of its Union Army. Ohio and Kentucky were overshadowed by what was happening in the East, and on the war's preeminent battlefront the news had not been so good.

In the summer of 1861, everyone spoke confidently of the war being over by Christmas. The three-month enlistments that the new recruits were given in the spring and summer were indicative of this optimism. However, after Major General Irvin McDowell's force was routed by the Confederates at Bull Run in July, there was a sense that the optimism had been misplaced. If the Union leadership and the population of the North had once seriously believed the war would be over by Christmas, they no longer did. Both sides spent their holiday season preparing for 1862 and a war that they realized could be a long one.

While Tom had seen action, the skirmishes in the West had been small ones. His older brother had first experienced combat at Bull Run, the signature field battle of 1861. With around 70,000 troops involved, and around 40,000 actively engaged, Bull Run had captured the attention of the press and public, while the campaigns in Kentucky were back page news, if that. George Armstrong Custer was with the 2nd US Cavalry Regiment at Bull Run, and while he *saw* the action he did not really experience it. He had watched as the great armies maneuvered. He had heard the cacophony and he had smelled smoke. His Company G was ordered to prepare for a cavalry charge to curb a Confederate move against Captain Charles Griffin's Battery D of the 5th United States Artillery, but the threat was perceived to have receded and the order to charge never came. By the time the Union Army realized that the Confederates had turned the tide, the only thing that McDowell could do was order his cavalrymen to help protect a general retreat by his entire force.

In the aftermath of Bull Run, as Tom was preparing to lie about his age to join the 21st Ohio, the 2nd US Cavalry was redesignated as the 5th US Cavalry, and Autie's Company G was attached to Brigadier General Philip Kearny's New Jersey Brigade. Under Kearney, though still a second lieutenant, Autie had served briefly as a staff officer, and he later had been detailed to serve as a courier for General McDowell. By the time that Tom was in his first battle at Ivy Mountain in November, Autie had departed Virginia on a furlough that would remove him from the battlefield until March 1862.

Coincidentally, Tom and the Tontogany Boys finally departed Bacon Creek on March 3, 1862, having spent the winter in camp, and not back home like Tom's officer brother. By now, the US Army's Department of the Ohio (later the Army of the Ohio), under Major General Don Carlos Buell, had been reorganized. Within it, the 21st Regiment, Ohio Volunteer

Infantry was assigned to the 9th Brigade which also contained the 2nd and 33rd Ohio, as well as the 10th Wisconsin Regiments commanded by Colonel (soon to be Brigadier General) Joshua Woodrow Sill. In turn, Sill's 9th Brigade was a component of the new 3rd Division of the Army of the Ohio, under Brigadier General Ormsby Mitchel.

In the fall of 1861, the 21st Ohio had been a defensive pawn on the chessboard of Kentucky. In the spring of 1862, it seemed to all as though they would be at last on the offensive, but the action for which they yearned would prove elusive. By the time they crossed the Cumberland River and marched through Nashville, it was already occupied, having been the first Confederate state capital captured by Union troops. Aside from reacting to occasional hit and run rains by Texas Rangers, who operated like a guerilla band, Tom and his regiment saw no combat.

In a letter home from Murfreesboro dated March 29, Liberty Warner complained of the Rangers, writing that these men who "bring up the rear of the rebel army. They burn or otherwise destroy everything that could be of any possible use to us. They lurk continually about the country, thieving about and watching the chance to slip in to our camp and spy."

As the regiment moved south toward Alabama, resistance was light and usually nonexistent. During the first week of April, the 21st Ohio marched 25 miles to Shelbyville, Tennessee, where they were—to their amazement—greeted warmly by the pro-Union citizenry. On April 11, the Union troops occupied Huntsville, Alabama, virtually without firing a shot. As at Shelbyville, Union sympathy ran high, and there was little enthusiasm for active resistance. The life of the men of the 21st Ohio, and the whole 3rd Division, was more like postwar occupation duty than what they had expected when the year began.

In early April, as General Mitchel's 3rd Division was enjoying their strange, almost eerie, detachment from the war, 150 miles to the west in Hardin County, Tennessee, 100,000 men were engulfed in the vast Battle of Shiloh, which would prove to be the bloodiest battle—to date—in

American history. Meanwhile in Virginia, George Armstrong Custer and his 5th US Cavalry were part of the Peninsula Campaign by the Army of the Potomac under Major General George B. McClellan. Autie himself even spent a month from early April to early May as an aide to McClellan.

In the war's western theater, Tom and the 21st Ohio saw nothing of the great battles that were taking place near them. At the end of April 1862, as 65,000 Confederates under General P.G.T. Beauregard were surrounded by twice as many Federals under General Henry Halleck at Corinth, Mississippi, the 21st Ohio was 100 miles away and might well have been on peacetime maneuvers.

From Huntsville on April 19, Liberty Warner had written that "the 21st will neither see Corinth nor battle without we are attacked. Our boys are fighting at Corinth like bulldogs. The slaughter is great on both sides. The news of victory sounds beautiful on the ear of a soldier . . . The forests are all clothed in green and a beautiful summer is already broke upon us. We pick greens and get onions, so we have a change of diet. I caught about 100 fish out of a little run."

A break from the routine came on April 23 when Warner, along with Tom Custer and other men of Company H, were detailed to escort a number of prisoners to the north.

"About fifty of them wanted to take the oath of allegiance and be permitted to go home but General Mitchel refused to let any go home that lived outside of territory not in our possession," Silas Canfield recalled. "Several from Kentucky and Tennessee were permitted to return home. Occasionally one would make an effort to appear cheerful but as a rule they were sober and quite crestfallen."

Canfield recalled that as the 21st Ohio marched into Athens, Alabama, on May 28, two citizens approached him and "complimented the officers and men of the 21st Ohio in high terms upon the reputation which had preceded them from Huntsville and pointing out their residences assured us their houses were open to the officers during the stay of the regiment in Athens."

Two days later, Liberty Warner wrote that "parts of the Division skirmish now and then with the enemy, but nothing of any consequence has transpired yet. And what is more, I do not know that there is any chance for it, although we would jump at the chance of getting a hack at them. The sesech [secessionist] cavalry keeps fooling around. They will get in a bumblebee's nest yet some of these days. Our boys would have no mercy on them at all in any case they should get them in their powers . . . There is talk of taking some men out of the Regiment and mounting them on horses to pursue those cowardly thieves."

Demonstrating his impatience with the lack of combat duty, he continued by saying that "we are beginning to get tired of this thing. It has hung on until we are now in fighting order and now we want to fight. We feel as if we had hung around the table some time and now we want to eat. If there is any fighting, we are ready. We have loaded our guns too long." It had to have been especially frustrating for Tom Custer, knowing that his big brother was in the thick of the action in Virginia.

Over the summer, Colonel Jesse Norton was replaced at the head of the 21st Ohio by his former second in command, Lieutenant Colonel James M. Neibling. He was in charge when General Buell ordered a number of units, including the 21st, to pull back to Nashville to defend the city against possible action by General Braxton Bragg's Confederate Army of Mississippi.

Canfield wrote that as they moved north on August 29, "the bushwhackers were upon us and our immunity from rebel attack was ended, but we saved our wagon trains and arrived at Nashville on the 2nd of September."

The 21st Ohio again made contact with the enemy on the evening of October 6 about 5 miles south of Nashville. As the Confederates withdrew after the initial clash, the Ohio men gave chase, running into a considerable enemy force at LaVergne. Canfield recalled that "a sharp skirmish ensued but the enemy were driven. They made another stand before we reached the position assigned us but the delays caused by the attacks delayed the column so that most of the enemy escaped. In this affair which consisted of several brilliant skirmishes the enemy lost forty to fifty killed and wounded."

By contrast, Tom's older brother had just been with McClellan through the Battle of Antietam, in Maryland, on September 17, the bloodiest single day's battle in United States history. The combined casualty toll had exceeded 22,000.

Amid the autumn leaves, Liberty Warner and Tom Custer at last had the opportunity to "get a hack at" the enemy that had been nipping at their heels for months. After LaVergne, the 21st Ohio was involved in a series of engagements in the 10 miles that separated Nashville from Wilson's Bend on the Columbia River.

November brought a reorganization of Union forces in the area. Buell was replaced at the head of the Union Army of the Ohio by Major General William Rosecrans, who straightaway renamed it the Army of the Cumberland. Within this organization, the 21st Ohio, along with the 37th Indiana, the 74th Ohio, and the 78th Pennsylvania, were combined into the 3rd Brigade under Colonel John F. Miller. In turn, the 3rd Brigade was part of the 2nd Division, commanded by Brigadier General James Scott Negley.

Meanwhile, Braxton Bragg had reorganized his own Confederate Army of Mississippi as the Army of Tennessee, and gathered—by Bragg's own accounting—37,712 troops in the vicinity of Murfreesboro in preparation for a major assault on Nashville. On the day after Christmas, Rosecrans led the 43,400 troops of the Army of the Cumberland, organized into three columns to confront him.

Nagged by Confederate skirmishers and by cold, thick ground fog, the 21st Ohio, as part of Negley's 2nd Division, marched in the center of the three columns, covering the same ground that they had traveled nine months earlier in the sunny days of early spring. For Tom Custer, Liberty Warner, Christopher Grundy, and the Tontogany Boys, it was a dreary reminder of the cold and damp of Bacon Creek and winter quarters, and of the fact that they had now marched for nearly a year without a major battle.

At first light on the morning of December 31, just a few miles from Murfreesboro, on the banks of the West Fork of the Stones River, which meandered through the battlefield, Rosecrans finalized plans to strike the Confederate right flank. But Bragg struck first, launching a powerful attack, first against the Union right, then across the whole line.

After nearly fourteen months of seeing only occasional combat action, Tom Custer was suddenly thrust into his first major battle since Ivy Mountain in November 1861, and one of the biggest battles of the war to date.

"A cornfield was in front of the 21st Ohio," recalled Silas Canfield of their position at around 8 a.m. when the battle was joined, "and as soon as the rebels came in range, the infantry opened a deadly fire on them. More persistent courage on the one hand, or greater coolness on the other could hardly be displayed . . . Men fell at every step and still they pressed forward."

The cornfield was to the north of the Wilkinson Turnpike, about 4 miles northwest of Murfreesboro, and roughly half a mile west of the river. With their backs to a cedar forest, Tom Custer and the 21st Ohio now faced the 2nd Division of the Confederate Army of Tennessee on Polk's right wing, commanded by Major General Jones M. Withers.

Regarding the regiment's closing in on the Confederate line, Canfield wrote, "When the enemy was only about thirty yards distant the order was given to fix bayonets but about this time they broke and fled followed by a volley as a parting salute. It was said the bayonets were used on some parts of the line but not on the left of the regiment. Our front clear we had a chance to view the ghastly sight."

Through the day, Bragg made considerable progress, pushing the Union right back, though not overrunning it, and compressing it into the Union center where the 21st Ohio was positioned. As Canfield explained, "The enemy having passed us on both flanks, Colonel Neibling called out, 'Fall back, we are surrounded.' How we got back through the cedars, I can never tell except that we walked, we didn't run."

Tom and the Tontogany Boys spent New Year's Eve and the following day only about a mile north of where they had begun the battle, having withdrawn north to the Nashville Turnpike (later Nashville Highway) where it ran close to the Nashville & Chattanooga Railroad. On the Union right, meanwhile, Major General Alexander McCook's three divisions had been pushed back around 10 miles.

As the new year began, both Rosecrans and Bragg thought the Confederates were winning. There was some thought given to a Union retreat, but Rosecrans knew the battle was not yet finished.

Licking their wounds after taking considerable losses, neither side undertook any major action on the first day of 1863, and it was not until 4:00 on the afternoon of January 2 that the battle resumed. Preceded by an artillery barrage, Confederate Major General John C. Breckinridge led an assault against the Union left flank, commanded by Major General Thomas Crittenden. They overwhelmed Brigadier General Horatio P. Van Cleve's 3rd Division, which anchored the Union line along the West Fork of the Stones River. The day before, Tom and the 21st Ohio had been positioned about a mile west and across the river from the scene of the Breckenridge assault, with Brigadier General Thomas J. Wood's 1st Division between them and the west bank of the river. However, they had been pulled out to guard a supply train, and missed the initial Confederate attack.

As Canfield recalled, the Union troops east of the river "terrified at the onslaught of the rebels, delivered their fire and retreated in haste and great disorder. Men and horses a commingled mob, horses with riders and horses without, men with guns and men without all, making haste to escape the enemy pursuing vigorously and pouring a destructive fire into the retreating mass."

"My God," said Colonel Neibling. "It was the most heartrending sight I ever saw."

Meanwhile, General Negley and Colonel Miller shifted troops from the center to staunch the hemorrhage. This included Tom Custer's regiment, which the day before had enjoyed a respite from the line, having been picked to guard the supply train. Now, they found themselves fording the bitter cold river to place themselves in front of a Confederate charge that was rampaging down upon them from the high ground above.

In Canfield's recollection, Negley and Miller endeavored to "instill calm courage into the men, Colonel Neibling instructing the 21st Ohio to measure out the sulphurous regions to the rebels by the acre, and Colonel Moody urging the 74th Ohio not to be out done by the 21st." Supported by Union artillery, the 21st and 74th succeeded in halting Breckinridge's advance.

Tom Custer had not tasted victory, but he shared in the satisfaction of having prevented the other side from savoring one.

On January 3, as the battle continued, reinforcements and supply trains reached Rosecrans from Nashville, replenishing some of the heavy losses suffered over the preceding days. Among the front line units relieved by fresh troops was the exhausted 21st Ohio. By the end of the day, Bragg, who had no such reserves to reinforce his depleted command, realized that the battle was lost and began the Confederate withdrawal.

On January 5, Rosecrans reoccupied Murfreesboro, but chose not to pursue the retreating Bragg, allowing him and his army to fight again another day. Strategically, however, the battle ensured that Nashville, as a major transportation hub, would remain under Union control for the remainder of the Civil War.

Of the 21st Ohio at Stones River, General Negley of the 2nd Division wrote that "without a murmur they made forced marches over almost impassable roads, through drenching winter rains, without a change of clothing or blankets, deprived of sleep or repose, constantly on duty for eleven days, living three days on a pint of flour and parched corn. Ever vigilant, always sacrificing their lives with a contempt of peril, displaying the coolness, determination and high discipline of veterans, they are entitled to our country's gratitude."

The total number of casualties on the two sides at Stones River was around 24,000, or around thirty-one percent of the troops engaged, with battle deaths numbering around 3,000. The official casualty figures for the 21st Ohio were twenty-one killed in action, 109 wounded—including Liberty Warner—and twenty-six missing.

After fifteen months in uniform, Liberty Warner and Tom Custer had seen their first large-scale battle. The experience haunted Warner's nightmares.

"Oh, the scenes of blood that I have seen," he would write on January 31. "I wish that they could cease, not that I fear it, but it so hardens a person, a dead man seems no more than a dead sheep or a log of wood."

If Tom Custer wrote a similar letter home describing his impressions of this massive conflagration, it does not survive.

CHAPTER 6

MONROE

In 1863, as Tom Custer and the 21st Ohio Infantry marched forth from the aftermath of Stones River, there began a series of changes at home. Indeed, these changes would culminate in a new definition of "home" as it applied to the Custer family. Before the year was out, and before Tom once again set foot north of the Ohio, his parents and younger siblings had moved from Ohio to Monroe, Michigan. The city that was home to Lydia Ann Reed, and the adopted home of George Armstrong Custer—though he had not actually lived there since he was a schoolboy—would henceforth be the nexus of the Custer family narrative.

Located in southeastern Michigan about a dozen miles north of the Ohio line, Monroe lies on the shore of Lake Erie and straddles the river that the Potawatomi people named Nummasepee, meaning River of Sturgeon. When French voyageurs came through in the early seventeenth century, they noticed the wild grapes along the shore and named it Riviere aux Raisins. Two centuries later, it was anglicized as the River Raisin and so it remains to this day. Present-day Monroe County was formed in 1817 and named for President James Monroe, who is said to have visited the area that year. The town of Monroe was platted in 1817 as part of the area around Navarre's original settlement which was known as Frenchtown for obvious reasons. Monroe was officially reincorporated as a city in 1837, the same year that Michigan achieved statehood.

Maria Ward Custer's daughter, Lydia Ann, had moved to Monroe in 1846 after having married David Reed. George Armstrong Custer had later lived with her while he was attending the Stebbins Academy in Monroe, and it was here that he met, albeit fleetingly, Elizabeth Clift "Libbie" Bacon, his future bride. By the time that he went off to West Point in 1857, Autie found himself drawn to Monroe, having lost interest in Rural Ohio. Lydia Ann, meanwhile, was already trying to coax Emanuel and Maria Custer to relocate to Monroe.

In October 1861, as winter drew near and as Tom was going into winter quarters in Kentucky, Autie came home from the battlefronts of Virginia. The "home" he chose was the Reed house in Monroe—*not* Emanuel and Maria's homestead on Tontogany Creek in rural Ohio. His biographers all mention that Autie was on sick leave, though there is no explanation of the malady, and his activities while on leave do not seem to be those of someone with a serious illness.

This October homecoming, in the crisp air beneath the kaleidoscope of autumn foliage, is remembered for the first of two major winter furlough turning points in Autie's life. Having met some friends at a tavern, Autie became appallingly drunk, and had to be helped back to Lydia Ann's home where he was staying. As the story goes, she closed the door, opened her Bible and delivered a homily of such convincing magnitude that it resulted in his pledging never to take another drink as long as he lived. It was to be a promise kept.

The second Monroe turning point in Autie's life, a year later, would involve Libbie Bacon. Her father, Daniel Stanton Bacon, was one of Monroe's most prominent citizens. He had arrived in the county from upstate New York in 1822. An ambitious man, he maintained an orchard, taught school, and studied law. Beginning in 1832 he was elected to a series of county offices. He even served in the territorial legislature. In 1837, the year of Michigan statehood, Bacon married 23-year-old Eleanor Sophia Page and became president of the Merchants & Mechanics Bank. In 1840, two years before Libbie was born, Daniel Bacon was elected as a Circuit Court Judge.

When Libbie was about nine years old, her parents enrolled her in the Young Ladies' Seminary and Collegiate Institute, a boarding school for girls, from which she graduated in June 1862.

Founded in 1828 by Reverend Erasmus James Boyd, the Boyd Seminary is important to the Custer family story because one of things that drew Emanuel and Maria into finally relocating to Monroe in 1863 would be to enroll daughter Margaret in the school. As Lydia Ann had actively lobbied Maria to let Autie attend the Stebbins Academy, she did the same for Maggie and the Boyd Seminary. As Custer scholar Dr. Lawrence Frost wrote, "It took more than two years to convince hardheaded Father Custer he could do better in Michigan . . . it took an offer to send sister Margaret to the Boyd Seminary." It took an offer to pay her tuition.

Monroe suited George Armstrong Custer—and by 1862, as his prominence as an overnight war hero began to emerge, it became apparent that he suited Monroe. He was making a name for himself. In the spring of 1862, during the Peninsula Campaign, he served as an aide to Major General George Brinton McClellan, who commanded the Army of the Potomac. In May, he led four companies of the 4th Michigan Infantry in a daring reconnaissance mission across the Chickahominy River that saw the first capture of a Confederate battle flag in the war. This earned him a temporary promotion to captain, but it was only the first of a long series of actions that would establish his reputation for daring and initiative—as well as recklessness.

In November 1862, after Antietam and the March to Warrenton, as things began to quiet down for the winter, Autie went home on furlough. As was the case the winter before, "home" did not mean Tontogany Creek, but a holiday season with Lydia Ann and David Reed on the River Raisin.

By now, he had fully embraced his Michigan identity to the extent that an important part of his ambitious career plan for the coming year involved securing command of a Michigan volunteer cavalry unit.

His homecoming being the cusp of the holiday season, there were receptions and soirees being organized, and young officers home for the holidays in their blue uniforms were in high demand as guests at these events. Captain—albeit *brevet* Captain—George Armstrong Custer, as an aide to General McClellan, was certainly high on this list.

Brevet rank involved temporary, rather than permanent, promotions in rank given to officers temporarily serving in positions designated for higher-ranking officers. In many cases, the officer would receive the pay and allowances of his brevet rank as long as he held the assignment for which he was brevetted, after which he would revert to his permanent rank and pay grade. During the Civil War, many officers, Autie included, received promotions that took them several grades above their permanent ranks.

Custer biographers Lawrence Frost and Frederick Whittaker both made much of the irony of a blacksmith's son being catapulted into Monroe's high society. Whittaker commented that "Monroe was beginning to forgive 'Captain' Custer for not being born with a silver spoon in his mouth." In fact, far from having to "forgive" him, Monroe society had probably never even *noticed* him previously.

One of the holiday parties, held around the time of Thanksgiving, was hosted by Reverend Erasmus Boyd and his wife at their Young Ladies' Seminary. It was naturally attended by numerous recent graduates who naturally had their eyes on the handsome young officers with their sparkling brass buttons—just as the young officers had their eyes on the attractive young maidens of Monroe high society. Among the latter was the daughter of Judge Daniel Bacon.

It was the first time that she and Autie had spoken since that perhaps mythical encounter about eight years earlier when a twelve-year-old Libbie had shouted, "Hello, you Custer boy!"

In a later letter written by Libbie and shared with Marguerite Merington, there is a suggestion that David Reed may have arranged the introduction that night, though some authors suggest that the Reeds and Bacons were not in the same social circles, being Methodists and Presbyterians, respectively. Nevertheless, they were neighbors on the same street and Monroe was not so big as to preclude contact.

It was Conway "Connie" Noble, a contemporary and one-time would-be suitor of Libbie's—and whose sister Laura was one of Libbie's closest friends—who made the actual introduction. When he asked, "Shall I introduce Captain Custer?" Libbie would admit that "I assented merely to be rid of him . . . for I had taken refuge in 'Greenland's icy mountains.'"

"I believe your promotion has been very rapid?" Libbie asked, making small talk.

"I have been very fortunate," Custer replied.

As he would later recall in florid prose, "My heart could have told her of a promotion far more rapid in her power only to bestow. How I watched her every motion, and when she left . . . in that throng of youth and beauty she had reigned supreme . . . when she left Armstrong Custer went home to dream . . . I was not ignorant of her father's proclivities, of the well-nigh insurmountable obstacles."

Though it was off to a slow start, this began the romance, marked by the gradual wearing down of her father's disapproval, that led to their marriage and to Libbie's becoming a sort of Custer family scribe, responsible for a great many insights into the lives of other family members, especially Tom.

Nevin Custer had also been courting. By the time that Autie reconnected with Libbie in the soiree season of 1862, Nevin was a newlywed. "I got to know Ann North pretty well—her father's farm ran close to ours." Nevin Custer said of his wife. "I married her when I was twenty. Folks married younger then, yuh know."

Born on November 12, 1843, in Tontogany, Ann was the daughter of William L. North and Matilda Skinner North, who had come west from south central Pennsylvania earlier in the century.

Having failed in his efforts to enlist in the grand cause of the Civil War, Nevin was the first of the Custer boys to be married. The wedding took place on October 30, 1862, as Tom was skirmishing with Texas Rangers south of Nashville and as Autie was campaigning in Maryland in the wake of the Battle of Antietam.

Emanuel and Maria probably attended the wedding, though the Wood County Library has no newspapers from this time period in which to look up an item about the nuptials. A record does exist of the oath that Emanuel swore on October 28 to confirm that Nevin and Ann were not first cousins and could therefore legally marry.

Nevin and Ann settled down on the farm previously owned by a man named George Fulmer, which was located immediately to the north of Emanuel and Maria's place on Tontogany Creek. Their first child, Claribel Custer, was born in New Rumley on September 5, 1863, not far from where both Nevin and Ann had been born.

It was in 1863 that Emanuel and Maria finally made the move to Monroe. Citing correspondence between Lydia Ann and Autie in his own collection, Lawrence Frost suggests that the two had been working together for some time to nudge the older Custers toward Monroe.

"With the older boys gone, their parents were not doing too well on their farm," observed Frost. "George had been trying to induce them to move to Monroe County and buy a farm there, so he wrote Ann. The country wasn't as pretty as it was in the rolling farmlands of Harrison County, for Monroe could offer no hills. It could offer soil that was highly productive, and it was near the Reeds."

Wrote Autie, "I am thinking of them and always have an anxiety and fear that they will not be able to buy a farm where they can get along comfortably." This correspondence, which had begun while George Armstrong Custer was a West Point cadet, continued after he was commissioned, and as he saw action in the first battles of the Civil War.

Nevin's having moved on to a farm of his own probably caused Emanuel to think twice about continuing to operate his own farm, but Lydia Ann's continued lobbying for 11-year-old Maggie to attend Erasmus Boyd's Seminary was probably the catalyst.

Lydia Ann and her husband even went so far to help Emanuel and Maria financially in making the move. In a letter to Autie cited by Lawrence Frost, Emanuel wrote, "You know that place we looked at for $1,000. We bought it for $800, $600 down and $200 borrowed from David Reed." Their previous residence, the farm on Tontogany Creek, was not sold until two years later. Presumably, without David Reed's loan, the move would not have been possible.

The price of their new two-story home on the northeast corner of Third and Cass Streets in Monroe came as a bit of a shock to Emanuel. In another letter to Autie, his father complained that "Monroe is an expensive place to live. Greenbacks do not go far."

Apparently, after their parents moved to Monroe, fourteen-year-old Boston Custer spent at least part of his time helping his older brother on his farm in Wood County, Ohio.

"It was a dead old time on the farm during the war," Nevin recalled in 1910. "Boston and I did the chores and spent our spare time looking for news from the front. Course we read how Autie was tearing things up and how he'd been made captain and put on General McClellan's staff. He was a great boy to write letters home and I tell yuh we certainly read 'em, those days."

CHAPTER 7
HOMETOWN HEROES

THERE HAD BEEN no Christmas goose for Tom Custer in 1862, only salt pork and hardtack. He had not seen a family Christmas since 1860. Unlike those which Autie was attending, there were no New Year's Eve soirees with punch and brandy for Tom to greet the arrival of 1863, only the vicious bloodbath at Stones River.

"There is a condition of depression and enervation which come upon men after a great battle that took possession of our regiment when it went into camp after Stones River," wrote Silas Canfield of the state of morale in the 21st Ohio Infantry in the cold and gloomy early days of 1863. "The scenes of death and desolation which had been witnessed, together with hardships and privations of the campaign, crowded hard upon patriotism."

Though Stones River was seen in the long term as a strategic victory, it was then perceived as a tactical draw. The Union troops were in possession of the battlefield, the textbook definition of victory, but Braxton Bragg's Army of Tennessee had escaped intact with no greater rate of casualties than had been suffered by William Rosecrans's Union Army of the Cumberland.

Both morale and discipline problems dogged the men of the 21st Ohio as they wiled away their time in winter quarters at Murfreesboro. Even with a trickle of replacements, the regiment's personnel strength ebbed to 593 in February 1863, down from 718 a year earlier and 696 before Stones

River. The cold and damp of the winter in a crucible of infectious disease added to the list of those unfit for combat. Liberty Warner was in a hospital in New Albany, Indiana until March. Payroll records, meanwhile, indicate that Tom Custer's Company H had the lowest number of men present, just nineteen, compared to a regimental average of twenty-six.

By late April, that number was reduced by one. Tom Custer was moving on.

Out of the shadows of the Stones River aftermath, Tom had emerged into the light of the favor of Brigadier General James Negley. He commanded the 2nd Division of General George Thomas's XIV Corps, of which the 21st Ohio was a component.

It was on April 20 that the general invited the infantry private out of the ranks, put him on a horse and ordered him to serve as his personal courier. Though still on the roster of the 21st Ohio, Tom Custer would now find himself in a very different kind of war. Instead of marching as part of his regiment, or at least a company-strength unit, he worked more or less alone.

It is the aspiration of soldiers, indeed of members of any hierarchical organization, to be noticed with approval by those of higher rank. And so it was for Tom Custer with Negley. Years later, in a letter to Tom's sister-in-law, Libbie Custer, Negley would bear "testimony in unstinted words to the courage and fidelity of the lad," and call him "a splendid soldier."

Meanwhile, Tom called Negley "a huge, handsome man who radiated good will without losing firmness."

At Stones River, Negley's 2nd Division had been in the center of XIV Corps. In June 1863, it was in the vanguard of the XIV Corps—still part of Rosecrans's Army of the Cumberland—in a Union offensive known as the Tullahoma, or Middle Tennessee, Campaign. The objective was to drive southeast from Nashville, through Tullahoma, toward Chattanooga and into northwestern Georgia. The objective was to defeat General Braxton Bragg's Confederate Army of Tennessee, or at least push it out of the state.

The Tullahoma Campaign was an immense tactical success. President Abraham Lincoln wrote that "the flanking of Bragg at Shelbyville, Tullahoma and Chattanooga is the most splendid piece of strategy I know of."

General David Stanley of IV Corps—with whom the Custers would cross paths in the West in 1873—wrote that "if any student of the military art desires to make a study of a model campaign, let him take his maps and General Rosecrans's orders for the daily movements of his campaign. No better example of successful strategy was carried out during the war than in the Tullahoma campaign." It was Tom Custer who carried these orders for the daily movements between Rosecrans and Negley.

Of course, the Tullahoma Campaign must be mentioned in the context of the wider war, for it concluded in the first week of July, and therefore coincided with two of the greatest Union victories of the year, and arguably of the Civil War. These were Ulysses S. Grant's victory at Vicksburg on July 4, and George Meade's decisive defeat of Robert E. Lee the day before at Gettysburg. While Tom rode with orders for Negley, his older brother, recently promoted to brevet brigadier general, led the spectacular cavalry charges that made him a hero and earned him the undying attention of the national media.

Unfortunately, in the glow of Vicksburg, Gettysburg, and the "most splendid" victory in the Tullahoma Campaign, there came a stunning Union defeat. Rosecrans paused rather than pursuing Bragg into the north Georgia mountains, allowing the Confederate general time to regroup.

September saw a rematch in which Bragg launched his counteroffensive from northwestern Georgia toward Chattanooga. The Confederates outmaneuvered Negley's 2nd Division, including Tom Custer's 21st Ohio, almost trapped them at a place called McLemore's Cove, then swept past them on September 11. The two armies met in the Battle of Chickamauga, which took place between September 18 and 20 on Chickamauga Creek, a few miles from Chattanooga. The battle forced Rosecrans to retreat into defensive positions in Chattanooga, and resulted in the biggest Union defeat in the West during the Civil War.

Among the 1,657 Union solders who died in the Chickamauga was Tom Custer's old friend and comrade, his fellow "Tontogany Boy" from Company H, Liberty Warner. The man whose letters home have provided such a vivid picture of life inside the 21st Ohio during the first year and a half of the war, would pick up his pen no more. Liberty Warner, who might have gone on to be one of the remembered chroniclers of the Civil War, was one of just eleven men from the 21st Ohio to be lost at Chickamauga.

Rosecrans was relieved from his command after Chickamauga, and so too was Negley—after his 2nd Division collapsed into disarray on September 19 during the height of the battle.

In the aftermath, General Ulysses S. Grant assumed command of all Union forces in the West. Having sacked Rosecrans, he replaced him with General George Thomas, who had become known as the "Rock of Chickamauga" when his XIV Corps stood its ground during the general Union collapse at the Battle of Chickamauga. Grant's subsequent Chattanooga Campaign, which culminated in the Union victory in the Battle of Missionary Ridge on November 25, reversed the setback at Chickamauga and left the Union in undisputed control of Tennessee.

As Grant prepared for the climax of the campaign at Missionary Ridge, young Private Thomas Ward Custer, the former courier for the discredited Negley, was assigned to ride as Grant's escort. Nothing is known of Tom's personal interactions with Grant, as his brief time with the general is known only from a line in his service record and in a secondhand mention by Emanuel Custer in a January 1864 letter to Autie that was shared with me by George A. Custer IV. However, Negley carried memories of the teenage private for decades. In the 1880s, he recalled Tom in a conversation with Libbie Custer, after which she reported that "he went back over twenty years and told me what a splendid soldier he had found our Tom. The praise one brave man gives another, irrespective of station, shone from his eyes, while he bore testimony in unstinted words to the courage and fidelity of the lad."

As Tom Custer's fifth magnitude star was now in its ascendancy, lifting him out of the ranks to rub shoulders with greatness, the first magnitude star of George Armstrong Custer shone more brightly than anyone who watched him depart for West Point in 1857 could possibly have imagined. His exploits in combat, meticulously considered despite the appearance of foolhardiness, had earned him both a stellar reputation among his fellow soldiers, as well as media notoriety. His triumphs against the odds had led to the coining of the phrase "Custer's luck" to explain his impossibly avoiding death on numerous occasions. Wearing colorful uniforms and a foppish hat, and with his mustached face framed by his long reddish blond hair, he was hardly one to go unnoticed—either while leading his troops into battle or being considered as potential copy by war reporters.

In June 1863, while Tom was embarking on the Tullahoma Campaign, his brother was 500 miles to the northeast in the Shenandoah Valley in pursuit of Robert E. Lee's Army of Northern Virginia as the Confederates marched into Maryland bound for a daring drive into Pennsylvania. By this time, Autie had come under the wing of Major General Alfred Pleasonton, one of two general officers—the other would be Philip Sheridan—who became important mentors, and who would do a great deal to advance his professional career. Pleasonton had seen Autie in action, and appreciative of his aggressive determination and boundless energy, made him an aide.

"I do not believe a father could love his son more than General Pleasanton loves me," Autie wrote to Nettie Humphrey, a friend of Libbie's in Monroe who had become his pen pal. "He is as solicitous about me and *my* safety as a mother about her only child. You should see how gladly he welcomes me on *my* return from each battle."

He went on to say that Pleasonton's usual greeting after a skirmish was, "Well, boy, I am glad to see you back. I was *anxious about you.*"

In June 1863, in the wake of the Union defeat in the Battle of Chancellorsville in May, Pleasonton was named to replace Brigadier General George Stoneman as commander of the Army of the Potomac Cavalry Corps. In turn, Pleasonton named Autie to command the 2nd Cavalry Brigade of the Corps' 3rd Division. Composed of the 1st, 5th, 6th, and 7th Michigan Cavalry regiments, as well as a battery from the 2nd United States Artillery, the brigade was known as the Michigan Cavalry Brigade or simply as the "Wolverines," after the Michigan state mascot. Having yearned to lead a volunteer cavalry regiment from his adopted home state of Michigan, he now commanded not one, but *four.*

With this command, the fresh-faced, twenty-three-year-old brevet captain earned a promotion—signed off by Secretary of War Edwin Stanton— becoming a Brevet Brigadier General George Armstrong Custer. Not unnoticed by the media, he quickly earned the nickname "Boy General."

On June 30, one day after his promotion, he and his Wolverines tangled with the Cavalry Corps of the Army of Northern Virginia, which was led by Confederate cavalry legend General J.E.B. Stuart. This skirmish, near Hanover, Pennsylvania, was inconclusive, but it served as a prelude to the coming Battle of Gettysburg.

Unfolding over the first three days of July 1863, the battle that took place at the small town of Gettysburg, Pennsylvania, is often seen as the turning point of the Civil War. The hard-won Union victory thwarted the effort by Robert E. Lee's Army of Northern Virginia to invade and march into the North. It was the Civil War's most costly battle, leaving 50,000 casualties over three days, more than double those of the bloody day at Antietam.

Gettysburg was also the battle that made George Armstrong Custer a household name and an enduring icon of nineteenth-century popular culture. On July 2, Custer personally led a contingent of the 6th Michigan Cavalry to bait a trap that snared a sizable Confederate force. On the following afternoon, Gettysburg's climactic moment, Lee launched a massive, all-out assault on the Union lines, with J.E.B. Stuart leading a massive flanking maneuver with 6,000 cavalrymen. Custer led his heavily outnumbered Wolverines in a series of cavalry charges that culminated in their thwarting J.E.B. Stuart in his determined assault against the Union rear along Cemetery Ridge.

With a shout of "come on, you Wolverines!" Custer personally led the outnumbered 1st Michigan Cavalry into Stuart's cavalry. In the viscous fighting, Custer had his horse shot out from beneath him, but quickly found another. Repeating his battle cry, he led the Wolverines like a hammer, delivering repeated blows until the numerically superior Confederate force began to crumble, and with it, the plan to rip into the Union rear with Stuart's cavalry.

"Custer, added to unflinching bravery, has excellent judgment, and is universally esteemed by his brother officers," effused a front page story in the *New York Herald* for August 4. "He is a man of mark, and would shine in any military sphere."

Was it "excellent judgment" or Custer's luck? It didn't matter. Tom Custer's big brother was a national hero. Having discovered Autie, James Gordon Bennett, Jr. of the *Herald* would champion and interpret his career for the rest of his life, helping to mold him into the heroic figure that nineteenth century popular culture came to know and love.

For the Boy General, whose Custer's luck had saved his life in numerous battles and skirmishes, there was one victory which he sought above all others. When he wrote Judge Daniel Bacon asking for Libbie's hand in marriage, the old man replied with a long and difficult letter. Summarizing the mood of so many fathers of daughters, he explained that "you cannot at your age in life realize the feelings of a parent when called upon to give up and give away an only offspring . . ."

Having painfully conceded one more victory, the quest of Libbie's hand, to his future son-in-law, Bacon added his congratulations for that of Gettysburg, telling Autie that "as a Michigan man I cannot but feel gratified at your well-earned reputation which is now fully established."

Meanwhile, Autie hoped that his own parents would like Libbie. In a letter written on December 22, Lydia Ann had told him that "I think they all love Libbie and all things will be right."

Apparently, the engagement came as a surprise for much of the family. In a later letter, Lydia told Autie that "Nevin said he had a letter from you and was perfectly surprised to hear of the matter. None of the family seemed to think you was going to get married for a number of years."

For the first time in three years, George Armstrong Custer did not return to Monroe to spend Christmas, remaining instead at the Michigan Cavalry Brigade's headquarters near Washington, a city where his prominence was now being widely celebrated.

The homecoming for the hero of the Wolverine Brigade was timed for dramatic effect. After much to-and-fro, including talk of a Christmas wedding—which Libbie rejected—the date was set for February 9, 1864.

George Armstrong Custer left Washington for Monroe by train in late January, accompanied by members of his Michigan Cavalry Brigade staff who were from Monroe. These included Jim Christiancy, Jacob Greene, and George Wilhelmus Mancius Yates. The latter would remain a loyal member of the Custer inner circle, and would be with the Custers at the Little Bighorn a dozen years later.

At some point on their journey, they were joined by Tom Custer. According to Talcott Wing, they "met on the cars," though Wing does not explain at which station Tom boarded the train. Given that they were coming from opposite directions, it is possible that they may have met Autie's train as he and his entourage arrived in Monroe.

The brothers had not seen one another since the summer of 1859, when Tom was just fourteen and his older brother was on break from West Point.

As Wing put it, "During that time Tom had grown to manhood, and little resembled the pale stripling the General had left in the Ohio home." Nor had Tom seen his parents since he had enlisted in 1861.

Realizing that Tom was hardly recognizable as the skinny teenager who had enlisted three years before, the two hardened veterans reassumed their bygone roles as childish tricksters, and concocted a prank to play upon their parents. As Wing wrote, "When they met their father at his home, Tom was introduced as Major Drew, and went unrecognized, but the General immediately informed his mother who her soldier son was, and she enjoyed the mystification of the family as well as the older brother."

Custer scholar Dr. Lawrence Frost adds that when Nevin was introduced to "Major Drew," he too failed to recognize his younger brother, a situation which greatly amused their mother.

Nevin and Ann would have brought their daughter, Claribel, who turned five months old just four days before the wedding, and who was the first grandchild shared by Emanuel and Maria. Given that Tom and Autie were back together and with the whole family, the wedding served as an occasion for a family reunion. In addition to the four brothers and Maggie, Lydia Ann was there, with her three children, fifteen-year-old Marie, seven-year-old Emma, and little five-year-old Harry Armstrong, known to the family as "Autie."

David Kirkpatrick, Maria's son and Lydia Ann's older brother, may have made the trip from Wood County, Ohio. If so, he would have brought his wife, Nancy, and their children, three-year-old Emma and baby John.

Family correspondence around the time of the wedding indicates, among other things, the difficult economic straits in which Emanuel and Maria found themselves. Compared to Judge Bacon and his wife, the well-heeled parents of the bride, the parents of the groom were virtual paupers. It will be recalled that Emanuel had to borrow money from David Reed to buy their house in Monroe, but the letters show that he could not even afford a coat.

In her December 22 letter, Lydia Ann had told Autie that "your paw says you are the only child he could depend on for help," and asking him to send her $20 so that she could help buy an overcoat for Emanuel.

Confirming receipt of the money, she wrote on February 2 that "Grandpa was very much pleased when I gave him the money and told him you sent it to get him an overcoat. He says he needs a dress coat very much. . . . Our folks seem to feel much better about your getting married than they did at first. I told them I thought they would like Libbie."

The wedding took place on the evening of February 9, with Judge Bacon escorting his daughter down the aisle of the Monroe Presbyterian Church at a little past 6:00. Reverend Erasmus James Boyd, Libbie's old schoolmaster, presided with the assistance of Reverend D.C. Mattoon.

On the morning of February 11, the newlyweds embarked for New York City by way of Buffalo, Rochester, and a visit to Autie's alma mater at West Point. From there, they traveled on to Washington, DC. On the train to Washington, the newlyweds ran into General Ulysses S. Grant who was en route to a meeting with President Lincoln, who was about to promote Grant to serve as general-in-chief of the entire Union Army.

Autie set Libbie up in the city, where she would officially reside for the coming year. However, she insisted on spending time with him as he returned to the Michigan Cavalry Brigade at their quarters near Brandy Station, Virginia, 60 miles to the southwest. Throughout their married life, she showed more interest in accompanying her husband into the field than in being left behind. For the young bride, enamored with her young husband, the colorful Boy General, as well as with the uniforms and pageantry of an active military post, Brandy Station was a thrilling place to be—and this was a thrilling moment to be there.

Grant, meanwhile, established his own headquarters in northern Virginia, and brought in General Philip Sheridan to command the Cavalry Corps of the Army of the Potomac. In turn, Custer's Michigan Cavalry Brigade became an important part of Sheridan's operations.

Beginning in May, Grant's 1864 offensive actions in Virginia consisted of two parallel north-to-south operations. The first, known the Valley Campaigns, was through the Shenandoah Valley generally between Winchester and Lynchburg. The other, known as the Overland Campaign, ran through the heart of Virginia roughly between Fredericksburg and the area around the Confederate capital at Richmond. Custer's Wolverines would participate in both.

Tom Custer had left Monroe on a cold day in mid-February to go back into the field himself. Though his enlistment had expired at the end of the 1863, he succumbed to the prospect of a $100 bonus and a promotion to corporal, and he had reenlisted in the 21st Regiment, Ohio Volunteer Infantry, on January 1, 1864.

Now wearing the two stripes of a corporal, Tom was still technically part of the 21st Ohio Volunteer Infantry, but he went back to his duty as a solo courier and escort, to which he had been assigned for most of 1863. Specifically, he was now assigned to General John McAuley Palmer, who commanded XIV Corps in General George Thomas's Army of the Cumberland.

In May 1864, as Autie and the Army of the Potomac were getting underway in Virginia, the Army of the Cumberland was combined with two other field armies, those of the Ohio and of the Tennessee. This organization became the Military Division of the Mississippi and was placed under the command of General William Tecumseh Sherman for a massive Union offensive into Georgia against the Confederate Army of Tennessee, commanded by General Joseph E. Johnson. Known as the Atlanta Campaign, Sherman's assault was designed to cut the Confederacy in half.

The campaign succeeded, but it was not easy going. Tom was with Palmer at the Battle of Kennesaw Mountain on June 21, 1864, when Union forces suffered a serious setback on the approaches to Marietta, Georgia, and remained at his side as XIV Corps—with the 21st Ohio still assigned—marched into Atlanta in late July.

In Virginia, where Grant was driving his two prongs southward into Virginia, Phil Sheridan was reassigned from one to the other, from the Overland Campaign to operations in the Shenandoah Valley. Given command of the Army of the Shenandoah on August 1, 1864, Sheridan, who, like Alfred Pleasonton, had developed into a fan of the Boy General, brought Autie's Michigan Cavalry Brigade into his new fold. As the campaign developed, Sheridan would promote Custer to brevet major general, and elevate him to command the 3rd Division of the Army of the Shenandoah.

In a series of contests from Berryville and Front Royal to the Third Battle of Winchester, Custer and the Wolverines shown like a star. In a letter to Libbie on August 21, he bragged that "imagine my surprise as I watched the retreating enemy to see every man, every officer, take off cap and give 'Three Cheers for General Custer!' It is the first time I ever knew of such a demonstration except in the case of General McClellan. I certainly felt highly flattered."

While one is tempted to take this as a swaggering exaggeration, only one day later the *New York Daily Tribune* published an article observing, "Future writers of fiction will find in Brig. Gen. Custer most of the qualities which go to make up a first-class hero and stories of his daring will be told around many a hearth stone long after the old flag again kisses the breeze from Maine to the Gulf. With a small little figure, blue eyes and golden hair which will persist in curling loosely around his head . . . Gen. Custer is as gallant a cavalier as one would wish to see."

Like James Gordon Bennett's *New York Herald*, the *Daily Tribune* (the word *"Daily"* was dropped after 1866), would follow the charismatic Custer's career—and send correspondents to follow him into the field—using every opportunity to promote him as the sort of heroic character that readers loved. And of course, there was a snowball effect as other papers, not to be outdone, joined in.

It was not that he was undeserving of the accolades. At the Battle of Cedar Creek on October 19, the climax of the 1864 Shenandoah Campaign, Custer spearheaded a stunning victory over the Confederate Army of the Valley, commanded by Lieutenant General Jubal Early.

The twenty-five-year-old hometown hero from Monroe could hardly have ended the year in a more heroic fashion—brevetted to major general and leading an entire division in dramatic victories whose almost theatrical spectacle was eagerly chronicled by war correspondents and enthusiastically consumed by their readers.

At that same moment, nearly 600 road miles to the south and west, a nineteen-year-old hometown hero who was claimed by Monroe, but who had never lived there, was in action against the Confederates outside Atlanta.

Corporal Thomas Ward Custer of the 21st Ohio Infantry, having participated in the capture of Atlanta in September, was now engaged in defending the Union positions against Confederate attempts to cut Union supply lines north of Atlanta. However, the Union counterattack pushed the men in gray westward into Alabama.

October 23, 1864, only four days after his famous older brother's moment of glory at Cedar Creek in Virginia, Tom was just across the Georgia line in Gaylesville, Alabama, when he received word that he had been permanently detached from the roster of the 21st Ohio Volunteer Infantry in order to join his older brother's Michigan Brigade.

The following day, October 24, as the news of Cedar Creek reached them, Nevin Custer and his wife Ann greeted their firstborn son. They named him George Armstrong Custer.

CHAPTER 8

BROTHERS IN ARMS

Since the beginning of the war, and indeed since George Armstrong Custer first departed Ohio for West Point, he and Tom had dreamed and fantasized about serving together as brothers in arms. So too had their father. In a January 7, 1864, letter shared with me by George A. Custer IV, Emanuel told Autie that he had just heard from Tom, telling about his role "in Gen. Grant's escort," after Missionary Ridge in November 1863. He went on to say that "I have just thought of this plan." Father Custer's idea was that if Tom could "have his choice of what regiment to go into it would be a good plan for him to join one of your regiments . . . I have given my opinion about it. You know more about it than I do. I would like if Thomas could make that if there is any chance if it would not interfere with your other arrangements about getting him a commission. If he could get both it would be a good thing." The subject would certainly be a topic of conversation when they were all together in Monroe a month later.

From the moment he was promoted to brevet brigadier general and given command of the Michigan Cavalry Brigade in the summer of 1863, Autie had begun to look for the appropriate slot within the organization into which to bring Tom aboard as a junior officer. Though nepotism raised no eyebrows in the nineteenth-century armed forces, getting the two of them together was still a complex manipulation of the bureaucracy—such as the transfer of an individual from a volunteer regiment of one state to that of another. It was a complicated process even for the commander of a bri-gade—or in Custer's case, the commander of the 3rd Division—because the leaders of the volunteer regiments maintained control of personnel matters and because there were only so many openings for officers.

Autie had first lobbied Lieutenant Colonel Russell Alexander Alger, com-mander of the 5th Michigan Cavalry—and a future Michigan governor. Alger rebuffed his entreaties, maintaining that there was already a waiting list of veterans within the regiment who should be given the right of first refusal when opportunities arose for of filling vacancies. It should be men-tioned here that Autie's older half brother, Henry C. Custer, was serving with the 5th Michigan, though they apparently had no contact during the war. Of course, it might have been awkward because Henry's division com-mander was a half brother who was eight years younger than he.

On October 3, according to a memo in the collection of the University of Michigan's Bentley Historical Library, Autie received a positive response from Colonel George Harvey Kidd, who commanded not only the 6th Michigan Cavalry Regiment, but who exercised direct command over the Michigan Brigade after Custer had been moved up to 3rd Division command.

On November 8, 1864, after a short visit to his parents' home in Mon-roe, Thomas Ward Custer was commissioned as a second lieutenant in Company B of the 6th Michigan Cavalry. By his service record, he was twenty-one years old. In fact, he was just nineteen.

Shortly after Tom reported for duty with Kidd's regiment, he was detached to serve as an aide-de-camp to his brother. It was not as though he was inexperienced in this role, having served in a similar capacity for series of officers going back to the day seven months before when James Negley plucked him out of the infantry ranks.

Winter quarters for the Michigan Brigade were in northern Virginia between the city of Winchester and Cedar Creek, the site of their final victory of 1864. As was to be her custom, Libbie Custer left the relative comfort of her Washington hotel room to spend the winter sharing the tent of the brigade commander. Autie's commanding officer, General Phil Sheridan, made an exception for Libbie in December when he ordered the wives of the other officers to leave to camp and relocate to Washington or elsewhere.

Libbie and her husband did not have long in the tent. Robert and Sarah Glass, prosperous residents of Winchester, invited the couple to board at Long Meadow, their spacious mansion located about 4 miles south of Winchester. Here, Tom was a frequent caller, generously welcomed by Libbie.

Custer scholar Dr. Lawrence Frost observed that since her own brother had died when she was five, and "having no exposure to a brother during her childhood, 'brother' Tom's presence in the camp was a pleasurable sensation." In a letter in Frost's collection, Libbie wrote home that her and the General "could not help spoiling him owing to his charm and our deep affection." Thereafter, in her correspondence, she never referred to Tom as a brother-in-law, but as her "brother."

The story that she told of the reunion of her husband and brother, and of later "official" encounters is amusing, but it also provides an insight into the deep brotherly bond between Tom and Autie.

"When Tom came in to report he was the most formal of them all standing at attention and using a tone of voice that betrayed no signs of anything but the strictly disciplined soldier," she reported. "The two called each other 'Sir' and until I had become accustomed to this I used to think that Tom had surely been offended by some dereliction and I prepared to take his side and plead his cause whatever might be the right or wrong of the case. As soon as the report was made and the commander had said, 'I have no more orders, sir, for the present,' Tom flung his cap off, unbuckled his saber and the two were calling each other by their first names and with some teasing words in the midst of a scuffle as vigorous and rollicking as when they were boys on the Ohio farm of their childhood."

With regard to her husband, she recalled, "It was a long time before I became accustomed to the instantaneous transformations from the overflowing exuberance of the boy to the grave, dignified manner of the commanding general when he was suddenly arrested in a frolic by the appearance of an officer who came to make an official report."

Sometimes, when he became absorbed in his work and spoke to Libbie in the "quick, authoritative tone of official life," she would salute and ask, "Is that a military order or a request?"

She would later remember the "peals of laughter that followed at my affronted air and the apology that immediately ensued."

Years later, in her essay in Theophilus Rodenbough's anthology about Civil War heroes, Libbie reflected upon Tom's character, as she observed it during that winter in Winchester.

"His manners and self-culture became a serious study with him," she wrote. "He not only aimed to be a perfect soldier, but he was determined to take up his studies, interrupted by his early enlistment. Even in those busy times he bought himself school-books, and pored over them with patience in the evenings. He seemed to have come through unscathed by the coarseness of his surroundings as an enlisted man; for though the best blood of our land was often in the ranks, there was a large element of law-lessness, beside, among the soldiers."

In contrast to the experience of Tom and Autie during the previous three winters, the duration in winter quarters was both shorter and punctuated by combat action—which saw the Custer brothers together in battle for the first time. Sheridan had ordered Autie to lead a cavalry operation that was intended as a distraction to lead Confederate Lieutenant General Jubal Early to divert some of his troops away from his effort to destroy railroad infrastructure north of Charlottesville.

The Custers and their small detachment departed Winchester on December 19 and camped near Lacey Spring, about 60 miles to the south-west. The diversion succeeded in diverting, but otherwise it was not a stel-lar moment. The Union troops were ambushed in their camp at dawn by raiders from the 5th Virginia Volunteer Cavalry Regiment commanded by

Autie's former West Point classmate, Brigadier General Thomas Lafayette Rosser. After the skirmish, the enemy withdrew and Autie withdrew his own contingent to Winchester.

The Custers—the three of them now functioning more or less as a family unit—had hoped to withdraw to Washington for Christmas to meet Libbie's father, Daniel Bacon, and his wife Rhoda. When permission for this was denied and the trip postponed into January 1865, the Bacons visited them in Winchester.

This is an illustration of the perception of relative safety enjoyed by the Union forces in winter quarters. So too was the gala surprise party that Sheridan hosted on January 15, the eve of their departure for the capital. The Custers remained in Washington only briefly before traveling on to Monroe by way of another short stop in New York City. The Custers visited New York frequently through the years, and Libbie eventually retired there as a widow. They were captivated by the cosmopolitan bustle of the place, but there were also practical reasons. To reach Washington, DC, they had to go through New York. The Michigan Central Railroad, which served Detroit and Monroe, was controlled by the powerful New York Central, and intersected with it at Buffalo. In later years, as Autie's notoriety grew, he was wined and dined by the press in the city, especially by the *New York Herald*, which he greatly enjoyed.

An early resumption of their part in the Civil War awaited them upon their return to Winchester. On February 27, 1865, Custer's 3rd Division went into the field as the spearhead of Sheridan's Shenandoah operations.

Grant's strategy for Virginia in 1865 involved a continuation of that pursued in 1864. The main component of the plan was for the Army of the Potomac to confront and destroy Robert E. Lee's Confederate Army of Northern Virginia while capturing the rebel capital of Richmond. Meanwhile, General William Tecumseh Sherman had marched from Atlanta to Savannah, successfully cutting the Confederacy in half by late December. He would now turn north through the Carolinas.

The strategic idea was that Grant and Sherman would be the hammer and anvil that would destroy the final fighting strength of the Confederacy. Sheridan, meanwhile, would continue operations to sweep the Confederate forces from the Shenandoah Valley. He would then merge with the parallel effort by the Army of the Potomac, while dispatching his cavalry to join Sherman's offensive. Tactically, the entire scope of operations was dogged by a period of heavy rail across the region which complicated matters for both sides.

For Tom and Autie, their position at the tip of Sheridan's spear cast them into the first and climactic battle of the 1865 Shenandoah campaign. On March 2, having encountered little resistance, they reached Waynesboro, Virginia, on the Shenandoah River 100 miles southwest of Winchester and about 35 miles west of Charlottesville. Confederate Lieutenant General Jubal Early had heavily fortified the town, but had failed to concentrate cavalry in its defense. This defensive error was quickly exploited by the fast moving Union cavalry. Autie's men on horseback slashed through a small contingent of Tom Rosser's 5th Virginia Volunteer Cavalry, and swept into town through a gap in the defenses.

By the time Sheridan arrived, the Custer brothers owned the town, and Early was in retreat—literally on foot and running for his life ahead of Custer's cavalrymen. Early was relieved of his command at the end of the month.

On March 3, the Custer brothers led the 3rd Division into Charlottesville, the home of the University of Virginia and the hometown of Thomas Jefferson. The night before, Sarah Strickler, a nineteen-year-old student at the Albemarle Female Institute in Charlottesville, confided in her diary that "everything is in an uproar tonight . . ." I do not think that Union troops will have any Charlottesville to take when they get here. The merchants will carry it off."

When Custer's men arrived, she observed, "The long expected hordes have come at last—they came shouting and galloping through town, waving their banners aloft."

A delegation from the university met with Custer's advance guard, hoping to save their institution from destruction. They included the rector, Thomas L. Preston; the faculty chair and a professor of chemistry, Socrates Maupin; Christopher "Cap" Fowler; and law professor John B. Minor. In his diary, Minor had written that "most persons think they will destroy the University . . . and we may not flatter ourselves that we shall escape the visitation."

In the afternoon, at around two o'clock, the committee met the first Union troops under a flag of truce.

"We announced to these men, who were accompanied by a dirty-looking lieutenant [Tom Custer], that no defense of Charlottesville was contemplated," Minor wrote, and "that the town was evacuated, and that we requested protection for the University, and for the town . . . Immediately afterwards, Gen. Custer passed in triumph, with three of our battle flags displayed."

The city was surrendered to the Custer brothers. Writing in *The Magazine of Albemarle County History* in 1964, John Brown and Anne Freudenberg observed that "a good looking officer [Tom Custer] rode up, who announced himself as Gen. Custer's adjutant." Lawrence Frost adds that the brothers were "met just outside of Charlottesville by a delegation of citizens led by the mayor who turned over the keys to the public buildings and the University of Virginia."

Brown and Freudenberg went on to say that "Custer moved his headquarters into the University of Virginia and by this intervention and requests of the people and a committee of the more important men of Charlottesville, the University of Virginia was saved from being burned."

By the end of the month, Sheridan's Army of the Shenandoah, with Custer's 3rd Division cavalrymen, had joined in Grant's Union noose that was being pulled tight around Robert E. Lee's besieged defenders inside Richmond and Petersburg. On March 31, the division was serving as a guard for its supply train and had reached the town of Dinwiddie Court

House, about 50 road miles from the Confederate capital at Richmond on its southern approaches, and about 20 miles from heavily defended Petersburg.

As they pressed northward in the heavy downpour, the Union troops were confronted by a Confederate force led by Generals George Pickett and Fitzhugh Lee. The 3rd Division lagged behind to protect wagons stuck in the mud, and was not immediately engaged. However, when the initial Confederate assault gained ground, Sheridan brought Custer's men forward to help hold the line, which they were able to do. Having done so, Autie, with Tom at his side, led an afternoon counterattack that forced Pickett back after a day of forward progress.

Tactically, the Battle of Dinwiddie Court House was a Confederate win, though the role played by the Custer boys was a glaring and significant exception. Strategically, it was overshadowed by the Battle of Five Forks, a rematch the following day between the same forces. Five Forks was strategically important because it controlled the Confederate supply line into the Richmond-Petersburg area, as well as the potential route of escape for Robert E. Lee's forces if the defense of the Confederate capital became untenable.

When Sheridan launched his follow-up attack at dawn on April 1, Custer's 3rd Division was on the left, opposite Pickett's right flank. Because of the heavy ground fog, there was much confusion across the front, but as the exhausted Confederates faltered, the momentum was with the attackers. This, combined with a Union breakthrough at Petersburg on April 2—after a siege of nearly three hundred days—marked the beginning of the rapid end of the Confederacy.

Having won a decisive victory over Jubal Early in the last major Shenandoah battle, having captured Charlottesville, and having saved the University of Virginia, the Custer boys in blue would now participate in the death knell of the Confederate capital. On the blood-stained fields south and west of Richmond, they were now poised for their starring roles in the final decisive month of the Civil War.

CHAPTER 9

NAMOZINE, APPOMATTOX, AND RENOWN

ON THE VIRGINIA battlefront, the climax of five hellish years was about to be written as a headlong chase between vast armies for 100 miles across the rolling hills and rain-swollen runs of Virginia's Piedmont.

As the University of Virginia's John Minor had written, "Nothing intervenes now between us and the Yankees, but the mud," and indeed the incessant rain and resulting muck were as much of an impediment to Union momentum as much of the Confederate armed resistance. Indeed, Autie wrote to his wife on March 30, 1865, that he had awaken from his slumber that day in two inches of water.

On April 2, General Robert E. Lee, general-in-chief of the entire Confederate Army, informed Confederate President Jefferson Davis that Richmond could no longer be defended and withdrew his troops westward, moving quickly to prevent their being cut off by Union forces.

Once the widely scattered Confederate units had escaped from Richmond and Petersburg, they organized into four principal columns that would proceed westward, generally in parallel with the Appomattox River. Lee intended them to rendezvous at Amelia Court House, 40 miles to the west, where they would unite into a single large force. Then, Lee would turn this force to the south, eluding the Union force, and ultimately link up with the Confederate forces under General Joseph E. Johnston in North Carolina.

Lee succeeded in withdrawing his forces, but as they rode westward, the Union forces under Lieutenant General Ulysses S. Grant were soon in pursuit, dogging them on their left, or southern, flank. The immediate Union goal was to prevent the Confederates from turning south, next to overtake them, and finally to defeat them in a decisive battle.

In the order of battle, Grant directly commanded three field armies: Major General George Meade's Army of the Potomac, Major General Edward Ord's Army of the James, and Major General Phil Sheridan's Army of the Shenandoah. The latter's Cavalry Corps was commanded by Major General Wesley Merritt and contained the Brigadier General Thomas Devin's 1st Division and George Armstrong Custer's 3rd Division. Custer's division was comprised of three brigades, Colonel Alexander Pennington's 1st Brigade, Colonel William Wells's 2nd Brigade, and Colonel Henry Capehart's 3rd Brigade.

Custer's division, having been on the Union left flank as Sheridan's army pushed north to Five Forks, was on the western edge of the Union line. As the momentum of the action turned forty-five degrees toward the west, the 3rd Division now found itself at the vanguard of the Union pursuit. For the Custer brothers, this was tailor-made for their kind of fast-paced cavalry action.

Of the four columns of Confederate troops retreating westward from Richmond and Petersburg, the Custers were opposite the southern column, comprised of Lieutenant General Richard Anderson's IV Corps and an amalgam of cavalry units commanded by Major General Fitzhugh Lee.

To slow the Union pursuit, Lee ordered Brigadier General Rufus Barringer to organize detachments of Confederate troops to pause, dig in behind hastily erected breastworks, and set up holding actions. Such was the case on the morning of April 3, when Custer's advance was interrupted in rural Amelia County, about a dozen miles north of Five Forks, from which the 3rd Division had begun their part of the Union pursuit. Leading the division's advance were the 1st Vermont and 8th New York Volunteer Cavalry Regiments, which were part of Wells's 2nd Brigade.

In a series of rapid moves, Wells's men attempted to outflank the Confederates, who, as planned, pulled up stakes, moved back and reestablished their line. This process repeated itself until the Confederates had withdrawn for about 5 miles up Namozine Road to the vicinity of the Namozine Presbyterian Church. Here, in an open area east of the two story, wood frame church building, the 1st and 2nd North Carolina Volunteer Cavalry Regiments, supported by a cannon, dug in for a fight.

When Wells ordered assaults by the 1st Vermont and 8th New York, Barringer ordered the 2nd North Carolina to mount up for a counterattack.

In many a battle over the preceding campaigns, the narrative tells of George Armstrong Custer audaciously attacking the Confederates in a dramatic mounted charge. However, the Battle of Namozine Church was Tom Custer's fight. That morning, riding with Wells at the head of the 2nd Brigade column, he spurred his horse forward to lead the cavalry charge.

With minié balls flying in every direction, Tom crested the rebel defenses and plunged into what was apparently the command staff of the 2nd North Carolina, because straight ahead of him was the standard bearer holding the regimental colors. Tom seized the 2nd's battle flag, and took charge of the situation, demanding the surrender of fourteen Confederates, including three officers.

Battle flags were high on symbolism because the flag represented—and had stitched on it—the lineage, honors, and victories achieved by the unit. Capturing an enemy battle flag was therefore considered to be the epitome of valor and heroism, tantamount to the seizure of the regiment itself. Of course, because the flag was held by the regimental command staff, capturing it was a metaphor for taking control of the regiment itself.

"You have already heard how God has blessed us with victory," Autie wrote to Libbie on April 4, presuming that news of the battle would reach

Washington before his letter. "The 3rd Division had the advance yesterday and was on the extreme left of our army. With my three brigades of cavalry I fought and whipped six brigades of infantry and two divisions of cavalry capturing nine caissons, one piece of artillery, and one battle flag. Tom in the most gallant manner led the charge of the 2nd Brigade and captured the battle flag of the 2nd North Carolina Cavalry, also the color bearer. He also captured two officers and twelve men. None of our men were near him . . . Tom is always in the advance."

For his action that day, General Phil Sheridan later promoted Tom Custer to the brevet rank of captain and awarded him the Medal of Honor.

More was yet to come.

Barringer withdrew his remaining forces from Namozine Church, having succeeded in buying time for the Fitzhugh Lee's withdrawal. Robert E. Lee's intended rendezvous of forces took place at Amelia Court House on April 5 as he had intended. However, with the Union troops pressing him hard, he was unable to turn south and was compelled to continue moving west. The speed of the Confederate retreat slowed, with the troops being exhausted, hungry, and dispirited by the rain and mud, and by the realization that they were in an increasingly untenable position.

By April 6, they had reached the vicinity of Farmville, about 40 road miles west of Namozine Church and 25 miles west of Amelia Court House. Here, they were overtaken by the Union forces in a group of individual, roughly simultaneous actions that are known collectively as the Battle of Sailor's Creek (aka Sayler's Creek).

This battle, in which nearly 20,000 Confederate troops faced around 25,000 Union troops, was the largest battle of the campaign and the climactic battle between forces under the direct command of Robert E. Lee and Ulysses S. Grant.

Sheridan's Army of the Shenandoah entered the battlefield on the southern side, opposite Confederate forces commanded by Lieutenant General Richard Anderson and Lieutenant General Richard Ewell. From east to west, he and Wesley Merritt, his Cavalry Corps commander, had the three divisions—Custer's 3rd Division, Devin's 1st Division, and Major General George Crook's 2nd Division from the Army of the Potomac.

The Custer boys first made contact with the enemy on the Union right in the vicinity of a place called Marshall's Crossroads. As the Confederates sought to construct defensive positions, Custer's mobile cavalry outflanked them, succeeding in capturing a train of supply wagons, some artillery, and nearly 1,000 troops.

Tom Custer, riding with Colonel Capehart at the head of the 3rd Brigade, as he had been riding with Wells in the lead at Namozine Church, was again at the tip of the spear and eager for action. After having seized the Confederate battle flag at Namozine church three days before, his appetite for that singular sort of glory had been whetted.

"Tom led the assault upon the enemy's breastworks, mounted, was first to leap his horse over the works on top of the enemy while they were pouring a volley of musketry into our ranks," Autie explained in a letter to his father-in-law, Judge Bacon. "Tom seized the rebel colors and demanded their surrender. The color-bearer shot him through face and neck, intending to shoot him through the head. So close the muzzle Tom's face was spotted with burnt powder. He retained the colors with one hand, while with the other he drew his revolver and shot the rebel dead. By this time our men were by his side and the fight was over."

With the adrenaline pumping, Tom was unfazed by his injury. Even with the prized banner in hand, he wanted to keep going.

"The damned rebels have shot me, but I got my flag," Tom told his brother when Autie walked up, his horse having been shot out from beneath him.

"With blood pouring from his wound he asked that someone might take the flag while he continued with the assaulting column," Autie recalled. "Only my positive order forced him to leave the field."

Lieutenant Colonel Edward Whittaker, Autie's chief of staff recalled that "Tom, on that day, fought like a lion."

"Custer's luck," that intangible beneficence that seemed to shield the older brother from serious injury amid hails of lead over the course of more than three years seems to have also swathed the younger Custer. It could have been so much worse. The bullet passed within an inch of his carotid artery. Even having missed that, it could have done severe damage—irreparable with 1865 medical technology—to his jaw. Of course, a slightly different angle would have sent the hot lead tumbling disastrously through his brain.

In a letter to Libbie written many years later, Colonel Capehart recalled the events of April 6, 1865, at Marshall's Crossroads, explaining in graphic detail that "I saw your brother capture his second flag . . . Having crossed the line of temporary works in the flank of the road, we were confronted by a supporting line. It was from the second line that he wrested the colors, single-handed, and only a few paces to my right. As he approached the colors he received a shot in the face which knocked him back on his horse, but in a moment he was upright in his saddle. Reaching out his right arm, he grasped the flag while the color bearer reeled. The bullet from Tom's revolver must have pierced him in the region of the heart. As he was falling Captain Custer wrenched the standard from his grasp and bore it away in triumph. For intrepidity, I never saw this incident surpassed."

For Tom Custer, and for many others, the Civil War ended that day in the Battle of Sailor's Creek. Current estimates by the National Park Service calculate 9,980 total casualties. In his 1883 memoirs, Confederate Major General Andrew Humphreys said that losses on his side numbered "not less than 8,000." Among the nine Confederate generals taken captive, Richard Ewell told Autie that "further fighting is useless; it is a wanton waste of life."

But the fighting *would* continue, albeit for just three more days.

Robert E. Lee's immediate objective became one of survival, of pressing forward for another 30 road miles to Appomattox Station, where a supply train waited.

It would be George Armstrong Custer's 3rd Division that delivered the checkmate of the Appomattox Campaign. By the afternoon of April 8, Lee and his vast throng had reached Appomattox Court House, just 3 miles short of their goal, when Custer's men outflanked them and rode into Appomattox Station. Though the Confederates attacked from the east, Custer's men captured the supply train and some artillery pieces, and began tearing up the track. Skirmishing consumed the remainder of the day, but it did so against rampant rumors on both sides that the war was about to end.

Realizing he was now cut off, Lee sent word to Grant, whose main force was still a dozen miles back, telling him that he was ready to talk.

On Sunday afternoon, April 9, the two leaders met at the home of Wilmer McLean, about twenty-five yards west of the actual courthouse in Appomattox Court House, to sign the documents surrendering the largest component of the Confederate Army. Other Confederate officers surrendered their units over the ensuing few weeks, but after Appomattox, the Civil War was essentially over.

George Armstrong Custer, who had ridden in the First Battle of Bull Run, the first great field contest of the war, was also present at the McLean house that day. So too, of course, was his boss, General Phil Sheridan. In the aftermath of the signing, souvenir hunters besieged Wilmer McLean. Among them, Sheridan gave him a twenty-dollar gold piece for the small table upon which the surrender had been signed. In turn, he presented it to Autie as a present for Libbie.

"Madam," he wrote in a short note. "There is scarcely an individual in our service who has contributed more to bring about this desirable result than your gallant husband."

George Armstrong Custer did indeed cast a long shadow, but in his own eyes, brother Tom was an heroic personality with whom history would be reckoned.

Thomas Ward Custer was the first soldier in American history to receive the Medal of Honor twice. Having earned his first on April 3, 1865, for his actions at Namozine Church, he would be awarded a second one for his part in breaking through the Confederate line in the Battle of Sailor's Creek three days later. Of the roughly 3,500 recipients of the nation's highest and most prestigious decoration for valor, only nineteen of them have earned two. Of course, it should be pointed out that during the Civil War, the Medal of Honor was the only decoration that existed for valor in combat, and that it was often awarded after actions for which a Distinguished Service Cross or Silver Star would be awarded in the years since they were created in 1918.

"Tom's conduct was gallant in the extreme and is spoken of by all in the highest admiration," George Armstrong Custer reported in a letter to his wife on April 7. "Won't Father Custer and Father Bacon be delighted to hear of Tom's gallantry? Do you want to know what I think of him? Tom should have been the General and I the Lieutenant."

Such was the level of the Boy General's respect for his little bother, who had turned twenty—or twenty-two by his erroneous service record—just three weeks before.

After forty-three months in uniform, he had earned both of his Medals of Honor in less than a week and in what amounted to the last week of the war. Tom had earned those medals, and he had stood in the company of household name generals—not the least of which being his own brother. As Autie had advanced to the brevet rank of major general, so too did Tom advance up the staircase of brevet rank. The nineteen-year-old corporal who was commissioned as a second lieutenant in November 1864, became a brevet captain five months later because of Namozine Church, and after that, his second Medal of Honor action resulted in promotions to brevet major, and ultimately to lieutenant colonel.

Along with the accolades, Tom had earned a thirty-day furlough, though because of the timing, there would be no war to which to return. The injury suffered at Sailor's Creek kept Tom Custer from the war's final hours. As Autie was marching down the stairs of the McLean House with the surrender table under his arm, Tom was nearly 50 miles to the east at Burkeville, Virginia, with a large contingent of ambulatory wounded, waiting for the train that would take them to the military hospital at City Point on the east side of Petersburg that had served the Union Army during the year-long siege.

He arrived at City Point on April 11, but did not stay long. According to correspondence between his bother and Libbie, who was living in Washington, Tom had official duties in the capital, and his older brother had insisted that he report to the US Army's Armory Square Hospital, directed by Dr. Willard Bliss.

"He will go to Washington with his flags to present them to the War Department," Autie wrote to Libbie who would be waiting in the nation's capital to greet her heroic "brother."

"He must be very careful as his wound is near the main artery," Autie advised. "Caution him against violating any regulation or orders concerning wounded officers while in the capital. He must go to Dr. Bliss's hospital. He must be very careful of himself. His wound is much like the mortal wound Sergeant Michow received at [the June 1864 Battle of] Trevillian Station."

On April 14, within a day or so of Tom's arrival, tragedy struck the capital when John Wilkes Booth put a bullet into the head of President Abraham Lincoln.

According to Marguerite Merington, Edward A. Paul, a *New York Times* war correspondent, reported being present in the aftermath "when the circumstances of Lincoln's assassination were being discussed in a military group."

"Why, Tom Custer was in Washington at the time, in charge of the battle-flags; he may have been in the theater that night," someone observed.

"Impossible," Paul replied, "Tom would have taken in the situation at a glance and the assassin would never have escaped."

Such was the reputation that Tom Custer had developed by this time. Autie was not the only of the Custer boys to have made a positive impression on the media—though there is no evidence that Tom was a theater enthusiast and that he would have been, or could have been, at Ford's that night.

If it had ever come to that, he would certainly have been a better choice to guard the president than Washington policeman John Frederick Parker, who was supposed to be outside the president's box, but who instead was drinking at a nearby tavern when John Wilkes Booth arrived to do his damage. Tom Custer, as described by Autie—by now a teetotaler—was "moderate in drink."

George Armstrong Custer was an awed champion of the young Medal of Honor hero. Having described Tom's almost foolhardy aggressiveness—a clone of Autie's from earlier Civil War fights in the actions that created the Boy General's media image a year or so earlier—Autie assured Judge Bacon, "You might infer that Tom lacks caution, judgment. On the contrary he possesses both in an unusual degree. His excellent judgment tells him when to press the enemy, and when to be moderate. Of all my staff officers he is quickest in perceiving at a glance the exact state of things. This trait frequently excites comment."

Could any endorsement have carried more positive weight than this?

Tom's actual Medals of Honor were among those formally awarded by Secretary of War Edwin Stanton in his office on April 24 and May 22.

"It is with profound grief that I cannot return to you the thanks of the late President," Stanton effused to the honorees on April 24, "who since you won these spoils has gone from the pinnacle of honor and glory in this world to the right hand of God, where, if it be permitted mortals to look upon what is passing in the world beneath, now sees transpiring in this chamber."

Tom Custer's career had taken him to a peak that all but few can imagine only in their dreams. On the morning after his second Medal of Honor ceremony, he rode with Autie at the head of the 3rd Division as they joined the other elements of the Army of the Potomac in the Grand Review of the

Armies. This massive triumphal parade through the nation's capital included 80,000 troops from the Army of the Potomac. The following day, the review continued with William Tecumseh Sherman leading an additional contingent of 65,000 troops from the Army of Georgia and the Army of the Tennessee.

"Custer's division, which had the advance, was the chief attraction and its appearance was the signal for vociferous cheers and continued applause," wrote a reporter for the *Cleveland Daily Leader*. With the conclusion of the Grand Review, Custer formally dismissed his division.

Tom Custer had come far since that day in 1861 when, as a kid of sixteen, he boarded the sluggishly rambling troop train that had taken him and his fellow recruits from the hills of rural Ohio into the cauldron of what was to be one of the bloodiest wars yet to scar the progress of the human race.

And Tom had survived. The newspapers had coined the term "Custer's luck" to describe Autie's improbable escapes from disaster, but as we have noted, it applied equally to Tom. The bullet that ripped through his face and neck at Sailor's Creek missed killing him by the width of a straight razor's blade.

CHAPTER 10

THE GENERAL, THE OLD LADY, AND THE SCAMP GO WEST

By ANY REASONABLE measure, the Custer boys in blue could have held their heads high if they had checked their blue uniforms on the evening of the Grand Review and had marched forth into the kinds of civilian careers that greet genuine war heroes. There was even serious talk of a Michigan Congressional seat for the Boy General.

However, there was still unfinished business.

The Grand Review should have tied up and tied off the business of the Civil War, providing a neat and conclusive end point, but it was more a blurry closing parenthesis than a firm, bold period. The Civil War had not ended with Lee and Grant at Appomattox on April 9—though the history books tell us that it ended "effectively" on that day. Nor did it end with Andrew Johnson's May 9 presidential proclamation that it was over.

Though all organized Confederate forces east of the Mississippi had formally surrendered by the end of May, unrest in Texas would be rampant for another fifteen months. In the meantime, there were rumors that the situation might be exploited by Emperor Maximilian of Mexico, the Austrian archduke who had been installed on a puppet throne created by Napoleon III of France. Therein lay the unfinished business.

Ulysses S. Grant, still the general-in-chief of the Union Army, ordered General Phil Sheridan to assemble a force to go south into Texas and western Louisiana to restore order and to thwart any cross-border invasion from Mexico.

Sheridan, who left Washington even before the Grand Review, had a great deal of personal fondness and professional respect for George Armstrong Custer, so he naturally picked him to lead the 2nd Division of Cavalry, one of the contingents of his new Military Division of the Southwest, which was forming up to go into Texas.

"While others hastened to discard the well-worn uniforms, and don again the dress of civilians, hurrying to the cars, and groaning over the slowness of the fast-flying trains that bore them to their homes, my husband was almost breathlessly preparing for a long journey to Texas," Elizabeth Bacon Custer would later write of her husband's decision. "He had accepted the offer for further active service, and gratefully thanked his chief for giving him the opportunity. I, however, should have liked to have him get some of the celebrations that our country was then showering on its defenders. I missed the bonfires, the processions, the public meeting of distinguished citizens, who eloquently thanked the veterans, the editorials that lauded each townsman's deed, the poetry in the corner of the newspaper that was dedicated to a hero, the overflow of a woman's heart singing praise to her military idol."

Though the bonfires and the processions beckoned seductively, Autie eschewed all that in favor of saddle and guidon. As Libbie put it, her husband "believed in what old-fashioned people term a 'calling,' and he himself had felt a call to be a soldier."

Thomas Ward Custer had by April 1865 clearly emerged from the shadow of his older brother. However, he would nonetheless choose for himself a position—perhaps predestined as early as in those days in Old Foster's one-room school in the Dining Fork—as the Robin-to-Batman sidekick to Autie, a role which he would embrace until his dying day on that hill in Montana.

In analyzing this choice, one should include consideration of the practical. As a West Point man with a media following, Autie had a lot of options. As a man without a high school diploma, whose entire short adult life had been in uniform, Tom had few civilian options, other than farming, which bore no allure for him.

At the end of May 1865, the Custer brothers boarded a train in Washington for Louisiana, en route toward the distant frontier. They were accompanied by Libbie, whose father had admonished her in numerous letters to "follow Armstrong everywhere." The three of them formed themselves into a dissimilar, but equilateral trio that would remain as a symbiotic unit for more than a decade.

Except for a few extended separations in the early 1870s, they would sojourn together for most of the coming eleven years, moving like nomads across the West, and gradually becoming part of the legends and lore of this vast region. Crossing the Mississippi River that summer, they opened this new chapter of their intertwined lives, a part of their story that would define their legacy as icons of the American West.

Within this tightly wound clique, each would play a role defined by stage names as though they were starring in some contemporary melodrama. By Libbie's telling, Autie was perpetually, throughout her long writing career, "the General," while he and Tom referred to her as the "Old Lady." The name, as she later explained in her book *Following the Guidon*, was not coined by her Custer boys, but by some Monroe youngsters when Libbie first began referring to herself as "Mrs." Custer. Though he had reverted to his permanent rank, Autie was still entitled to be referred to as "general," but the title had no relevance to his actual authority in any chain of command, nor in his seniority in the service.

Tom, meanwhile, was known affectionately as "our Scamp." This term was definitely coined by Libbie, though just as she always called her husband by his brevet rank, she also often referred to Tom as "colonel," referencing his brevet rank as a lieutenant colonel.

The "Scamp" moniker fit Tom's being cast as the prankster among their threesome, though in his unofficial hours Autie was nearly as comfortable in the role of jester as he was on the pedestal that Libbie and the wartime media had crafted for him. There would be a supporting cast, of course. Though many would come and go, Eliza Brown, the African-American cook whom Autie had hired during the Virginia campaigns, would remain a member of their entourage for the ensuing five years as they took up residence at various posts across the West.

Libbie provided an illustration of the "scampiness" of Tom Custer in her description of the first leg of their trip that month. It seems that the train was so crowded that many people had no seat, yet on their second morning, she discovered Tom in possession of two seats, "with his legs stretched comfortably on the seat turned over in front of him."

"You see," Tom explained, "two old codgers sat down in front of my pal and me, late last night, and went on counting up their gains in the rise of corn, owing to the war, which, to say the least, was harrowing to us poor devils who had fought the battles that had made them rich and left us without a 'red.' I concluded, if that was all they had done for their country, two of its brave defenders had more of a right to the seat than they had. I just turned to him and began solemnly to talk about what store I set by my old army coat, then on the seat they occupied; said I couldn't give it up, though I had been obliged to cover a comrade who had died of small-pox, I not being afraid of contagion, having had varioloid [smallpox]. Well, I got that far when the eyes of the old galoots started out of their heads, and they vamoosed the ranch, I can tell you, and I saw them peering through the window at the end of the next car, the horror still in their faces."

At this explanation by his brother, Autie reportedly "exploded with merriment."

Their journey took the three Custers to Alexandria, Louisiana, where Sheridan first made his headquarters. Sheridan's strategic design was to march west into Texas from Alexandria with Custer at the head of five regiments bound for the Houston area, while a parallel column under Wesley Merritt—like Autie, a brevet major general—marched toward Austin. In the beginning of the campaign, Sheridan imagined they would eventually link up and continue south to the Rio Grande, possibly, if the tactical situation warranted, continuing into Mexico.

In August, the Custer contingent made the march of nearly 300 miles westward to Hempstead, Texas, on the north side of Houston. Conditions under the hot Texas summer sun were trying. The troopers were at the end of a long and tenuous supply line, and morale was collapsing.

The bulk of the Union Army was made up not of regular US Army troops, but of volunteer regiments contributed by the states to defeat the Confederate rebellion. With this task accomplished, the men felt they should go home, not into occupation duty on the lawless plains of Texas. Discipline collapsed, men deserted, and those caught were executed.

Complicating matters for Custer was the fact that none of the regiments were from among the Michigan or other volunteer units that had served under him during the Civil War, and as such, they felt no loyalty to a man they knew only from his flamboyant media stereotype.

"They hated us, I suppose," wrote Libbie Custer. "That is the penalty the commanding officer generally pays for what still seems to me the questionable privilege of rank and power."

Many of the troops—as well as both Tom and Libbie—came down with mosquito-borne dengue fever, then aptly referred to as "breakbone" fever. Though Tom insisted that "nothing makes the Old Lady ill," she, as well as he, did suffer mightily.

Sheridan himself observed, "If I owned Texas and Hell, I would rent out Texas and live in Hell."

Gradually, Custer was able to establish order and discipline within his 2nd Division of Cavalry, though rogue elements of one regiment, the 2nd Wisconsin, remained particularly hostile. In late October 1865, he moved on to Austin and up the chain of command to become chief of cavalry for the Department of Texas. His command now included regular army, rather than solely volunteer regiments. Gradually, the Union show of force—combined with the general exhaustion of four years of war—took the wind out of the sails of the restlessness in Texas. Indeed, the farmers and ranchers around Hempstead and Austin, actually came to welcome the calming influence of the occupation force. The Custer boys and other Union officers even found themselves being invited to join the Texans in hunting trips, horse races, and other amusements.

In her description of the hunts in her memoir, *Tenting on the Plains*, Libbie related a tale of her "brother" Tom.

"Tom also shot a deer that day, but his glory was dimmed by a misfortune, of which he seemed fated never to hear the last," she recalled. "The custom was to place one or two men at stated intervals in different parts of the country where the deer were pretty sure to run, and Tom was on stand watching through the woods in the direction from which the sound of the dogs came. As the deer bounded toward him, he was so excited that when he fired, the shot went harmlessly by the buck and landed in one of the General's dogs, killing the poor hound instantly. Though this was a loss keenly felt, there was no resisting the chance to guy the hunter. Even after Tom had come to be one of the best shots in the 7th Cavalry, and when the General never went hunting without him, if he could help it, he continued to say, 'Oh, Tom's a good shot, a sure aim—he's sure to hit something!'"

By fall, the atmosphere had become sufficiently congenial that the Custer brothers invited their father for a visit. With his arrival, the whirlwind of practical joking that always seemed to prevail between the brothers quickly swept Emanuel Custer into its vortex.

Libbie described a situation in which "Father Custer" was seated near the fire, so that the smoke from his pipe would go up the flue. Autie came into the room and casually threw what appeared to be some waste paper in the fire. Suddenly there was a "wild pyrotechnic display," as he had added a handful of blank cartridges to his waste paper.

"These innocent-looking scamps faced their father and calmly asked him why he had jumped half-way across the room," Libbie recalled. "They often repeat this Fourth-of-July exhibition with fire-crackers, either tied to his chair, or tossed carelessly on the burning logs, when his attention is attracted elsewhere . . . No matter what trick they play, he is never phased. He matches them too, and I help him, though I am obliged to confess I often join in the laugh, it is all so funny."

At least it broke the monotony.

The boys also enjoyed teasing Emanuel with political discussions. Knowing that he was an ardent Democrat, they would bait him with Republican doctrine. They did so with faces so straight, that even Libbie was often taken in that they were serious.

As she explained, "The older man was never rasped or badgered into anger. He worked and struggled with his boy, and mourned that he should have a son who had so far strayed from the truth as he understood it. The General argued as vehemently as his father, and never undeceived him for days, but simply let the old gentleman think how misguided he really was . . . Tom connived with the General to deprive their father temporarily of his dinner. When the plate was well prepared, as was the old-time custom, the potato and vegetables seasoned, the meat cut, it was the signal for my husband to hurl a bomb of inflammable information at the whitening hairs of his parent. The old man would rather argue than eat, and, laying down his knife and fork, he fell to the discussion as eagerly as if he had not been hungry. As the argument grew energetic and more absorbing, Tom slipped away the father's plate, ate all the nicely prepared food, and returned it empty to its place."

But Father Custer, a scamp in his own right, was adept at turning the tables. After Christmas, when they traveled north by Mississippi steamer en route to Monroe for a visit and to return the elder Custer to his home, the boys arranged to surreptitiously relieve the old man of his pocketbook.

"Tommy and I had a stateroom together, and on one night in particular, all the folks had gone to bed in the cabin, and Tom was hurrying me to go to bed," Emanuel wrote in a later letter to Libbie. "He took the upper berth. I put my vest under the pillow, and was pulling off my boots, when I felt sure I saw something going out over the transom. I looked under the pillow, and my vest was gone. Then I waked Tommy, who was snoring already. I told him both my purse and vest were gone, and, as the saying is, I 'smelt the rat.'"

Emanuel suspected Autie, who denied everything, blaming the theft on "those shameless rogues" aboard the ship. On the third day after the robbery, the boys were gloating over their escapade, and as Libbie described it, they "incautiously exhibited the pocketbook. Suddenly the hand that held it was seized in the strong grasp of the wronged father, who, lustily calling for aid, assured the passengers that were thronging up (and, being strangers, knew nothing of the relationship of the parties) that this purse was his, and that he had been robbed by these two scoundrels, and if they would assist in securing their arrest and restoring the purse, he would prove all he said."

"For shame!" Father Custer shouted. "Stand there, cowards, will you, and see an old man robbed?"

The crowd of passengers intervened to restore the old man's property, and the outwitted Custer boys wound up paying for their father's passage and all of his room and board while he was "penniless" aboard the vessel.

He who laughs last, laughs best. As often as he was duped, Emanuel had the penultimate laugh—the last laugh being reserved for that in which father and sons *all* joined in the hilarity.

CHAPTER 11

ADJUSTING TO THE REGULAR US ARMY

THE TRIP UPSTREAM on the Mississippi steamboat was occasioned by a brief interregnum in the military careers of the Custer boys. Though sufficiently brief so as to figure only in passing in the timeline of their careers and their roles in the West, it marked a turning point.

During the year spanning the months at the middle of 1865 through the middle of 1866, the Union Army was undergoing a vast and far-reaching reorganization. The unrest in Texas, and other places within the former confederacy, notwithstanding, the demobilization had begun in the summer of 1865 even before the surrender of the last Confederate stragglers east of the Mississippi. From a peak strength of around 2.2 million men— the vast majority members of the temporary volunteer regiments linked to states—the head count of the Union Army declined rapidly. Through the first week of August 1865, 641,000 officers and men were discharged, and through November, another 160,000 were deleted from the rolls. Most of the remainder were discharged through the winter.

In the meantime, brevet rank advancements, necessary during the rapid expansion earlier in the war, were now expiring as officers were being mustered out of the volunteer regiments, and as the huge divisions, corps, and field armies were being deactivated. Regular US Army officers brevetted the much higher rank to lead volunteer regiments and volunteer brigades now reverted to their earlier permanent ranks.

Because the Union Army consisted primarily of volunteer regiments, the immediate postwar regular US Army was what historian Robert Utley described as a "mere skeleton." During 1866, as the number of volunteers dwindled to 11,000, the meat put back on the bone of the regular Army skeleton brought the personnel strength *up to* 30,000—though General-in-Chief Ulysses S. Grant had wishfully and unsuccessfully lobbied Congress for a US Army of 80,000.

George Armstrong Custer, a brevet major general of volunteers, reverted back to his permanent regular US Army rank of lieutenant colonel in February 1866. Tom Custer, meanwhile, who had risen to the brevet rank of lieutenant colonel of volunteers by the end of the war, was commissioned into the regular US Army in March 1866 as a first lieutenant.

Autie, who was in Washington, DC, got the news before Tom, who was in Monroe. In a letter that month to Libbie, also in Monroe, Autie asked her to "urge Tom to study his Tactics, Cavalry and Infantry. He was most fortunate in his appointment considering the number and rank of applicants. Several of those appointed Lieutenants in the regular army had been brevet Major Generals in the Volunteers . . . So the 'Custer luck' has again prevailed."

In fact, Tom apparently *had* studied tactics, for passing a written examination was a prerequisite for an officer's commission in the postwar Army.

However, in the near term, both of the brother officers found themselves without an assignment because the skeletal US Army had downsized so far that there was no immediate place for them. Gradually, though, the rebuilding would bring the US Army's field strength to forty-five infantry regiments, and ten of Cavalry.

In July 1866, Autie was assigned to the newly constituted 7th US Cavalry Regiment at Fort Riley in Kansas. Located about 130 miles due west of Kansas City, Fort Riley had been established back in 1853 as one of the posts that existed to provide security for the Santa Fe Trail. Now, it was one of the posts providing security for the construction of the Kansas Pacific Railway.

Lieutenant Colonel George Armstrong Custer, once the commander of entire divisions, now found himself second in command of a mere regiment. The apparent demotion seems not to have fazed him, because the regimental commander, Colonel Andrew Jackson Smith—himself a wartime brevet major general—had parallel duties as chief of the District of the Upper Arkansas and his frequent absences allowed Custer to run the show at Fort Riley. A quarter century older than Autie, Smith had his eyes not on the grand adventure of the American West, but on retirement.

Contrary to the popular myth, Custer never actually commanded the 7th Cavalry, though he would almost always act in that role on behalf of absentee colonels.

As had been the case in Texas, and all of Autie's future posts in the West, Libbie soon joined her husband. He had written to her from Kansas on May 2, "Come as soon as you can . . . I did not marry you for you to live in one house, me in another. One bed shall accommodate us both." Her father, who had passed away just a few months earlier, on March 18, 1866, had always counseled her to follow her husband wherever he went, and she had done so—even without his urging.

Indeed, as she wrote in *Tenting on the Plains*, his last words to her were "continue to do as you have done; follow Armstrong everywhere."

Meanwhile, Lieutenant Tom Custer of the regular US Army had found a home in the 1st US Infantry Regiment, then on occupation duty in the South. However, Autie made sure that this assignment was brief. He apparently pulled some strings with Secretary of War Edwin Stanton, who that year had told him, "I tell you, Custer, there is nothing in my power to grant I would not do, if you would ask me."

A few weeks later, Tom had his own permanent assignment to the 7th Cavalry, in which he would ride at his brother's side for most of the rest of their lives.

By November 1866, Autie and Libbie were together again with Autie's brother—and the Scamp whom Libbie referred to as *her* brother—cozily sharing quarters at Fort Riley. Initially assigned to Company A, Tom was sidelined for a time as quartermaster for the 7th Cavalry.

During Colonel Smith's routine absences, Autie's being in charge often proved awkward, as least as noticed by Libbie. As she wrote, he "had under him officers much older than himself. He was then but twenty-seven years of age, and the people who studied to make trouble used this fact as a means of stirring up dissension. How thankful I was that nothing could draw him into difficulty from that question, for he either refused to listen, or heard only to forget."

As for relations with that junior officer, Lieutenant Tom Custer, it was that form of childish foolery that made it seem as though time had moved neither tick nor tock since their preteen days in New Rumley—except that Libbie was now their playmate.

"The Custer men were given to what their Maryland father called 'toting' us around," she explained in her memoir *Tenting on the Plains*. "I've seen them pick up their mother and carry her over the house as if she weighed fifty instead of one hundred and fifty pounds. There was no chance for dignified anger with them. No matter how indignant I might be, or how loftily I might answer back, or try one of those eloquent silences to which we women sometimes resort in moments of wrath, I was snatched up by either my husband or Tom, and had a chance to commune with the ceiling in my airy flight up and down stairs and through the rooms."

She seemed to have enjoyed it every bit as much as her husband and the scamp.

Of course, there was a dark side to the dynamics of the threesome. While Autie had sworn off alcohol in 1861 and apparently never took another drink, Tom paid lip service to temperance, but on occasion he fell far from the proverbial wagon of sobriety. In a letter to his wife in May 1867, Autie complained that "Tom's conduct grieves me."

While the purpose of the 7th Cavalry at Fort Riley was the protection of the westward trails from interference from the Kiowa or Southern Cheyenne—as well as bandits drawn from the ranks of former Confederate soldiers and Union deserters. However, compared to what was taking place farther north in the territories of Montana and Wyoming, where Red Cloud's War raged through the winter of 1866–1867 and into 1868, that winter for the Custers at Fort Riley was tediously quiet.

"It is hard to imagine a greater change than from the wild excitement of the Virginia campaigns, the final scenes of the war, to the dullness of Fort Riley," Libbie wrote. "Oh! how I used to feel when my husband's morning duties at the office were over, and he walked the floor of our room, saying, 'Libbie, what shall I do?'"

In the spring of 1867, the monotony was finally broken when the 7th Cavalry was ordered into the field. General William Tecumseh Sherman, who had laid waste to Georgia during the Civil War and who now commanded the Military District of the Missouri, decided that there should be a cavalry show of force on the Southern Plains. To lead it, he picked Winfield Scott Hancock, a hero of Gettysburg and a wartime brevet major general who—unlike George Armstrong Custer with whom he shared those two attributes—was now a permanent major general in the regular US Army.

Hancock, in turn, picked the 7th Cavalry under Custer's acting command as part of his 1,400-man task force. Not among this group was Tom Custer, who had again been laid low by "breakbone" fever, who had to rely on his brother's letters for news of their trek across western Kansas and an inconclusive conference held with Cheyenne leaders at Fort Larned on April 12.

Tom, along with Libbie, finally joined the 7th Cavalry in the field on May 17 as the wide-ranging patrol continued its meandering, 1,000-mile sweep of the Plains. While Autie was on patrol, Libbie was transported to a succession of Kansas outposts, from Fort Riley to Fort Wallace, where she would await the arrival of his patrol as it passed through a particular fort for resupply. Tom, of course, joined his brother at the head of the 7th Cavalry column.

For three months, there was no significant confrontation with a Cheyenne war party, though tensions within the command resulted in numerous desertions, and arrests of some of the deserters. In one case, the officers sent in pursuit—including Major Joel Elliot and Tom Custer—found themselves in a firefight with a group of deserters. Three deserters were shot, one of them mortally.

"The first fight of the 7th Cavalry was at Fort Wallace," Libbie Custer wrote in *Tenting on the Plains* of hers and the regiment's baptism of fire. "In June, 1867, a band of three hundred Cheyennes, under Roman Nose, attacked the stage-station near that fort, and ran off the stock. Elated with this success, they proceeded to Fort Wallace, that poor little group of log huts and mud cabins having apparently no power of resistance. Only the simplest devices could be resorted to for defense. The commissary stores and ammunition were partly protected by a low wall of gunny-sacks filled with sand. There were no logs near enough, and no time if there had been, to build a stockade. But our splendid cavalry charged out as boldly as if they were leaving behind them reserve troops and a battery of artillery. They were met by a counter-charge, the Indians, with lances poised and arrows on the string, coming on swiftly in overwhelming numbers. It was a hand-to-hand fight."

A week later, on July 2, a 2nd Cavalry courier detachment under Lieutenant Lyman Kidder, carrying dispatches from Sherman to Custer was wiped out to a man by a raiding party comprised of Cheyenne and Lakota.

The site of the incident was discovered on July 12 by Will Comstock, one of Custer's scouts. This was the first time that Tom and Autie had laid their eyes upon the aftermath of the complete annihilation of a US Army contingent by the indigenous people of the Plains. It made a vivid impression.

"Every individual of the party had been scalped and his skull broken," Autie wrote in *My Life on the Plains*. "Even the clothes of all the party had been carried away; some of the bodies were lying in beds of ashes, with partly burned fragments of wood near them, showing that the savages had put some of them to death by the terrible tortures of fire. The sinews of the arms and legs had been cut away, the nose of every man hacked off, and the features otherwise defaced so that it would have been scarcely possible for even a relative to recognize a single one of the unfortunate victims. We could not even distinguish the officer from his men. Each body was pierced by from twenty to fifty arrows."

The Custers and their contingent reached Fort Wallace, 40 miles to the south, the following day. It was here that Autie expected to be reunited with both General Hancock and Libbie. Both had been there, but had moved on.

The trek continued, with much of the traveling being done at night to beat the heat. Driven by anxiousness about missing his wife, and without orders from Hancock, Autie made the decision to press on to Fort Harker, from which he could take a train to Fort Riley and Libbie's loving embrace. Undertaking a forced march, he and his men reached the fort in the wee hours of July 19.

Colonel Smith, the commander of the 7th Cavalry, happened to be at Fort Harker, but he was asleep when his regiment arrived under Custer's command. Autie awakened him to tell him that he was going to grab the next train to Fort Riley. Thinking that Autie was doing this under orders from Sherman, Smith allowed him to go. When the colonel discovered that his lieutenant colonel was acting on his own initiative, he was livid.

By some accounts, Smith wired Fort Riley to order that Autie be charged with deserting his regiment and that he be placed under house arrest pending a court martial. Custer Scholar Lawrence Frost, however, wrote that Smith ordered him back to Fort Harker, but that train schedules delayed his return for two days, and that the arrest order came from Hancock.

Ironically, Sherman shortly thereafter relieved Hancock of his command for his having failed to engage and defeat the Plains tribes in his lengthy patrol.

The ensuing proceedings against George Armstrong Custer moved slowly, and the court martial was not empanelled until September at Fort Leavenworth. In addition to desertion, he was charged with leading a forced march on the personal business of trying to reach his wife, and with the death without a trial of the deserter who died as a result of a shootout with pursuing troops. The prosecution called Tom Custer to testify, but his word was not sufficient to persuade the panel to acquit his brother.

Found guilty, Autie was suspended from rank and pay for a year. General Phil Sheridan, who had assumed Hancock's command as head of the Military Division of the Missouri, permitted the Custers to reside in officers quarters at Fort Leavenworth through the winter—and Tom once again moved into their household.

The winter snow drifting across the plains always curtailed the transit of wagon trains, and limited the efforts of the railroad construction crews. As had been the case during the previous winter, that of 1867–1868 was also a period of inactivity for the 7th Cavalry on the Kansas Plains. The Cheyenne, their annual buffalo hunts completed, also went into winter quarters.

Aside from missing out on a few hours of office work each morning, Autie's life was little changed. For Tom, the boredom was punctuated by periodic resumptions of his drinking jags. Jennie Barnitz, the wife of Captain Albert Barnitz, in letters collected into the volume *Life in Custer's Cavalry*, noted Tom's drinking, but insisted that he had managed to tame the beast that winter at Fort Leavenworth.

In the evenings, the social scene was punctuated by the occasional party or soiree. Sharing the fun was Libbie's cousin, Rebecca Richmond, who came south from Monroe to stay a while as the Custers' house guest. The possibility of a romance between she and Tom presented itself, but nothing materialized, and Tom remained unattached.

Perhaps it was because of his drinking, and perhaps it was because he had met someone else: Lucia Gregory Burgess, known as Lulie, whom he apparently met at Fort Leavenworth that spring. She was twenty years old and the daughter of John Burgess, a grocer in Jersey City, New Jersey. Those looking for romance in the scamp's life may find it in this relationship, for it would continue, albeit mainly at a distance, for the next several years.

When they parted on June 20, Lulie inscribed a small book entitled *The Words of Jesus*, "for Colonel T.W. Custer, 7th Cavalry." She also wrote her home address, anticipating his communication.

He continued to carry this book with him through those coming years, often scribbling marginal notes in it. Eventually, the book came into the possession of Custer scholar Dr. Lawrence Frost. In addition to writing several meticulously detailed books about the Custers, Frost, who died in 1990, was one of the twentieth century's most avid collectors of Custer ephemera. Today, parts of his collection not in private hands, are in the archives of the Monroe County Library in Monroe, Michigan.

CHAPTER 12

THE BLOODY ROAD
TO WASHITA

GIVEN THE FACT that the life of a cavalry soldier on the Plains was almost entirely one of relentless boredom punctuated only by the rare and usually fruitless pursuit of a raiding party, it would have been hard to predict that during 1868 the Custer boys in blue were marking the countdown to the most significant battle that they would experience between Appomattox and the Little Bighorn.

For Tom Custer, the year was like a replay of 1862 without the magnolias of Alabama—a year of routine camp life that would culminate in a violent climax. In 1862, it had been Stones River. Six years later, it would be the Washita River. Likely he had heard of neither river when their respective years began.

For Tom's older brother, it was the endless year of his suspension from duty, boredom incomparable to anything he had endured during the Civil War.

Beyond the walls, literal and figurative, that enclosed them, though, storm clouds were boiling up on the horizons all around. While George Armstrong Custer was sidelined by his enforced hiatus, major diplomatic initiatives were in play with the objective of altering the political landscape on the windswept Plains.

With the end of the Civil War, there had been a substantial increase in the number of emigrants moving across the Plains toward California and Oregon. At the same time, railroads were now being constructed to span the Plains with the goal of reducing transcontinental travel time from months to days. The Union Pacific, building westward from Omaha would meet the Central Pacific, building eastward from Sacramento, in Utah in 1869. Meanwhile, the former was not the only railroad being planned to lead westward from the Mississippi.

There had been a clash of cultures between the emigrants and the indigenous people of the Plains since the first wagon trains had crossed a generation earlier. However, after the Civil War, the scale of the intrusion upon the Plains—not to mention the technology represented by the steel rails—had mushroomed.

In 1851, the US government had negotiated the Fort Laramie Treaty with the Cheyenne and the other tribes of the Southern Plains, as well as with the tribes of the Northern Plains, especially the Lakota and the other Siouan-speaking peoples. This treaty called for free passage on the trails in exchange for compensation to the tribes in the form of goods transferred via agents of the Office of Indian Affairs. The treaty also defined the perimeters of tribal land, a concept that was alien to people for whom the vast open Plains were like an ocean over which they had always moved without a thought of arbitrary boundaries.

Subsequent treaties, such as the Fort Wise Treaty of 1861 amended the Fort Laramie Treaty to redefine boundaries and specify reservations. These were naturally opposed because the reservations were much smaller than the areas granted in 1851. There was also disagreement with treaties that had been signed by a handful of chiefs without consultation with the majority of the people. Most contentious in their opposition were the Hotamétaneo'o, or "Dog Soldiers." They were a band of militant Cheyenne who had been a defiant element within mainstream Cheyenne life since the late 1830s, and who were allied with similarly defiant Lakota bands.

The post-1861 round of conflict culminated in the infamous Sand Creek Massacre of 1864 in which a 700-man uniformed force led by Colonel John Chivington of the 1st Colorado Volunteer Cavalry undertook a dawn surprise attack against an encampment of about 100 lodges belonging to a Cheyenne group under the leadership of Black Kettle, as well as a few Arapaho lodges. Between 500 and 800 people, including women and children, had been killed. This disaster, recognized as such by the federal government, led to Chivington's resignation and strong official condemnation. On the Plains, it led to antagonism that boiled over into frequent skirmishes between Hotamétaneo'o and settlers.

After General Winfield Scott Hancock's inconclusive search and destroy campaign in the summer of 1867, the United States government again traded its stick for a carrot. In July of that year, Congress empanelled the Indian Peace Commission, charging it with the goal of negotiating further agreements with the people of the Plains.

By the terms of another round of treaties, including the Medicine Lodge Treaty of 1867 and a second Fort Laramie Treaty in April 1868, Plains tribes surrendered more land in exchange for reservations with fixed boundaries and federal aid. The Cheyenne were granted land in Kansas south of the Arkansas River, through which emigrant wagon trains were theoretically barred. However, this was complicated by the fact that the supplies that constituted their grant of federal aid were dispensed at Fort Dodge and Fort Larned, which were *north* of the Arkansas River.

Immediately south of this part of Kansas, and about 100 miles south of the Arkansas River in western Kansas, lay Indian Territory. Now part of Oklahoma, Indian Territory was an officially designated swath of land that had been set aside in 1834 as a "permanent" home for various tribes ejected from the southeastern United States under the Indian Removal Act of 1830.

In May 1868, as the weather warmed and as bands of Cheyenne, Kiowa, and Arapaho were once again on the move, the 7th Cavalry saw little action, although they patrolled deceptively quiet prairies against the backdrop of numerous stories of attacks, presumably by Hotamétaneo'o rather than by mainstream tribes, against wagon trains. In one incident that earned some media attention that summer, a woman named Clara Blinn and her two-year-old son Willie were captured. She managed to get a very poignant letter out via a trader in which she begged for rescue. Incidents like this, which were by no means isolated, were picked up by the media and became significant in forming public opinion throughout the West.

The absence of direct conflict between the US Army and the tribes on the Southern Plains ended dramatically on September 10 when a contingent of 3rd Infantry Regiment troops out of Fort Wallace crossed into Colorado in pursuit of a Cheyenne raiding party that had ambushed a wagon train.

They were ambushed by a group of Hotamétaneo'o warriors led by Woquini (aka Roman Nose) and forced to retreat to a sandbar on the Arikaree Fork of the Republican River, about 20 miles west of the Kansas-Colorado border. Greatly outnumbered, they were besieged for days, but managed to send for help. The Battle of Beecher's Island—named for Lieutenant Frederick Beecher, nephew of author Henry Ward Beecher, who died on the island—was immediately regarded as a milestone event in relations with the Plains tribes and a catalyst for renewed US Army offensive operations.

Tom Custer, who was in western Kansas with the 7th Cavalry at the time, was not tasked with aiding the efforts to relieve the troops at Beecher's Island, but he learned about the battle soon after.

George Armstrong Custer, who was with his wife in Monroe wiling away the final days of his year-long, court martial-mandated exile, heard about it from General Phil Sheridan, the tireless champion of Autie's professional career. Sheridan had gone to Sherman and had gotten Autie reinstated to active duty two months early. Now, Sheridan wanted him to lead the 7th Cavalry as the spearhead of a winter campaign to defeat the Cheyenne and allied tribes decisively.

For reasons of mobility, neither the US Army nor the Plains tribes campaigned in the winter, but this was precisely why Sheridan wanted to do it—to catch his enemy off guard and be in a good position to destroy stocks of supplies, thus limiting the tribes' ability to continue to conduct raids north of the Arkansas River. Indeed, Sheridan explicitly ordered Custer to take the 7th Cavalry 150 miles south of the Arkansas to the Washita River—*inside* Indian Territory—where the Cheyenne and Arapaho bands were known to spend the winter in technical violation of the treaties.

George Armstrong Custer was confident about his mission and anxious for action. In a letter of October 8 from the field, which is preserved at the US Military Academy, Autie's alma mater, he told Sheridan that "I can whip the Indians if I can find them and shall leave no effort untried to do this."

On October 2, 1868, less than a week after Autie had gotten a wire from Sheridan, he surprised Tom at the 7th Cavalry bivouac on Bluff Creek, south of Fort Dodge, Kansas.

Probably pleased to be in the field with his brother again, Autie mentioned numerous anecdotes involving the "Scamp" in his letters to Libbie during this period. In one, he bragged proudly of Tom supplementing the officers' mess by bagging a half dozen wild turkeys.

In another series of missives, he spoke of Tom losing two uniforms in less than a week. One incident involved Tom's dogs having cornered a skunk, with the result that Tom found himself "highly if not fashionably perfumed."

Tom turned this into a prank, positioning himself in a tent with fellow officers and blaming the odor on dogs attacking a skunk somewhere out in the night. He repeated the joke in several tents before it was determined that this "skunk" was actually the perfumed Scamp.

Another lost uniform incident came when Tom and a colleague were bathing unclothed in a stream. Their horses were spooked by an approaching party of Cheyenne, so the two naked soldiers leaped upon them and rode for safety—alive but embarrassed when they reached camp.

Within Indian Territory, the US Army maintained a presence at Fort Cobb, ostensibly to guard the fragile peace that prevailed in the absence of emigrant trails. Here, the 38th Infantry Regiment was commanded by Colonel William Babcock Hazen, who like Tom Custer, had been with XIV Corps of the Army of the Cumberland in the Battle of Stones River in January 1863. Hazen had led the 2nd Brigade of the 2nd Division on the left wing, while Tom was a few dozen yards away in the 3rd Brigade of the 2nd Division with George Thomas's force in the center.

Nearly six years later, Hazen had been tasked by Sheridan with visiting various Indian camps to explain that the Cheyenne, Kiowa, and Arapaho should leave Indian Territory and return at once to the reservations assigned to them by the Medicine Lodge Treaties, or be attacked by the 7th Cavalry.

On November 20, a delegation of Cheyenne and Arapaho were at Fort Cobb meeting with Hazen. Among them was Black Kettle, whose encampment had been decimated by Chivington almost exactly four years earlier in the Sand Creek Massacre.

According to documents now part of US Senate records, Black Kettle told Hazen, "The Cheyennes, when south of the Arkansas, do not wish to return to the north side because they feared trouble there . . . The Cheyennes do not fight at all this side of the Arkansas; they do not trouble Texas, but north of the Arkansas they are almost always at war. When lately north of the Arkansas, some young Cheyennes were fired upon and then the fight began. I have always done my best to keep my young men quiet, but some will not listen, and since the fighting began I have not been able to keep them all at home. But we all want peace, and I would be glad to move all my people down this way; I could then keep them all quietly near camp. My camp is now on the Washita, 40 miles east of the Antelope Hills, and I have there about 180 lodges. I speak only for my own people; I cannot speak nor control the Cheyennes north of the Arkansas."

Unfortunately for Black Kettle, at that very moment, the 7th Cavalry was making its way toward the place on the Washita River where his people were camped, following tracks in the snow that they identified as being that of a Cheyenne raiding party.

The US Army had reached Indian Territory the previous week. Sheridan had established his field headquarters, aptly dubbed as "Camp Supply," at a point about 25 miles south of the Kansas border, while the 7th Cavalry had continued due south from there.

On November 26, as Black Kettle was returning home after a difficult journey through deep snow, the 7th Cavalry's Osage scouts had located his camp on the south side of the Washita. They were probably unaware that farther downstream, there were additional encampments of Arapaho, Kiowa, and Cheyenne. Black Kettle's camp was selected for attack, essentially by the random chance that it was the first one to be located by the 7th Cavalry.

In preparation for leading his first major action since Appomattox, George Armstrong Custer rested his men by day, rousting them after dark to be in position to strike at dawn.

From the 7th Cavalry position west and upstream from the encampment, he divided his troops into four contingents. He dispatched two of these south of the river. Captain William Thompson commanded Companies B and F troops, while on his right, Captain Edward Myers led Companies E and I.

On the north side of the river, Major Joel Elliot, commanding Companies G, H, and M, would circle around and strike from the east, while on Elliot's right, Autie gathered Companies A, C, D, and K around him to strike straight into the heart of Black Kettle's encampment.

Tom Custer, as he had since before Sailor's Creek and Appomattox, and as he would in all of his battles for the rest of his life, rode with his brother.

As the barely discernable light of the dawn of November 27 first became visible on the eastern horizon, Autie, Tom, and their fellow officers gathered to look in the direction of the distant, slumbering Cheyenne camp. Among this small group was Captain Louis Hamilton, the grandson of founding father Alexander Hamilton. At age twenty-four, he was said to be the youngest captain in the US Army, but no one gathered there that morning could be called "old." Autie was twenty-nine and Tom Custer was twenty-three.

As they looked into the barely discernable landscape, they observed in the sky what Autie would later recall in *My Life on the Plains* as "something which we could only compare to a signal rocket, except that its motion was slow and regular. All eyes were turned to it in blank astonishment."

As he wrote, "slowly and majestically it continued to rise above the crest of the hill, first appearing as a small brilliant flaming globe of bright golden hue. As it ascended still higher it seemed to increase in size, to move more slowly while its colors rapidly changed from one to the other, exhibiting in turn the most beautiful combinations of prismatic tints."

"How long it hangs fire!" someone said. "Why don't it explode?"

"Rising above the mystifying influences of the atmosphere," Autie continued. "That which had appeared so suddenly before us, and excited our greatest apprehensions, developed into the brightest and most beautiful of morning stars."

Witnessed by many, this incident has developed into a mainstay of Custer lore. In reality a sighting of the planet Venus through atmospheric distortion that occurs with the ground fog that clings to the bottoms of river valleys on the Plains during winter nights, the incident has often been imbued with mystical and prophetic significance.

"Often since that memorable morning have I heard officers remind each other of the strange appearance which had so excited our anxiety and alarm," Autie wrote. "In less perilous moments we probably would have regarded it as a beautiful phenomenon of nature, of which so many are to be witnessed through the pure atmosphere of the Plains."

With the Custer boys and Louis Hamilton riding in the vanguard, the 7th Cavalry "approached near enough to the village now to plainly catch a view here and there of the tall white lodges as they stood in irregular order among the trees. From the openings at the top of some of them we could perceive faint columns of smoke ascending."

The encampment was so quiet that they thought it might be deserted.

As the commander prepared to order the attack, a shot rang out from somewhere, possibly from within the encampment. With this, Autie signaled the regimental band to strike up "Garryowen," the eighteenth-century Irish quickstep dance tune that had been adopted by the 7th as its regimental song.

Bugles sounded the charge, and from four opposing directions, the 7th Cavalry converged on Black Kettle's camp. For him, there had to have been the fearsome *déjà vu* of recalling Chivington's surprise dawn attack on his camp on Sand Creek four years, less two days, earlier.

As the battle began, Hamilton and the Custers, followed by the troopers of Companies A, C, D, and K, spurred their horses across the icy river, firing their Colt revolvers. The Cheyenne tumbled from their bedding. Some hunkered down for safety inside their lodges, but others grabbed their weapons and began what Autie called "a vigorous and determined defense."

Some returned fire from the cover of the trees, while others used the banks of the river itself as a rifle pit. Bullets hissed everywhere, many at point blank range. The one that struck Louis Hamilton in the heart was fired from so close a distance that it left powder burns on his jacket.

Captain Frederick Benteen, leading Company H, had a run-in with a fourteen-year-old boy who was later identified as having possibly been Black Kettle's son. The boy pointed his gun at Benteen, who gestured that he wouldn't shoot if the boy lowered his weapon. Instead, the boy fired four times, killing Benteen's horse with his third shot, before the captain returned fired, killing the boy.

"Seventeen warriors had posted themselves in a depression in the ground, which enabled them to protect their bodies completely from the fire of our men, and it was only when the Indians raised their heads to fire that the troopers could aim with any prospect of success," Autie recalled. "All efforts to drive the warriors from this point proved abortive, and resulted in severe loss to our side. They were only vanquished at last by our men securing positions under cover and picking them off by sharpshooting as they exposed themselves to get a shot at the troopers."

When the shooting subsided, Autie ordered his interpreters to tell the women and children that they would not be harmed.

The vigorous and determined defense put up by the Cheyenne cost the lives of twenty-one troopers, including Louis Hamilton. Once again, as throughout the Civil War, Custer's luck prevailed and Autie emerged unscathed. Tom suffered a flesh wound on his hand.

Estimates of Cheyenne casualties vary widely. In his report for Sheridan, penned the following day, Autie said he carefully surveyed the battlefield and counted the bodies of "103 warriors," a number that he later recalculated to at least 140. Most later estimates and calculations inconclusively provide numbers ranging between one and four dozen. Among the confirmed dead were Black Kettle himself and his wife, Medicine Woman, who were shot in the back as they tried to escape on horseback.

At about 10:00 that morning, as the battle was still winding down, the troops were surprised to see "a small party of Indians collected on a knoll a little over a mile below the village, and in the direction taken by those Indians who had effected an escape through our lines at the commencement of the attack."

At first, they assumed that these were those Cheyenne who had escaped, but as Tom and Autie studied them with binoculars, they could "plainly perceive that they were all mounted warriors; not only that, but they were armed and caparisoned in full war costume, nearly all wearing the bright-colored war-bonnets and floating their lance pennants. Constant accessions to their numbers were to be seen arriving from beyond the hill on which they stood."

The question was asked, "Who could these new parties be, and from whence came they?"

From interrogating their captives, they quickly ascertained that Black Kettle's encampment was merely one of many and that downstream there lay, as Autie recalled, a "succession of the winter villages of all the hostile tribes of the southern Plains with which we were at war, including the Arapahos, Kiowas, the remaining band of Cheyennes, the Comanches, and a portion of the Apaches; that the nearest village was about two miles distant, and the others stretched along through the timbered valley to the one furthest off, which was not over ten miles."

The 7th Cavalry burned the remains of Black Kettle's camp and prepared to withdraw before nightfall while simultaneously preparing to defend themselves if attacked. This plan was complicated by the fact that Major Elliot had led a seventeen-man detachment downriver in hot pursuit of a contingent of Cheyenne and had not returned. Lieutenant Edward Godfrey, who also rode in pursuit of escaping Cheyenne, recalled hearing him shout, "Here goes for a brevet or a coffin," as he rode out of sight.

Considering the situation a danger to the rest of his command under the circumstances, Autie decided to withdraw after a limited effort at a search. Many under his command, notably Benteen, were openly critical of Custer's decision, and would continue to harbor animosity toward their leader for what they perceived as his having abandoned Elliot.

Custer decided on making a show of force while getting the rest of the 7th Cavalry out of harm's way. Citing "that maxim in war which teaches a commander to do that which his enemy neither expects nor desires him to do," Autie feinted toward the other Indians as though to attack, "throwing out a strong force of skirmishers, we set out down the valley in the direction where the other villages had been reported, and toward the hills on which were collected the greatest number of Indians."

The 7th Cavalry had entered battle under careful discipline of band and bugles, and withdrew from the field under a cloud of uncertainty—albeit with an apparent show of force that convinced their opponents to pull back.

Later, under cover of darkness, the 7th Cavalry column made a hard left turn from their eastward course, reconnected with their supply train, and marched 80 miles north to Camp Supply.

By December 2, the 7th Cavalry had held a memorial for Captain Hamilton, and Custer had reported in person to Phil Sheridan. On December 7, the 7th Cavalry departed Camp Supply for a return visit to the scene of the battle on the Washita. Sheridan wanted to see it for himself and they all wanted to ascertain what had happened to Elliot and his command.

The troops reached the battle site three days later by heading toward a cloud of ravens and other scavengers swirling above it. While they were inspecting the charred remains of Black Kettle's camp, some of their Osage scouts reported finding a trail made by horses with horseshoes—cavalry horses, possibly made two weeks earlier by Elliot's men.

It was Tom Custer who first spotted the remains near a small stream that flowed into the Washita. The others arrived soon after.

Autie described the "stark, stiff, naked, and horribly mutilated bodies of our dead comrades," adding that, "no words were needed to tell how desperate had been the struggle before they were finally overpowered."

In his subsequent report, Sheridan wrote that they were "horribly mutilated," but had not been scalped. He added that the piles of spent cartridges indicated that "every man had made a brave fight."

Having buried the deteriorating bodies, Sheridan and the men of the 7th Cavalry continued downstream to inspect the other Indian encampments that had by now been abandoned. In a former Kiowa camp, they closed the circle on the search for Clara and Willie Blinn. She had been shot in the face at close range, while her badly emaciated two-year-old son had his skull crushed. Their bodies were recovered and later buried at Fort Arbuckle.

Sheridan saw Washita as a turning point. In a letter to his wife on December 6, Autie reported that his commander had called it "the most complete and successful of all our Indian battles."

The attack on Black Kettle's Washita encampment, and an ensuing controversy over whether the attack had been too aggressive, became the subject of national media attention. On December 22, the *New York Times* described it under a headline reading, "The End of the Indian War." The paper mentioned "the charge that Gen. Custer massacred a band of peaceful Indians," but added "the truth is, that Gen. Custer, in defeating and killing Black Kettle, had put an end to one of the most troublesome and dangerous characters on the Plains."

In fact, he was neither.

In his own final report on the campaign, widely excerpted in the national media in April 1869, Autie congratulated the US Cavalry for being able to "endure the inclemencies of the winter better than the Indians," and concluded with the assertion that "this I consider is the end of the Indian war."

Those who saw Washita as a decisive victory and an "end"—whether it was Sheridan, Autie himself, or the *New York Times*—were right insofar as the 7th Cavalry in Kansas was concerned. The regiment would remain deployed there until the spring of 1871 with neither a major, nor even a middling, hostile encounter with the Cheyenne.

In the larger context of the ongoing war between the two civilizations across the Great Plains, however, Washita was merely a milepost on a narrative that had decades left to run.

CHAPTER 13

THE SONS OF THE MORNING STAR ON THE PLAINS

THE STRANGE AND distorted appearance of Venus on the eve of the Washita battle is often associated with the famous nickname that was later bestowed upon George Armstrong Custer, though it was actually bestowed retrospectively. Evan Connell, author of the Custer biography *Son of the Morning Star*, wrote that it was in Dakota Territory five years later when the Arikara, not the Cheyenne, christened him "Son of the Morning Star," or "Child of the Stars."

"At least that is how he might have received the name," Connell wrote. "Maybe the Crow scout White Man Runs Him, who also was known as Son of the Morning Star, conferred this—his own name—upon Custer. Whether a Ree [Arikara] or a Crow first called him that, Son of the Morning Star must be regarded as a child of Dakota Territory; but symbolically it seems right to say he was born at dawn in Oklahoma beneath the bright soft light of Venus. No matter how he got the name, he liked to be called Son of the Morning Star."

If one were to have looked at the Son of the Morning Star through the prism of those such as Phil Sheridan or the *New York Times*, it would seem that recognition and reward were his for the asking after Washita. Perhaps it was time for his wartime brevet rank as major general to be made permanent. At least a promotion to the permanent rank of colonel was in order, was it not?

But the opposite came to pass. When Colonel Andrew Jackson Smith, the nominal commander of the 7th Cavalry, retired from the service in April 1869, the job should naturally have gone to George Armstrong Custer, the man who had led the regiment in its most famous battle. Instead, though, it went to Lieutenant Colonel Samuel Sturgis of the 6th Cavalry, who was promoted to colonel and brought over to the 7th. Like Custer, he had been a brevet major general during the war.

The controversy that had clung to Custer since his court martial was taking its toll. A year later, Autie sought the post of Commandant of Cadets at West Point, his alma mater. Instead, the job went to Brigadier General Emory Upton, who had been at the Point at the same time as Autie, and who graduated with the Class of May 1861.

Instead of watching Autie spiral upward and outward within the US Army hierarchy, as might have been expected, Autie and Libbie—as well as the everpresent brother Tom—remained in the West, inextricably bound as a threesome until they numbered three no longer.

The 7th Cavalry had spent the early months of 1869 on patrol across Indian Territory, with Tom having led a contingent south to the Red River on the border with Texas. By April 8, 1869, they had circled back to Fort Hays in central Kansas, and had set up camp about 2 miles away on the banks of Big Creek. Here, Libbie would join her two Custer boys in what she called a "village of white canvas nestling so peacefully in the bend of a sinuous stream." This place would remain the home and the base of operations for the 7th Cavalry until the spring of 1871.

One wonders what might have become of Tom had Autie and Libbie retired to West Point. He would probably have remained with the 7th Cavalry, and might have—as he did at Namozine and Sailor's Creek—achieved for himself some independent glory. In the summer of 1869, the Cheyenne nicknamed him "Mouksa," which translates as "Buffalo Calf," perhaps an appropriately subordinate name when considering him in relation to his more prominent brother. However, if he had remained in the West if Autie had gone east, would he have staked out an independent reputation?

Tom was, after all, also bathed in the light of Venus on the Washita River, so could he not also have been called *a* Son of the Morning Star? As it was, however, he remained in the shadow of the light cast by the Morning Star and he therefore remained as the Scamp, a role for which he was certainly suited.

An illustration of this can be drawn from an anecdote which Libbie recorded in *Following the Guidon.* Almost immediately after the 7th arrived at Fort Hays, there was an effort made at erecting semipermanent accommodations, or as Libbie put it, "to exhibit our triumph over circumstances, our ingenuity at inventing conveniences, and to elicit praise from each other for doing so much with so little."

Soon after her arrival, Tom invited her to visit his tent, which he had decorated as the nineteenth-century cross between a man cave and an anthropological museum. He showed her a dizzying collection of "shields made of the toughest part of the buffalo hide, and painted with warlike scenes; necklaces of the foreclaws of the bear; warbonnets, with the eagle feathers so fastened that they stood out at right angles when worn, and extended from the head to the heels; and, alas for my peace of mind, there seemed to be scalplocks everywhere!"

She added, "Our brother Tom always had an ample collection of these Indian mementos, and it made his tent or quarters in garrison very uncanny, in my estimation. But if the war bonnet, shield, or bearclaw necklace could be bought or traded for, or captured in an Indian fight, it was like possessing one's self of the family diamonds."

All of this was a mere prelude to her description of "Tom's next most valuable possession . . . a box of rattlesnakes."

As she explained, "being very agile and extremely quick, he never failed to bag his game. When he discovered a snake with seven or more rattles he leaped from his horse, called his orderly to take off his coat and tie up the end of the sleeve and hold it for the prisoner. Then, with a well-aimed and violent stroke with the butt of the carbine he pinioned the reptile near the head, and holding it down with one hand, seized it by the back of the neck, lifted it from the ground, dropped it into the sleeve, tied it again, and swinging into the saddle, joined the column as unconcerned as if the seven rattles were not threatening vengeance behind him."

This menagerie existed, according the Scamp, explicitly for *her*.

"Well, Old lady, I have some beauties to show you this time, captured them on purpose for you," he would tell her at the end of a campaign.

"I appreciate the honor," she told him, resorting to subterfuge to escape this form of hospitality. "But I will see the reptiles some other day."

"I might as well have argued with the snakes themselves for all the good I accomplished," she recalled. "The insecure cages were patched-up hard-tack boxes, and the snakes had to be lifted out to exhibit them . . . I only begged before the performance began to take up my place on the bed and oh, how I bemoaned the lowness of it! The agonizing thought was forced upon me that at that very moment a snake might be lurking under the low camp-cot, or, worse still, wriggling under the blankets on which my trembling toes then rested. Then, with skirts gathered about me for a sudden flight, with protruding eyeballs, I shook and gasped as the box-lids were removed, and the great loathsome objects stretched up to show their length, a chance being given to each one to shake his rattles in rage."

Despite her professions of horror, she seemed to have maintained a lurid fascination with the experience, going into great detail when "words of regret from Tom awoke no answering emotion in me when he found himself minus one snake. What was a source of regret to him was an occasion of horror to me; there was not a vestige of the snake remaining; it had not escaped; it was a victim of reptile cannibalism, for the larger of the two had eaten his smaller comrade, and not even a rattle was left!"

In turn, she suggested that Tom ought to "keep all of his snakes together instead of in separate boxes; and I contended that this was nothing more than a measure of justice to them, as they must miss the sort of companionship, a craving for which is said to exist throughout the animal kingdom."

"If you think, Old Lady," he replied," that after all the trouble I have been to, to catch these snakes to show you, I am going to make it easy for them to eat each other up, you are mightily mistaken."

The signature wildlife of the nineteenth-century Great Plains of North America was not, of course, rattlesnakes, but the American Bison, still universally known in the West as the "buffalo." Tom and Autie, like many officers stationed on the Plains after the Civil War, avidly pursued the sport of hunting these massive creatures, and the meat thereby derived was a welcome change to the salt pork and hardtack of typical Army field rations.

The spectacularly vast herds, which had begun to diminish by the 1870s through overhunting by the indigenous people and newcomers alike, had become the stuff of legend throughout the world. During 1869, because of Autie's continued media notoriety, he was now routinely sought out as an escort for foreign celebrity delegations who came to the United States for buffalo hunts. They had all heard of him. The Boy General of the Civil War still made good copy, and since Washita he was now also being heralded as an "Indian fighter."

In fact, it was the paucity of the latter activity in Kansas that year that made celebrity hunts possible. One of these hunts involved a pair of English lords who were amusingly upstaged by an Ohio teenager named Sallie

Tallmadge. Libbie mentioned the episode in a September 19 letter to her friend Laura Noble in Monroe, but it seems to have faded from the annals of Custer lore until Ms. Tallmadge's brother Frank Tallmadge penned the article "Buffalo Hunting With Custer" for the January 1929 issue of *Cavalry Journal*. Custer scholar Dr. Lawrence Frost later discounted the tale as apocryphal, writing that "it is inconceivable that Custer would permit a seventeen-year-old stranger to participate in such a dangerous sport."

However, a September 25, 1869, article in the *Lawrence Daily Journal* from Lawrence, Kansas—of which Dr. Frost may have been unaware—describes what the headline touted as "A Belle Among the Buffalo." The article tells the story of a "young lady, fresh from school, with the bloom of young desire and purple light of love mantling her cheek, in the full flush of roseate health and beauty, who refused the offer of her wealthy and indulgent parents to make a summer tour of the Eastern fashionable places of resort for tourists and travelers, and comes to Kansas . . . and creates a greater sensation in killing buffalo than if she had married a Vanderbilt or had 'done up' all the fashionable round of pleasure at the Eastern watering places."

With Tom and Autie in the lead, the hunting party departed Fort Hays on September 7 and made camp on the Smokey Hill River after a ride of 16 miles. Their massive entourage numbered well over 200, including Colonel Sturgis and a sixteen-piece contingent from the 7th Cavalry regimental band. The guests of honor, as reported by the *Journal*, were "Lords Berkeley-Paget and Henry Waterpark, of the British Peerage, the latter a scion of the Wellesley family."

T.W. Tallmadge and his teenage children, as highly placed as they may have been in Columbus, Ohio society, were apparently mere additions to the VIP list.

The *Journal* reported that on the first day of the hunt, Paget bagged three buffalo, and Waterpark four. Autie claimed eight. Tom's tally, from among the additional fifteen that were brought down, was not reported.

After having watched from atop a nearby hill, most of the ladies of the party returned to Fort Hays, "satisfied with the exciting scene they had witnessed from afar off."

Sallie Tallmadge declined. "She was tired of being merely a 'looker-on in Vienna,'" reported the *Journal*. "And remained with her father, brother and Mrs. Custer at the camp. Her wish to join the next day's gallop was gladly gratified by the officers, and a dark, blooded bay of Custer's was placed at her disposal."

"Mounted upon the beautiful creature, she must have been indeed the glorious picture we are told she was," effused the *Journal*. "There were one hundred and thirty men, and one lady, apparently a very Joan of Arc, leading that armed band."

As Autie gave the word, "the entire party charged upon and scattered a herd of buffaloes that appeared to the westward. Foremost in the wild dash the fleet courser of Miss Tallmadge bore her, until she found herself upon the track of a huge bull. Full five miles of the prairie the bay spurned beneath his heels before the side of the old fellow was reached. Two quick, well-directed shots from a Colts revolver, that Miss Sallie carried, brought the bison to a halt. The big bull settled slowly to his knees, bellowed and rolled over—dead! Col. Cook, whose gallantry and admiration had kept him from joining separately in the chase, and who had followed close upon the track of Miss Tallmadge, now expected to see her stop satisfied. Not so. Her blood was up. Quick as a flash she wheeled and made for a second quarry, another sharp gallop, three shots, and the thing was over."

As she told her fifteen-year-old brother Frank, after her first kill, she "looked around for applause. No one was in sight but my escort and his orderly, whose testimony would never do. So later in the day I killed another when everybody could see."

As tokens of his appreciation, Berkeley-Paget gave both Tom and his brother a .44-caliber Galand & Sommerville revolver in a polished wood presentation case. I became personally acquainted with Tom's pistol just before it was sold at auction in 1995 for $77,000.

Three years later, Autie—but not Tom—served to escort another buffalo-hunting European nobleman in the person of Grand Duke Alexei Alexandrovich, the fourth son of Russia's Tsar Alexander II. In the January 1872 hunt, the master of ceremonies was Old West legend William F. "Buffalo Bill" Cody, though Alexei became fast friends with Autie, who accompanied him on later parts of his American "grand tour."

In the meantime, another Old West icon figured into the lives of the Custer boys and the "Old Lady" in 1869 and 1870. When they arrived at Fort Hays, the newly elected city marshal of nearby Hays City—and the sheriff of Ellis County—was James Butler Hickok, better known by his nickname, "Wild Bill" Hickok. A gambler and gunfighter, Hickok had already attracted some media attention, especially for the tall tales told by and about him. He had worked as a teamster for the Union Army in Missouri during the Civil War, and thereafter served as a lawman in a series of jurisdictions.

"The town of Hays City, near us, was a typical Western place," Libbie wrote of the colorful locale where the Custers crossed paths with Wild Bill. "The railroad having but just reached there, the 'roughs,' who fly before civilization, had not yet taken their departure . . . The carousing and lawlessness of Hays City were incessant. Pistol shots were heard so often it seemed a perpetual Fourth of July, only without the harmlessness of that pyrotechnic holiday. The aim of a border ruffian is so accurate that a shot was pretty certain to mean a death, or, at least, a serious wound for someone. As we sat under our fly in camp, where all was order, and where harmony reigned, the report of pistol shots came over the intervening plains to startle us."

With her gift for understated humor, she added that "I should not have heard much about these things had not the men delighted to shock the three women in camp with these tales of bloodshed; and, besides, it was rather difficult to keep us in ignorance of much that occurred in the town, as our soldiers were, unfortunately, engaged in many an affray with the citizens."

Of Libbie's impressions of Hickok, one cannot help but blush.

"Physically, he was a delight to look upon," she wrote. "Tall, lithe, and free in every motion, he rode and walked as if every muscle was perfection, and the careless swing of his body as he moved seemed perfectly in keeping with the man, the country, the time in which he lived. I do not recall anything finer in the way of physical perfection than Wild Bill when he swung himself lightly from his saddle, and with graceful, swaying step, squarely set shoulders and well poised head, approached our tent."

As the Custer boys discovered on the Plains their passion for hunting rattlesnakes and buffalo, the Old Lady discovered a passion for the human wildlife of the Plains. Had her general not been close at hand, there is little doubt that Libbie, had she found herself in Kansas by some other means, would have thrown herself at Wild Bill—or if not him, one of his fellow plainsmen.

"The impression left upon my mind by the scouts of which Wild Bill was the chief was of their extreme grace," she effused. "Their muscles were like steel, but they might have been velvet, so smooth and flexible seemed every movement. Wild Bill reminded me of a thoroughbred horse. Uncertain as was his origin, he looked as if he had descended from a race who valued the body as a choice possession, and therefore gave it every care . . . Among the white aborigines of the plains, the frontiersmen and scouts, there have long existed fine specimens of physical development that one seldom encounters among people who live an indoor life."

Indeed, Libbie may well have indulged a wandering eye that winter at Fort Hays and Hays City. Counterintuitively, Tom and Autie went home to Monroe for Christmas in 1869, though Libbie did not. The fact that Libbie and Autie were apart during this holiday season, as well as the following Christmas, and his explicit renunciation of gambling during the latter Yuletide, have led some to suspect trouble in the paradise of the wedding bliss of Autie and Libbie.

Custer biographer Louise Barnett, for example, described this period as "the crisis in the Custer marriage," while Marguerite Merington curiously chose to include no letters for the entire intervening year in her extensive and detailed compendium of their correspondence. On the other hand, Dr. Lawrence Frost, in his book *General Custer's Libbie*, mentioned the separations, but indicated no particular friction.

In fact, these separations were initiated in both cases by Autie having been away on Army business, though he did stay away longer than absolutely necessary. In November 1869, a month after the 7th Cavalry had gone into winter quarters at Fort Leavenworth, Kansas, Phil Sheridan, now a lieutenant general and the commander of the Military Division of the Missouri with responsibility for all the Great Plains, had summoned Autie to his headquarters in Chicago—which was the catalyst for his going east that winter. Among other things, Sheridan wanted to insist personally that Autie attend the reunion of the Army of the Potomac in Philadelphia in April.

According to Frost, Autie "enjoyed every moment he was in Chicago," attending the theater and celebrating his thirtieth birthday on December 5. In turn, Sheridan, who was ill at the time and apparently unable to travel, ordered Autie to continue on to Washington on further official business.

Before going to the capital, Autie chose to take the time to spend Christmas with his parents. Meanwhile, Tom, who had been granted a twenty-day furlough from Fort Leavenworth, joined his brother, and together, they arrived in Monroe on December 13. While Autie returned to Libbie after his visit to Washington, DC, Tom requested and was granted a three-month leave extension.

When Autie rejoined Libbie just ahead of the New Year, Tom was absent, but they were soon joined by a Custer face not previously seen on the Plains. The Custer boys' sister Maggie, who had just turned eighteen on January 5, 1870, arrived at Fort Leavenworth in the company of Julia Thurber, one of Libbie's Monroe friends. Also visiting Leavenworth at this time was Rebecca Richmond, Libbie's cousin, who was now living in Grand Rapids, Michigan.

In her diary, quoted at length by Lawrence Frost in his biography of Libbie, Ms. Richmond spoke enthusiastically of a "Grand Masquerade," of dance halls "gracefully festooned" with red, white, and blue bunting, of fine music, of "highly polished cutlasses" and of soirees that lasted until six o'clock in the morning. Such was Maggie's introduction to life on a frontier army post—although by this time, Leavenworth, with its proximity to Kansas City and the national railroad grid, had put its days of being on the "frontier" well behind it.

In the course of the Leavenworth festivities, a taste for Army life in the West had apparently taken its hold on the little sister of the Custer boys in the person of an attractive young sergeant named James Calhoun. As Margaret Custer spun her way through the winter's social season, they had apparently caught one another's eye and a romance had begun.

The son of well-to-do Cincinnati merchant James Calhoun, Sr. and his wife Charlotte Sanxay Calhoun, young James had enlisted in the Union Army during the Civil War. After the elder Calhoun died in 1864, it had greatly vexed his widowed mother when James decided to stay in the service, and along with his younger brother, Frederick, to make military careers for themselves rather than joining the family's wholesale grocery business.

According to an official biography on the website of the library of Jefferson County, Indiana, where their mother retired after her husband's death, "one can only surmise the distress Charlotte Calhoun must have suffered seeing her boys turn from a merchant life to life on the frontier, exposed to every danger present and indigenous to the area."

When he first met Maggie, Calhoun was with the 21st Infantry Regiment, which had recently been assigned to Camp Grant in Arizona. He had started his postwar military career in the West in 1867 with the 32nd Infantry at Camp Warner in Oregon, and had gone to Arizona after the 32nd was merged into the 21st during a round of US Army consolidations.

The plan for the Custer family in the spring of 1870 had been for Maggie to be escorted back to Monroe by Autie and Libbie en route to the Army of the Potomac reunion in April. However, when the 7th Cavalry was ordered to deploy once again to Fort Hays, the Philadelphia trip was cancelled, so Maggie and Julia returned to Monroe on their own. Traveling more than 750 miles across six states was a daring exercise for city girls with limited exposure to the world beyond their immediate environs.

Meanwhile, it illustrates the contrast between the level of refinement prevailing east of Leavenworth and Kansas City with the lack thereof epitomized by the lawlessness of Hays City and points west. It perhaps only added to the aura of Hays, that the city's marshal, Wild Bill Hickok, had shot and killed several men in gunfights during his tenure as a lawman.

In one case in July 1870, he tangled in a barroom brawl with a pair of 7th Cavalry troopers.

"In our ranks were just as lawless men as were found in Hays City, but the strict discipline of military life soon subdues the most violent spirits," Libbie rationalized. "In the town, however, with restraints removed, the bluff and the bully showed forth in his true colors. A little of the very bad liquor sold there turned an obedient soldier into a wrangling boor. Three desperate characters, planning to kill Wild Bill, decided that no one of them stood any chance if the scout was left the use of his arms; not only was his every shot sure, but he was so lithe and quick, and so constantly on the alert for attack, that it was next to impossible to do him any injury."

In this incident, a man named Jeremiah Lonergan jumped Hickok, and pinned him to the floor while another, John Kyle, attempted to shoot him. Hickok then, as Libbie wrote, "drew his pistol from the belt, fired backward without seeing, and his shot, even under these circumstances, was a fatal one."

Lonergan was wounded, Kyle was dead. The men of the 7th Cavalry promised revenge, and in the town, they were beyond military control.

"It was impossible for General Custer to interfere in such a contest," Libbie bemoaned. "His jurisdiction did not extend to the brawls of the town; the soldiers off duty were not punished, unless the citizens found something so flagrant, and proof of the dereliction so positive, that the offence must be investigated by a court-martial."

Was Tom Custer part of this or other drunken brawls in Hays City? Such rumors, including his having been arrested by Hickok, circulated well into the twentieth century, some even reported in the pages of pulp magazines. These included one especially grisly tale of Tom having shot a horse in a Hays saloon when it refused to jump onto a table. There are, however, no known nineteenth-century accounts to corroborate any such mischief by Tom.

Wild Bill left Hays City in the spring of 1871 and moved on to Abilene and beyond for more of the adventures that made him one of the characters who helped define the archetype of the Western folk hero. The Hays years were the formative period of this archetype, which prevailed at the apogee of American popular culture through the halcyon days of the Western motion picture genre at the midpoint of the twentieth century. It can certainly be said that Wild Bill's place in this pantheon of folk heroes was due in no small part to his skill at relating his own adventures in an entertaining, if embellished, way.

The same was true of George Armstrong Custer. He had been well known to readers of major newspapers since the Civil War, and had begun in 1867 to publish articles in the sportsman's journal *Turf, Field and Farm*.

Though these were written under the pseudonym "Nomad," he used his own name for a popular series of articles entitled "My Life on the Plains," that would begin to appear in *Galaxy* magazine in January 1872, and which was published in book form under that title two years later.

CHAPTER 14

A SCATTERED FAMILY

FOR THE MEMBERS of the extended Custer family, the year of 1871, and the shoulders of this year extending into the two adjacent years, was a time of change. It was not so much a family turning point, though a case for that could be made, but a time of altered trajectories, a time when the pieces on the board of interlocking lives were moved and repositioned.

For the General, the Old Lady, and the Scamp, it was an interruption in their close-knit bond, a moment of scattering, an interregnum between their period of snug symbiosis in Kansas, and the snug symbiosis that was to form once again in Dakota Territory.

In 1871, after having been together more or less continuously since the end of the Civil War, the threesome scattered, with Autie and Libbie apart for more extended periods, and Tom almost entirely absent from their group for the better part of two years. This disruption of the family unit was not so much a matter of their own motivations. Autie's absence from Libbie at Christmas in both 1869 and 1870 can be attributed not to choices he made, but rather to outside events that necessitated US Army redeployments.

For Tom Custer in 1871, the disruption was to be the temporary breakup of the 7th Cavalry in 1871 to address unrest in the former Confederacy.

After having been based in Kansas for four years, with its attention directed westward, the 7th was pulled eastward, back across the

Mississippi. The rise of the Ku Klux Klan and increasing violence against black former slaves and white former abolitionists across the South was perceived by the federal government as being tantamount to armed insurrection against the authority of the United States.

In 1870 and 1871, Congress passed the Enforcement Acts, designed to suppress the anarchy by sending in US Army troops to back up the US Marshals who were tasked with keeping the peace and maintaining order. The 7th Cavalry was dispatched from Fort Hays by train on May 23, 1871, bound for Louisville, Kentucky. Rather than being deployed as a single regimental unit, individual companies were detached at Louisville and scattered to various locations throughout the South.

When the elements 7th Cavalry were disbursed at the end of May, Colonel Samuel Sturgis established his regimental headquarters in Louisville, and assigned Lieutenant Colonel George Armstrong Custer to command Company A at Elizabethtown, Kentucky, 50 miles to the south. Coincidentally, "E-Town," was only about 20 miles from the old Camp Jefferson at Bacon Creek, where Tom Custer's 21st Ohio had spent the first winter of the Civil War a decade earlier.

This time, however, Tom was headed nearly 600 road miles farther east. His Company M, along with Companies G, H, and L of the 7th Cavalry, were assigned to Darlington County, South Carolina. Autie had conspired—and failed—to try to get Tom assigned to Nashville, 500 miles closer to E-Town.

The Custers approached Captain Frederick Benteen, who commanded Company H, which had been assigned to Nashville, and proposed a trade. In an exchange of correspondence in the 1890s, Benteen told fellow 7th Cavalry veteran Theodore Goldin that the Custer Brothers told him that he would have his pick of an assignment if Company M could have the Nashville post so that Tom could be closer to Autie. When Benteen checked with Sturgis for confirmation, Sturgis said that this was not true. The

Custer Brothers' scheme was thwarted, and the wedge between the Custers and Benteen was driven deeper.

Tom Custer and Company M remained in Darlington County through the summer and into the fall, relocating to Spartanburg on October 18, 1871. Here, they joined a contingent of three other 7th Cavalry companies under the overall command of Major Marcus Reno, who had just been transferred into the 7th after a career as a judge advocate and provost marshal at various posts in the South and West. Though these were tense times for the US Army in South Carolina, the regiment was not directly challenged and the most action that Tom saw was serving arrest warrants.

While Tom was in South Carolina, Autie saw little of his new post in Kentucky. Having situated his men and rented a substantial house for themselves in Elizabethtown, he and Libbie traveled up to Monroe. They wound up spending the entire summer there, except for an extended visit to New York by Autie in July. George Armstrong Custer did not finally take up residence in E-Town until September 21, nearly four months after he had first been assigned there.

Tom Custer's personal life outside the close-knit threesome was often punctuated by stories of his associations with various women. While most of these are known from fleeting innuendo rather than specific affirmation, some are worth mentioning because they are part of the lore of the Scamp. Tom was not shy about his numerous liaisons. In *Tenting on the Plains*, Libbie had written that "Brother Tom" had spent the summer of 1866 in Monroe "skipping from flower to flower, tasting the sweets of all the rosebud garden of girls in our pretty town. I had already taken to myself a good deal of the mothering of this wild boy, and began to worry, as is the custom of mothers, over the advances of a venturesome woman who was no longer young and playing for high stakes . . . Lad as he was, he escaped, and preserved his heart in an unbroken condition during the summer."

If one particular story is to be believed, one member of "the rosebud garden of girls" was Rebecca Minerd of Wood County, Ohio. Born in June 1850, she was the youngest daughter of Samuel and Susannah Minerd, who lived on a farm on Tontogany Creek, less than a mile west of Nevin Custer's farm, and she had a son whom she named Thomas C. Custer. The date of his birth is unrecorded, but in the 1880 Census, he was listed as being a nine-year-old "grandchild" living in the household of Samuel and Susannah, which would place his birth in 1871 or 1872. Throughout his life, Tommy Custer would be known routinely—by members of the Minerd family, by neighbors, and in the occasional newspaper reference—as the son of Thomas Ward Custer and the nephew of the illustrious George Armstrong Custer. There is no evidence that either man ever acknowledged any relation, and the Custer family never recognized Rebecca's assertion. Whomever his father, Tommy died childless in 1896 and was buried in an unmarked grave.

As there were rumors about Tom, there were rumors about Autie and a young Cheyenne woman named Mo-nah-se-tah, the daughter of Little Rock. In November 1868 she was seventeen or eighteen years old and living in Black Kettle's encampment on the Washita River when it was attacked by the 7th Cavalry. As discussed by both Autie and Libbie in their published writings, she was taken into custody along with others by the US Army and spent the winter with the 7th Cavalry. According to Cheyenne oral history and stories repeated often by Frederick Benteen of the 7th, among others, she had a second child with distinctively light hair at the end of 1869. This boy, named Yellow Bird, was described in various eyewitness accounts later, and is cited by authors from Stephen Ambrose to Evan Connell as possibly having been fathered by Autie, though an alternate theory holds that *Tom* Custer was his father. As with Tommy Custer, the paternity of Yellow Bird was never ascertained nor documented.

Tom Custer's true love, however, appears to have been Lucia Gregory Burgess, whom he had met in 1868. During the first part of 1872, he was on leave for nearly four months, spending most of his time with this grocer's daughter in her home town of Jersey City, New Jersey. They talked about, and even planned for marriage, and in his will, he made Lulie the beneficiary of half of his meager estate—the other half going to his mother.

They discussed her coming to visit him in the field as Libbie did with Autie, but poor Lulie was increasingly frail. She suffered from tuberculosis, then called consumption because of the gradual withering and weight loss associated with those who suffered its symptoms, and she was bedridden much of the time. They saw little of one another after those months together in the spring of 1872, but they maintained contact, and they continued plans to one day be husband and wife. He even went so far as to refer to her as "your aunt Lulu" in letters to his niece, Emma Reed. It was not to be. In 1875, the tuberculosis finally overtook her.

Tom would never marry, and officially, he had no children. Nor did his oldest brother. Indeed, Nevin was the only one of the four Custer boys to have confirmed descendants.

By the summer of 1871, Custer family life in Monroe centered on four households. There was that of Mother and Father Custer, of course, and that of David and Lydia Ann Reed. Meanwhile, Libbie's widowed stepmother, Rhoda Pitts Bacon, still lived in the home at the corner of Monroe and Second Streets where Libbie had grown up, though the house was clearly not the same without the commanding presence of Judge Daniel Bacon.

Finally, Nevin Johnson Custer and his wife Ann North Custer, and their four children made the long considered move to Monroe from their farm on Tontogany Creek in Wood County that summer.

On August 22, 1871, Autie and Nevin jointly purchased a 116-acre farm for $5,820 from a man named Nelson Jarboe. It was a long, narrow ribbon of land located in Frenchtown and fronting the north side of the River Raisin opposite downtown Monroe that included a house that had been built in 1850. This house was located just north of a dirt road paralleling the river that was known locally as "River Road." Nevin and Ann would remain here for the rest of their lives and would raise their children here.

For many years, and up to the present time, the property was known as the "Custer Farm." In 1916, when the road was paved, it was renamed as "General Custer Road," though this was later changed to "North Custer Road." The address of this house which had been Nevin's home now bears the address of 3048 North Custer Road. A second house, with the address 3029 North Custer Road, was built across the road in 1935 and was occupied by members of the family for many years.

Nevin's oldest child, Claribel, had been an infant when she and her parents had attended the elaborate wedding of Autie and Libbie in 1864. She would turn eight in September while her famous uncle was still in Monroe and buying property with her father.

Nevin and Ann's oldest son had been born on October 24, 1864, just as Monroe was learning of Uncle Autie's daring defeat of Jubal Early in the Battle of Cedar Creek. The boy, named George Armstrong Custer after his uncle, was now six.

Maria Matilda Reed Custer was born in Tontogany on September 18, 1867. Through the years, there have been various versions of her name. By the 1870 Census, she was "Miriam," but in 1880, she was "May." Throughout the rest of he life, she would spell her name as "May," though it is occasionally (and probably incorrectly) seen written as "Mae." Lula B. Custer had been born on January 15, 1870, in the home of the late Judge Bacon, where Libbie Custer had grown up, and was now a toddler. As May was sometimes identified as "Mae," Lula's name was sometimes written as "Lulu," though this was apparently not a reference to Tom's fiance, Lulie Burgess.

For Emanuel and Maria, Father Custer and Mother Custer, the period of scattering that centered upon 1871 involved not a change of place, for they had been and would live out their lives in Monroe, but a change of those family members with whom they were surrounded. Maggie, whose education at the Boyd Seminary had been the reason for their having relocated permanently to Monroe, turned eighteen on January 5, 1870, and was off to explore the world—beginning with her trip with Julia Thurber to Fort Leavenworth to visit her oldest brother and Libbie. She apparently never returned to finish her studies at Boyd's. As Charmaine Wawrzyniec at the Monroe County Library told me, "I suspect Maggie did not graduate from the Boyd Seminary . . . Maggie's name does not appear in any of the Boyd Seminary Commencement Announcements from 1858 to 1875."

Though she was to come and go physically during those two years of family repositioning, she had, in her mind, clearly moved on from Monroe. Meanwhile, as noted previously, Nevin and Ann Custer, who been building an independent life for themselves in Wood County, Ohio, were on the threshold of moving *to* Monroe.

Boston Custer, the youngest brother, who turned twenty-two in October 1870, remained in the shadows. Little is known of his activities between the Civil War and 1870. He was just short of fifteen when his parents moved to Monroe in 1863, but there are no records of his having graduated from school in that city. In his introduction to a slim volume of Boston's post-1870 letters, Tom O'Neil noted that during the Civil War, George wrote Judge Bacon to ask him to speak with Boston about going to school. Noting this, Charmaine Wawrzyniec points out that O'Neil gave no source for this. She went on to add that "the only source we have for general school attendance is the end of year articles in the local paper. I checked several years and did not see Boston listed as graduating."

In painting his picture of Boston Custer, O'Neill wrote that "Boston at first glance might appear to be a 'shiftless sort' who never seemed to hold what we would call a steady job."

However, there is no evidence that Boston was an undue burden to his parents or siblings, nor that he incurred any unusual indebtedness. Nor is it true that his apparent lack of a "steady job" meant that he was never gainfully employed. In his teens, he had helped out on Nevin's farm, and he had worked for brother-in-law David Reed, who had a freight business.

The fact that Boston Custer did not enlist in the US Army did not mean that he had none of the fire for adventure that drove Autie and Tom to pursue military careers. He came of age in a different era. By the time Boston was old enough to enlist, the Civil War was over and the US Army was rapidly downsizing. He did later follow his brothers as a civilian contractor, applying skills that he had learned on the farm and in the freight business as one of the packers and foragers who were employed by the 7th Cavalry in the field.

When exactly he began contracting with the US Army is unclear, though a March 24, 1871, letter to his fourteen-year-old niece Emma Reed—daughter of beloved half sister Lydia Ann Reed—is datelined Fort Hays, Kansas, where Autie and Tom were posted at the time. In a July 1871 letter to Libbie, Autie mentioned that "Bos" had sent home almost half of his monthly Army paycheck, adding "I am proud of the way he is beginning life."

In this letter to Emma, Boston assured her that "I am well and getting along well, I am having a very pleasant time and all the Officers are very kind to me and do all they can to make it agreeable for me. I have just come from Lieut. Rouseau's room where we have been enjoying a smoke together. He calls for me just before going to his meals and we walk over to the mess room together. I tell you he is a first rate fellow although he is an old Bachelor."

In Boston's letters, we also find a rare glimpse of a rare view of the Custer half-siblings who are rarely, if ever, mentioned by Custer biographers. The conventional wisdom is that the Monroe Custers had little or no contact with the family of their half brother Brice William Custer, Emanuel's son by his earlier marriage to Matilda Viers, whom we first met in Chapter Two. However, Boston seems to have known them intimately. In his October 14, 1874, letter to Emma Reed, he mentions Brice, as well as "Ry" Custer and "Marvy" Custer, who are presumably Maria Stockton Custer and Marvin Samuel Custer, Brice's wife and son. Apparently, Boston had *lived* with Brice for an extended time, as had Marvy in the home of Emanuel and Maria.

"Yesterday I received a letter from Ry Custer saying she wanted me to pay for my board at once as she heard from the General that I was in Dakota [and earning money]," Boston wrote. "And that she had to make a payment on her piano the first of November and said as soon as I sent her fifty dollars my board would be paid for."

He then complains that "I don't see how she could well ask for such a thing when she and Marvy were at our house twice and as long each time and did not pay anything which was all right but she thinks I will send it to her by Express and Brice won't know anything about it—but I intend to write Brice saying I enclosed fifty dollars to Ry for my board."

That relations were strained is indicated by Boston griping that Ry "had the cheek to sign herself Your loving Sister."

As Ry wrote again in November asking for money, there was apparently no immediate resolution to this disagreement.

George Armstrong Custer may have been stymied in his efforts to have brother Tom posted nearby during his Kentucky posting, but he did succeed in getting James Calhoun situated at a comfortable distance. During the previous winter, Calhoun was transferred out of the 21st Infantry and reassigned to the 7th Cavalry effective on January 1, 1871. He was promoted to first lieutenant eight days later. When the 7th redeployed to Kentucky in May, Calhoun was with Company C, which was bivouacked at Bagdad, just 50 road miles east of Louisville. They later moved much farther east to North Carolina, being based at Lincolnton and Charlotte.

By now, Maggie's future husband had earned a nickname within the regiment, that of "Adonis of the 7th," a reference to the hypnotically handsome hero of Greek mythology who was adored by women. This reference is counterintuitive of most accounts of his actual disposition. He was apparently never regarded as having been a womanizer. While the mythological Adonis may have had the eye of countless women, the nineteenth century Adonis of the Plains had eyes only for young Maggie.

Calhoun was so quickly and graciously welcomed into the Custer family that when Nevin and Ann's second son was born on November 14, 1871, they named him James Calhoun Custer. At the time, Calhoun was still Maggie's fiancé.

The wedding of Margaret Emma Custer and Lieutenant James Calhoun, who was known as Jim, though he is occasionally mentioned in family correspondence as "Jimmi," took place at the Methodist Church in Monroe on March 7, 1872. Both families were there, headed by Mother and Father Custer on one side, while the groom's widowed mother, Charlotte Sanxay Calhoun came in from Madison, Indiana. She had retired here from Cincinnati after her husband had died in 1864, and lived there with her daughters Mary and Charlotte.

Tom Custer was there, in the midst of one of his extended series of furloughs from his duties with Company M. The Monroe County Marriage Book confirms that he signed as a witness to the marriage. Autie attended, of course, fresh from having joined Buffalo Bill Cody for several weeks guiding Russian Grand Duke Alexei Alexandrovich on a buffalo hunt and a subsequent tour of the Plains that had also taken him south to New Orleans for Mardi Gras.

As a footnote to the happy day, Frederic Sanxay Calhoun, the groom's twenty-four-year-old brother met Emma Reed, the bride's sixteen-year-old niece and Boston Custer's frequent correspondent that day. These two would marry seven years later on February 24, 1879.

After the wedding, Maggie and her new husband joined Autie and Libbie at the headquarters of Company A in Elizabethtown. Like Libbie, Maggie was determined to accompany her husband on his future deployments.

Libbie had always imagined that the threesome of herself and the Custer brothers would be rounded out by another woman, naturally assuming that this woman would be Tom's future wife. In *Tenting on the Plains* she had written that "I knew Tom would live with us always if he could manage to do so, and my prospective sister-in-law would be my nearest companion."

Instead, the sister-in-law who would be her nearest companion was Autie and Tom's sister.

CHAPTER 15

LIFE AS *WASICHU* OUTSIDE THE STATES

Tom Custer was away on furlough on Christmas Eve in 1872 when his Company M of the 7th Cavalry Regiment pulled up stakes in Oxford, Mississippi, its last duty station in the former Confederacy. After a year and a half of being scattered throughout the South on occupation duty, ten companies of the 7th were to be reassembled once again as a single unit and returned to the West. Even as he bade farewell to his own lady, Lulie Burgess, the Scamp knew that his life would once again be intertwined with those of the General and the Old Lady.

For Autie and Libbie, the new orders for the 7th seemed to come suddenly, with their westward destination a surprise. Wrote Libbie, "Not an hour elapsed after the official document announcing our change of station had arrived before our house was torn up. In the confusion I managed to retire to a corner with an atlas, and surreptitiously look up the territory to which we were going. I hardly liked to own that I had forgotten its location. When my finger traced our route from Kentucky almost up to the border of the British Possessions [Canada], it seemed as if we were going to Lapland."

It was not literally Lapland, but Dakota Territory, specially Fort Rice on the Missouri River, 200 miles south of the British Possessions and about 25 road miles south of Edwinton, the small settlement that would later become

Bismarck, North Dakota. By the measure of the times, it was, depending upon one's way of looking at things, either in the middle of nowhere or in the middle of the great adventure that was the American West of the nineteenth century.

Even compared to Fort Hays in Kansas, their earlier duty station on the Plains, it was distant and remote. Kansas had been a state for a dozen years. Dakota Territory would not achieve statehood—as two states—for seventeen years. As a territory, Dakota was referred routinely at the time as being "outside the states," as though it was a foreign land.

In Kansas, by the 1870 US Census, there were 45 people for every 10 square miles. In Dakota Territory, there was just one. Of course, this data did not include the indigenous people of the Plains, who were not considered citizens of the United States, but of their respective tribes. In Kansas, they were outnumbered, but in Dakota Territory, they outnumbered the newcomers. In Dakota Territory, the dominant tribe was the Sioux, who called themselves, Dakota, Lakota, or Nakota depending upon the nuances of their specific dialects of the Siouan language. They did not call themselves "Sioux" and did not like the term because it was derived by the French in the seventeenth century from the derogatory Ojibwa word *nadouessioux*, meaning "little snakes."

In turn, the Sioux referred to the encroaching immigrants from the distant East, the so-called "white men," as *wasichu*, which means "the ones who steal the fat," or "the ones who steal the bacon."

The three groups, especially the Lakota, had been the dominant superpower on the Northern Plains for generations and still considered themselves as such. The immigrants from the distant East numbered barely 14,000, while the best estimates of the Lakota population averaged around 18,000. In 1866, Newton Edmunds, the former governor of Dakota Territory, had counted 20,790 members of the group known collectively as the Sioux.

This is not to mention other tribes of the territory, such as the Arapaho, Arikara, or the Northern Cheyenne, who were also present in substantial numbers. While the Northern Cheyenne were allied with the powerful Sioux, many tribes that had traditionally been intimidated and dominated by the Sioux, still remained at odds with them. An example was the Arikara—pronounced at the time as "Arikaree" and often abbreviated as "Ree"—some of whom were employed by the US Army as scouts. Indeed, George Armstrong Custer's most reliable Indian scout was an Arikara man named Bloody Knife.

While Fort Hays was reachable in reasonable comfort by rail, Fort Rice could be accessed only part of the year by steamboat on the Missouri, or by traveling overland on horseback or by horse-drawn vehicles.

However, the *rails* were coming.

The Northern Pacific Railway had been chartered as America's second transcontinental railroad after the joint effort of the Central Pacific and Union Pacific, which had begun service between Omaha and Sacramento in 1869. The Northern Pacific had languished until 1870, when financier Jay Cooke—the man who had bankrolled the Union during the Civil War—became involved and helped jumpstart the railroad. With construction now running briskly, the plan was to build the Northern Pacific route between Minnesota, where it connected with the national rail grid, and Tacoma on Puget Sound. By June 1872, the rails had reached into Dakota Territory at Fargo, and a year later they would reach Edwinton, which the railroad soon renamed after German Chancellor Otto von Bismarck in a public relations effort aimed at luring German settlers.

The new mission of the 7th Cavalry would be to augment the 22nd US Infantry Regiment in Dakota Territory, and to help ensure the safety of the survey parties that would locate the route for the rails. Once again, the regiment would serve under Lieutenant General Phil Sheridan as part of his Military Division of the Missouri, that swath of nearly a million and a half square miles in the midsection of the United States.

The sparsely populated western reaches of Sheridan's domain were not, of course, a blank slate upon which a rail line could be inscribed. They had been the scene of constant strain between their traditional inhabitants and westward streaming *wasichu* ever since the first wagon trains had begun crossing in the decade or so before the Civil War. The simmering tensions in the region had boiled over into Red Cloud's War, a far-reaching, two-year conflict named for the powerful Lakota leader who led the allied Lakota, Arapaho, and Northern Cheyenne forces.

The Fort Laramie Treaty of 1868 had ended the war with the granting of a "Great Sioux Reservation" comprising the southwest quadrant of Dakota Territory, and a recognition of the dominance of the Lakota and their allies, even at the expense of people such as the Arikara and the Crow (Absaroka or Apsáalooke), who lost land to the Lakota that had previously been granted to them by treaties. It was generally understood that the area of Dakota and Montana Territories west of the Missouri River and south of the Yellowstone River would be off limits to the *wasichu* indefinitely. The US Army went so far as to abandon a line of forts along the Bozeman Trail and to grant the Lakota defacto autonomy in southeastern Montana Territory.

Along with the establishment of reservations, there came the promise of government assistance in the form of food and other supplies, dispensed by the government's Indian Bureau, which was intended to compensate for the reduced area of available hunting grounds.

Back in the "States," far from the reality "on the ground" out west, public opinion favored accommodation with the Plains tribes, who assumed that their traditional way of life was fading forever, and that embracing *wasichu* culture was their hope for survival, and that all efforts should be made to aid in this process.

Elected in 1868, President Ulysses S. Grant undertook a "Peace Policy" toward the indigenous people of the West, observing in his December 1871 State of the Union Address that "the policy pursued toward the Indians has resulted favorably . . . many tribes of Indians have been induced to settle upon reservations, to cultivate the soil, to perform productive labor of various kinds, and to partially accept civilization. They are being cared for in such a way, it is hoped, as to induce those still pursuing their old habits of life to embrace the only opportunity which is left them to avoid extermination."

With the government assistance came Indian Bureau agents—explicitly civilian, not military—charged with dispensing the aid. With the agencies and the accompanying bureaucracy, there came schools, whose role it was to introduce native youth to *wasichu* culture. Around the agencies there also sprang up trading posts and sutler's stores at which the Indians could purchase or trade for other *wasichu* goods and wares not dispensed under the terms of treaties. Often, these goods were sold at exorbitant prices.

Meanwhile, nongovernmental agencies, mainly church groups, also became involved in bringing the perceived benefits of *wasichu* culture to people whose lives were inevitably changing. The Quakers were especially active, and they became an important element of Grant's Peace Policy, being commissioned to manage many of the agencies. All of this was altruistic in its intent, but it was not always perceived as positive—neither by the people it was intended to help nor by the *wasichu* living in the West.

For many *wasichu*, the Quakers were seen as naive do-gooders whose belief that they could negate centuries of tradition and transform the native people to infuse them with *wasichu* values, was unrealistic. For example, photographs exist of Autie and Maggie lampooning the Quaker peace commissioners in an amateur theatrical production while they were stationed in Dakota Territory.

Some Indians embraced the reservation paradigm, but others rejected it and referred to these people disdainfully as "Agency Indians." Men such as Red Cloud, who signed the treaties and became Agency Indians, readily admitted that they did not speak for everyone, and they had alerted the *wasichu* to this fact. That the *wasichu* continued to believe that Red Cloud was the Lakota chief of chiefs would be the source of a great deal of trouble in the coming years.

There were still many among the various tribes who had not signed the treaty, and who did not subscribe to it at all, and they saw it as their right to continue to come and go as they wished and to not live on the reservations or depend upon the largesse of the United States government via the agencies.

Two notable Lakota dissenters in particular had begun to achieve a notoriety among the *wasichu*. Sitting Bull of the Hunkpapa Lakota was a charismatic, widely respected leader and shaman. Crazy Horse, meanwhile, was a skilled warrior who had cleverly outmaneuvered and outfought the US Army during Red Cloud's War. Like Red Cloud, he was a member of the Oglala branch of the Lakota.

For a while, the vast Dakota and Montana expanses outside the reservation were so sparsely populated by *wasichu* that it did not really matter, but five years had now passed since the treaty had been signed and the Northern Pacific was coming. As the Lakota and the others would soon learn, the railroad surveyors had identified the ideal route westward from Dakota Territory across Montana Territory—and it would cut through the valley of the Yellowstone River. This was an area over which the Lakota and Crow people had sparred for generations, and an area that neither would be pleased to share with steel rails and locomotives.

In the spring of 1873, as open warfare between the Lakota and the Crow raged along the Yellowstone to the west, the rails neared the Missouri from the east, and the 7th Cavalry approached from the south. In March, the 7th had come north from Tennessee and Kentucky on Mississippi River steamers. They assembled at Cairo, Illinois, from which they traveled by train westward to Yankton in the southeastern corner of Dakota Territory. Some of their equipment was loaded onto ships to be carried north on the Missouri River, while in early April, the majority of the regiment mounted their horses for the 500-mile overland march roughly paralleling the river.

"All were well mounted," Libbie recalled. "The two years' station in the South had given them rare opportunities to purchase horses. The General, being considered an excellent judge, had, at the request of the officers, bought several from the stables of his Kentucky friends." Maggie, who was accompanying her husband on an overland march for the first time, would ride the entire way on horseback.

"Our first few days were pleasant," Libbie wrote. "The General had invited two officers besides his brother Tom, and his brother-in-law, Mr. Calhoun, to mess with him. We had a tableful, and very merry we were, even in the early morning. To joke before daylight seems impossible, but even at breakfast peals of laughter went up from the dining tent."

Though the beginning of the trip was pleasant, a late spring blizzard struck with what Libbie described as "a dull, gray morning and stinging cold in which the wind cut our faces and stiffened the flesh until it ached . . . No camp-fire would burn, of course, in such a gale, but I remembered thankfully the Sibley stove that we always carried."

From peals of laughter to stinging cold it was a rude introduction to life as an Army wife for Maggie Calhoun. For troops used to the relatively quiet and genteel life as an occupation force in the South, it was a rude reawakening to life on the Plains.

Also reawakened were old animosities between those who found themselves in the inner circle of George Armstrong Custer's mess tent, and those, such as Frederick Benteen, who disliked him and who found the difficulties of the march grist for their rancor. So too did the presence of Libbie and Maggie disgruntle the men who had no female companionship—especially in light of what Libbie described provocatively as "our little [romantic] detours by ourselves as we neared the hour for camping each day . . . We left the higher ground to go down by the water and have the luxury of wandering through the cottonwood-trees that sometimes fringed the river for several miles."

As the 7th wound its way north, encounters with the Lakota at their numerous riverside encampments were not always congenial. Libbie wrote apprehensively in *Boots and Saddles* that "Stakes had been set in the ground, with bits of red flannel fastened on them peculiarly. This, the guide explained, meant warnings from the tribes at war to frighten us from any further advance into their country. Whether because of the coolness of the officer, or because the warriors knew of the size of the advancing column, we were allowed to proceed unharmed."

There were moments that Libbie described herself as being "perfectly cold and numb with terror," but fortunately these moments did not turn violent.

The danger to the women was twofold. There was peril from death or capture by the Lakota, as well as the possibility of being killed by the soldiers to prevent their capture. As Libbie explained, "Without discussing it much in my presence, the universal understanding was that anyone having me [or Maggie] in charge in an emergency where there was imminent danger of my capture should shoot me instantly. While I knew that I was defended by strong hands and brave hearts, the thought of the double danger always flashed into my mind when we were in jeopardy."

Shortly after they finally reached Fort Rice, a vexing, but certainly more benign predicament arose. The steamer arrived carrying their personal belongings. They quickly discovered that all of their baggage—from Autie's collection of books to all of the "silken finery" of Libbie and Maggie—had succumbed to mildew.

James Calhoun was livid. Wrote Libbie, "Our sister's husband . . . was dignified and reserved by nature, but on that occasion the barriers were broken. I heard him ask Margaret to excuse him while he went outside the tent to make some remarks to himself that he felt the occasion demanded. There were furious people on all sides, and savage speeches about the thoughtlessness of those who had left our property exposed to snow and rain, when we were no longer there to care for it. I endured everything until my pretty wedding-dress was taken out, crushed and spotted with mildew."

CHAPTER 16

WASICHU ON THE YELLOWSTONE

By June 1873, the Northern Pacific had reached Bismarck, and its survey-ors now prepared to begin their formal survey of the rail route westward along the banks of the Yellowstone River. Because nearly 500 miles of the Yellowstone sliced through territory claimed by the Lakota and criss-crossed by Lakota hunting parties, the surveyors would need a security detail, and this was to be the 7th Cavalry.

Ten companies of the 7th, its main strength, were at Fort Rice. Two companies, D and I, had been detached to serve as the military escort for the Northern Boundary Survey Commission on the Canadian border in northern Dakota Territory, and would not return to the fold until the cam-paigns of 1876. This detachment, which also included several infantry companies, was commanded by Major Marcus Reno of the 7th.

The regimental commander of the 7th Cavalry was still Colonel Samuel Sturgis, but he was on detached duty and not present in Dakota. Lieu-tenant Colonel George Armstrong Custer, as he had been in Kansas, was the effective commander of the unit.

Getting underway in the predawn hours of June 20, the Yellowstone Expedition, as it was called, was an immense undertaking. According to the official US Army report, there were 353 civilians, most of them employed by the Northern Pacific, around two dozen Arikara scouts under

Bloody Knife, and 1,530 troops. The latter included nineteen infantry companies drawn from the 8th, 9th, 17th, and 22nd Infantry Regiments, in addition to ten companies from the 7th Cavalry. The overall military operational commander was Colonel David Sloane Stanley of the 22nd, with Custer as his second in command.

The two officers did not like one another, and expressed this opinion in letters to their wives. Autie called the colonel "cold blooded, untruthful and unprincipled," while Stanley said that Autie was "universally disliked by all the officers of his regiment excepting his relatives and one or two sycophants." Certainly he had his detractors, Frederick Benteen for example, and he did surround himself with relatives.

Both men had been brevet major generals during the Civil War, but they seem to have had little else in common. While Custer was an outspoken teetotaler, Stanley was a heavy drinker. According to his correspondence, Stanley complained of Custer's nonchalance in displaying deference to senior officers—especially, as was the case with Stanley, when such officers issued orders while drunk. In one instance, they got into an argument that resulted in Stanley ordering Custer to ride at the rear of the column. The following day, after sobering up, Stanley rescinded the order and apologized.

Autie took advantage of his commander's contrition by elevating one of his relatives, First Lieutenant Tom Custer, to assume temporary command of the 7th's Company B.

Coincidentally, the chief engineer for the Northern Pacific on the Yellowstone Expedition turned out to be Thomas Lafayette "Tex" Rosser, a friend and West Point classmate of Autie's who had left the Academy in 1861 to join the Confederate Army as a cavalry officer. Like both Stanley and Custer, he had risen to the rank of major general. The two had last met while operating on opposing sides at the Battles of Trevillian Station and Tom's Brook in 1864. The two old compatriots were delighted to pick up their friendship where it had been interrupted by the inconvenience of the Civil War.

Also present in the vast entourage was Lieutenant Colonel Frederick Dent Grant, West Point Class of 1871, whose rank—far higher than most men with less than two years in uniform—was seen as a result of his being the son of President Ulysses S. Grant. Though young Grant was a modest and unpretentious man, his rank was the object of grumbling from junior officers with a great deal more seniority.

For Tom Custer, the early days of the Yellowstone Expedition were notable for the immense numbers of pronghorn antelope. According to Custer scholar Dr. Lawrence Frost, Tom and others succumbed to the urge to hunt the animals as they traveled. Far from being a detrimental deviation, the hunting provided welcome fresh meat to feed the huge multitude of hungry men. Frost added that in the fusillade of gunfire, one of Tom's dogs—which often accompanied him in the field—was killed. It was not the first Custer canine to be the victim of friendly fire in a hunting mishap.

According to a letter from Autie to Libbie written a week into the expedition, which found its way into the possession of Marguerite Merington, Tom's successes in the hunt also prevailed in the card games that were ongoing in the evenings, and he sent $225 in winnings to Libbie to put into his bank account.

Tom's biggest victim at cards seemed to have been his new brother-in-law, James Calhoun, whom Frost described as a "compulsive," albeit unlucky, gambler. According to his letter, Tom gave the poor man no respite.

While poor James was losing his metaphorical shirt, his wife was packing her own belongings to travel east. Within a week of the departure of the Yellowstone Expedition, both Libbie Custer and Maggie Custer Calhoun had departed from Fort Rice. There were, it seemed, no accommodations for the women at Fort Rice—the only exception to the rule seeming to be for the post commander's wife.

"I was willing to live in a tent alone at the post, but there were not even tents to be had," Libbie Custer wrote. "Then we all looked with envious eyes at the quarters at Fort Rice. The post was small, and there were no vacant rooms except in the bachelor quarters. These are so called when the unmarried men take rooms in the same house and mess together. No opportunity was given us to wheedle them into offering us a place. Our officers hinted to, but they seemed to be completely intimidated regarding women."

At least with the Northern Pacific having just arrived in Bismarck, Mrs. Custer and Mrs. Calhoun would not have to repeat the long journey back to Yankton. Nevertheless, the riverboat trip upriver turned out to be "wretchedness itself," with the ladies being "nearly devoured with mosquitoes at once. Only the strongest ammonia on our faces and hands served to alleviate the torment."

Having returned to Monroe by way of St. Paul, the two army wives traded the detachment of being outside the States for the detachment of being in a place where no one had any idea what it was like in the West. As she recalled in *Boots and Saddles*, "My idea was that the whole country would be almost as absorbed as we were, how shocked I was to be asked, when I spoke of the regiment, 'Ah, is there a campaign, and for what purpose has it gone out?'"

Beyond the States, and beyond the limit of ignorance of their very existence, in a place where the boundary between Dakota Territory and Montana Territory was as meaningless as it was invisible, the Yellowstone Expedition reached the Yellowstone River on July 15, 1873. Tom Custer was part of the advance party who was the first to see this river that William Clark had traveled nearly seven decades earlier on his return from the Pacific Coast, and whose environs remained virtually untouched and largely unseen by the *wasichu* in all that time.

Tom and the others scanned the river for a sign of their own civilization, and at last, at the mouth of Glendive Creek in Montana Territory, they spied the steamboat with which they were to rendezvous for much needed supplies—and upon which Tom Custer and Jim Calhoun, among others, would spend the night. Once provisioned, the huge armada of the land turned toward the southwest, following the Yellowstone upstream.

They well knew that the Lakota rode the rolling hills of the Yellowstone country, but it was not until early August, after more than a month, that the troops saw them. At twilight, they appeared, fired a few shots, then vanished. The next day, the troops passed a forlorn and isolated burial site. Attempts by a few troopers to loot artifacts were halted by Stanley, who thought it in bad taste. It was also a defilement that was the epitome of sacrilege and for the superstitious among the expedition, a portent of inevitable misfortune.

As the Yellowstone Expedition continued upriver, a contingent of about ninety 7th Cavalry troops rode ahead on point. Autie, naturally wanting to be at the forefront of any possible action, was in the lead with Tom at his side. On August 4, about 25 miles downriver from the place where the Rosebud River—then called Rosebud Creek—flows into the Yellowstone, a small number of Lakota launched a hit and run strike on the cavalrymen. Tom and some men from Company B took the bait and gave chase, not immediately realizing that the Lakota tactic was to lure them into an ambush.

Tom thought better of his pursuit and reversed course just as a much larger number of Lakota, approximately 200, spilled from the cover of some cottonwoods in the river bottom to spring their trap.

According to Paul Hutton in *The Custer Reader*, Tom took charge of the situation, ordered his men to "prepare to fight on foot," and put them into a defensive position. He ordered them to fire in volleys, and "aim low" to shoot the horses from beneath the attackers. Autie, meanwhile, also dismounted the rest of the command and arranged them into a defensive position in the cover of the banks of a dry river channel parallel to the Yellowstone.

The Lakota besieged the troops for about three hours, attempting without success to infiltrate some other warriors into the 7th Cavalry rear. At the appearance of a dust cloud that indicated the approach of the rest of the Yellowstone Expedition troops, the Lakota broke off their attack and withdrew. Under Autie's orders, Tom led a pursuit, but after several days it was apparent that the Lakota had extended their lead and would not be overtaken by the cavalry horses that had grown exhausted after the long march from Dakota Territory.

When the remainder of the expedition caught up, it was learned that the 7th Cavalry vanguard was not the only place where an attack had occurred. Another smaller Lakota party had attacked and killed three members of the expedition.

Unaware of any Lakota in the area, several small clusters of soldiers and civilians had wandered away from the expedition and had ridden down to the Yellowstone to water their horses and to cool off from the heat of the day.

Two of the *wasichu* were a civilian sutler named Augustus Baliran, and the 7th Cavalry's senior veterinary surgeon, Dr. John Honsinger, the first veterinarian assigned to the 7th Cavalry since the Civil War. Samuel Barrows, a correspondent for the *New York Tribune* who was riding with the 7th Cavalry that summer, called Honsinger "a fine-looking, portly man, about fifty-five years of age, dressed in a blue coat and buckskin pantaloons, mounted on his fine blooded horse. . . . No man of the regiment took more care of his horse than he. It was an extra-professional care—a love of the horse for his own sake."

When the Lakota struck the cavalry column, Baliran and Honsinger heard the shots in the distance. Despite warnings from Arikara scouts, the two men had persisted in the belief that the shots heard in the distance were being fired by 7th Cavalry troopers who had run into a herd of deer or antelope, and were merely doing some hunting.

As they rode toward the river, the two men were joined by a pair of soldiers, Privates John Ball and M. Brown. They rode into a Lakota trap. They rode into it so oblivious that Honsinger had the reins pulled from his hands as he was dragged from his horse. Only Brown survived.

When the bodies were recovered, it was noted that Dr. Honsinger's large gold pocket watch was missing. More than a year later, this timepiece would reappear and would figure in a significant incident involving Tom Custer.

As the Yellowstone Expedition continued in the aftermath of the fighting, George Armstrong Custer pulled all ten companies of the 7th Cavalry—including the regimental band—as well as one company of the 22nd Infantry, to form the leading edge of the Yellowstone Expedition as it continued upstream. Several Custer insiders now held company commands, including Tom Custer with Company B and James Calhoun with Company C, as well as Myles Moylan with Company A and George Yates with Company F.

The battle, the biggest experienced by the Custer boys and most of the 7th in the nearly five years since the Washita, was merely a prelude to what was to come a week later.

Within that week, the expedition reached the vicinity of the Rosebud, near the present location of Custer, Montana. The Arikara scouts had explained that the Lakota liked to camp along the Rosebud, so the anticipation of further trouble hung heavy in the air, which boiled with temperatures around one hundred degrees.

The 7th Cavalry vanguard camped on the north side of the Yellowstone, opposite the mouth of the Rosebud in an area later known as Pease Bottom. They awoke to gunfire at dawn on the morning of August 11. Covered by riflemen across the Yellowstone from the troopers' camp, hundreds of Lakota forded the river and undertook to outflank the cavalry through gullies that ran perpendicular to the Yellowstone.

From his position on a bluff overlooking the scene, Autie gave the order to counterattack, asking the band to play "Garryowen." Capturing the mood of the moment, a "special correspondent" for the *New York Tribune* reported. "'Forward!' shouted the commanders, and away they went 'pell-mell,' the horses seeming to share the eagerness of the men. There was no scattering or flagging. Every man keeps in his place. On they go like a whirlwind."

Among them was Autie's brother.

"Tom Custer plunging down the ravine on the right," the report continued. "Ditches, gullies, hills, cannot stop them . . . Lieut. Custer on the left led his men on furiously."

In a somewhat humorous anecdote—though it wasn't funny at the time—the reporter added that one of the troops had told him that Tom Custer was "a terrible rider . . . I saw him fly over a ditch about 15 feet wide. The man after him missed it, and horse and rider rolled into the gully."

As had happened around ten times previously, Autie had his horse shot out from under him in the attack, but he quickly remounted and led a charge against the Lakota force that had outflanked the 7th. Surprised by this unexpected turn, the Lakota broke and withdrew. The Custer boys and their regiment pursued for about 3 miles before breaking off their chase.

The earliest published description of the battle appeared in the *Tribune*, penned by their "special correspondent" who had witnessed the fighting firsthand. The story was datelined August 19, but not published until after the Yellowstone Expedition had returned from the field. The paper published at least three articles on what was then dubbed "The Yellowstone War," between September 8 and 12.

One of the *Tribune*'s headlines told the outcome with the phrase "Rout of the Sioux," though the attackers had gotten away unvanquished.

In its continuing coverage, *New York Tribune* named the fight variously as "the Battle of Tongue River" or as "the Battle of the Bighorn," the latter being accurate, as the Tongue is actually 90 miles downriver from the site.

Today, it is called the Battle of Pease Bottom. Whatever the case, it was a larger battle than the one a week earlier. The troops numbered about 500, compared to ninety, while the estimated number of Lakota was around 400, double that of August 4. Three men of the 7th Cavalry were killed, and four were wounded. Estimates put Lakota losses in the same vicinity.

Though casualties were minimal, the number of participants made it a significant battle. Historically, it is important because both Sitting Bull and Crazy Horse were present, although this was apparently not known to the *wasichu* at the time. Contemporary accounts mention Gall, who was, like Sitting Bull, an important Hunkpapa Lakota leader.

The *New York Tribune* mentions that Gall's horse, like Autie's, was shot out from under him, but that he quickly "leaped on a fresh horse and got away." All three of these Lakota leaders were again present at the Little Bighorn three years later, though Sitting Bull would not actively participate in that battle. At the Bighorn, rather than at the Little Bighorn, was the only time that the Custer boys faced Sitting Bull in battle—but they didn't know it.

The Lakota were, however, probably aware that they were fighting George Armstrong Custer that day. His reputation had spread far and wide on the Plains since Washita, and he was quite visually distinctive with his buckskin jacket and colorful scarves. As he had during the Civil War, he wore his blond hair so long that it spilled across his shoulders. For this reason, he was known variously by the nicknames "Yellow Hair" or "Long Hair." Tom Custer, who was known to be Long Hair's younger brother, was called "Little Hair" by the Lakota and Cheyenne.

The Yellowstone Expedition continued upriver from the Bighorn, but for less than a week. By August 16, 290 miles upriver from the mouth of the Yellowstone, they had reached Pompey's Pillar, a sandstone bluff where William Clark carved his name in 1806—making it one of only two instances of physical evidence of an exact site visited by Lewis and Clark Expedition. Stanley then ordered his own expedition to reverse course, and they began the long trek back, a march that was unblemished by further skirmishes with the Lakota.

Elements of the expedition, including the cavalrymen of the 7th, circled north into the valley of the Musselshell River, while the main elements returned the way they had come. The 7th Cavalry reached Fort Abraham Lincoln at Bismarck, which was to be their new home, on September 21. Two days later the Yellowstone Expedition was officially deemed concluded after spending ninety-five days in the field and covering more than 900 miles.

Much to their surprise, the participants in the expedition now received the unfathomable news that the reason for their journey had evaporated while they were gone. Less than a week prior to their return, Jay Cooke had gone into bankruptcy, plunging the future of the Northern Pacific Railway as a transcontinental road into limbo.

The railroad continued to exist, and it continued to run between Bismarck and the Twin Cities, but its continuing expansion was over. It would be six years before it was able to resume its westward construction or to make use of the survey data accumulated in the summer of 1873.

While the expedition had been out of communication with the outside world and completely out of touch with the States, the nation had moved perilously close to economic disaster. Cooke's dramatic failure precipitated the Panic of 1873, which hit the economy with the sledgehammer of Cooke's financial demise, on September 18. It would last until 1879 and be felt around the world—though not so much outside the States in the Montana and Dakota Territories.

CHAPTER 17

THE CUSTER CLAN IN THE WEST

By 1873, THE scattered fragments of the Custer family's nomadic wing would form into a cohesive much larger unit than the tightly wound threesome that emerged after the Civil War. This unit would soon evolve as a gradually expanding, but no less tightly wound, extended family that came to be known as the "Custer Clan."

As they had been in Texas and Kansas, the General, the Old Lady, and the Scamp were together again, now at Fort Abraham Lincoln in Dakota Territory, across the Missouri River from Bismarck, which would be their home for the coming three years. The threesome was now united with young Maggie, the kid sister of the Custer boys, and her husband James Calhoun. Boston Custer, who had come and gone at Fort Hays, was also a permanent member of the fold now, and eventually nephew Autie Reed would come west.

Meanwhile, James Calhoun's sister Charlotte—known as "Lottie"—had married Major Myles Moylan of the 7th Cavalry in October 1872, and they were part of the Clan. Like Boston Custer, James Calhoun's twenty-six-year-old civilian younger brother, Frederic Sanxay Calhoun, showed up at Fort Lincoln, where he was employed doing odd jobs. Fred later joined the US Army, and through strings pulled by George Armstrong Custer, he was given a commission as a second lieutenant in March 1875. However, he was assigned not to the 7th Cavalry but to the 14th Infantry.

The hierarchy of the Custer Clan formed like a series of concentric rings orbiting the original trio. In the innermost circle, of course, were Maggie and Boston. Jim Calhoun, the brother-in-law, was an outsider among insiders, an ember beside a fire. Though he was readily swept up in their activities, he had a hard time keeping pace with the raucous relationship between Autie and Tom, whose brotherly bond had been formed over decades. Incessant teasing had always prevailed among the Custer boys—including Boston—and it was second nature to them. However, when Calhoun was suddenly thrown into this fraternal maelstrom, his taciturn personality in the shadow of their boisterous assertiveness put him off balance, and his slowness with comebacks made him an easy butt of jokes and pranks. Of course, the fact that Calhoun had stumbled so badly in his evolving series of card games with Tom on his first field campaign after joining the Custer Clan got him off to a bad start.

Other Army officers in the orbit of the inner circles included men who had been part of the 7th Cavalry "family" since 1866, and were, one supposes, the Custer "sycophants" to whom Colonel David Stanley referred so derisively at the time of the Yellowstone Expedition.

These included old friends of Autie and Tom from Monroe, such as Captain George Yates and his wife Annie Gibson Roberts Yates. There was Lieutenant Edward Settle Godfrey of Kalida, Ohio, who like Tom Custer, had lied about his age to join the 21st Ohio Infantry in 1861. He had left the regiment before Tom joined so they did not meet until after Godfrey had graduated from West Point in 1867.

Among the others were Captain Algernon Emory Smith of New York and his wife Nettie Bowen Smith, as well as Lieutenant William Winer Cooke, whose surname was and is often misspelled without the "e." Cooke was a Canadian from Ontario, who had come south in 1863 to enlist in the Union Army, and who sported prominent "Dundreary" sideburns. Another foreigner in the Custer Clan who had immigrated to fight for the Union Captain Myles Keogh of Ireland's County Carlow. He had served in the Papal States Army of Pope Pius IX and as a Vatican Guard in the early 1860s before crossing the Atlantic to join in the Army of the Potomac. He was on George McClellan's staff at Antietam, and with Alfred Pleasonton's Cavalry Corps, albeit in a different division than Autie, at Gettysburg.

On the periphery of the Custer Clan were their servants. In the background, but mentioned frequently and fondly in Libbie's recollections and her memoirs was Mary, her African-American cook. She had joined the household in 1869 after the departure of Eliza Brown, who had been with Autie since the Virginia campaigns during the Civil War, and who had been with the Custers in Texas and Kansas. Mentioned only occasionally, such as in letters from Boston Custer to Emma Reed in the summer of 1874, is Ben, Tom's African-American servant.

Tom Custer remained at Fort Lincoln while Autie took the train east to collect Libbie shortly after the Yellowstone Expedition ended. The General and the Old Lady lingered in the east for several weeks. They visited friends in Detroit and Kentucky, and attended a reunion of the Army of the Tennessee in Toledo in late October 1873, at which President Grant and General William Tecumseh Sherman were guests of honor. General Phil Sheridan, also a headliner, had insisted that his old cavalry protégé, George Armstrong Custer, also attend.

As they traveled west to Fort Lincoln in November, Autie and Libbie were accompanied by Libbie's friend Agnes Bates, who had been bitten by the lure of life on the frontier. She was one of a diverse group of both civilians who traveled to Dakota on extended visits and who became part of the Custer Clan.

In *Boots and Saddles*, Libbie called Aggie a "joy forever," and remembered that she "submitted without a word to the rough part of our journey."

Libbie's ulterior motive in bringing her friend out to Fort Lincoln was her belief that the young woman might find a suitable husband among the 7th Cavalry officer corps. Libbie had always believed that matrimony had a calming, civilizing effect on the frontier Army posts.

Parting from Mother and Father Custer on the platform in Monroe was growing increasingly difficult. They were in their late sixties, and Maria was in ill health. Psychologically, the idea of having three sons—and now their *only daughter*—residing outside the States was a trying affair.

"Such partings were the only occasions when I ever saw him lose entire control of himself, and I always looked forward to the hour of their separation with dread," Libbie wrote of her husband's reaction to leaving his parents. "For hours before we started, I have seen him follow his mother about, whispering some comforting word to her; or, opening the closed door of her own room, where, womanlike, she fought out her grief alone, sit beside her as long as he could endure it. She had been an invalid for so many years that each parting seemed to her the final one. Her groans and sobs were heartrending. She clung to him every step when he started to go, and exhausted at last, was led back, half fainting, to her lounge."

Libbie continued, noting that "the General would rush out of the house, sobbing like a child, and then throw himself into the railway carriage beside me completely unnerved . . . At our first stop he was out of the cars in an instant, buying fruit to send back to her. Before we were even unpacked in the hotel, where we made our first stay of any length, he had dashed off a letter . . . full of the prophecies he never failed to make, of the reunion that he felt would soon come."

Their trip was aboard the last westbound train of the season. The winter blizzards had already begun. After a harrowing crossing of the icy Missouri River, they were greeted by Maggie and Tom. Libbie's recollection of her arrival at the cavalry post reads like a Christmas romance story. She wrote that "Our brother, Colonel Tom, met us, and drove us to our new home. In the dim light I could see the great post of Fort Lincoln, where only a few months before we had left a barren plain. Our quarters were lighted, and as we approached, the regimental band played 'Home, Sweet Home,' followed by the General's favorite, 'Garryowen.'"

After a season of construction work, Fort Lincoln now had seven new detached duplex houses for officers, the most desirable of which was reserved for Autie, as the defacto regimental commander and the senior officer at the post. In a letter to his wife on September 10, he had written that Captain George Dandy, the quartermaster, said that "no quarters being built in the Department of the Missouri compare with those being prepared for six troops—and the Commanding Officer's house is described as 'elegant.'"

The quarters were large enough that Aggie Bates could have a separate bedroom. The other half of this building would be occupied by the Calhouns. In early February 1873, a fire started in a defective chimney and the house burned down. It was quickly rebuilt.

Tom Custer stayed for a while in a spare bedroom at the home of his brother and sister-in-law, but later moved to another duplex. Soon after, Boston Custer made his appearance as a more or less permanent part of the Custer Clan, alternating his own residence between the homes of Libbie and Autie, or Tom's. In a September 1874 letter to Emma Reed, that "since I have been out here I have paid for my board and Tom one hundred dollars and the General twenty five."

Life within the walls of Fort Lincoln, at least for the officers and their families, was as congenial as at the posts in Kansas where the regiment had previously been stationed. Just as in Kansas, there were long periods of uninterrupted garrison life in which the armed combat mission of the regiment was just a distant abstraction.

When spring came, they planted gardens—even Tom Custer dabbled in gardening—and there were parties, dances, and even theatrical programs. There was always music, as most people liked to sing. While at the Boyd Seminary, Maggie Calhoun had become a skilled pianist, and she easily fell into the role of musical accompanist for the Custer Clan.

The presence of civilian visitors from "the States"—distinct from the civilian contractors whose caste paralleled that of the enlisted men—came to stay for lengthy periods of time, providing an aura of the "civilization" for which many of those within the officer corps felt nostalgic.

Aggie Bates was not alone among the civilian outsiders. Katherine Fougera, in her book *With Custer's Cavalry*, mentioned a woman named Kate Garrett, whose sister was married to one of the officers. Kate was apparently the object of Tom Custer's flirtations and teasing, but nothing serious seemed to develop from it. She became engaged to another officer and Tom departed in early April 1874 for six weeks, presumably visiting his fiance, Lulie Burgess, in New Jersey.

For the extended family of Custer boys, life at Fort Lincoln was almost like the old days in the Dining Fork. In a letter to his niece, seventeen-year-old Emma Reed, the daughter of his half-sister Lydia Ann Reed, Boston wrote, "Tom and I have lots of fun together and he and I come up to the Post every night together after sundown on the Roll Call."

In his extensive correspondence with Emma, he referred to her affectionately as a "young brat," also alternating between such salutations as "My little Sweetness" or "My little Chucklehead." He signed his letters "your affectionate brother," though technically he was her uncle.

Boston's role in the business of the 7th Cavalry in Dakota Territory, like his role during his time with the regiment in Kansas, was on the periphery. Never a soldier, he was among the groups of civilian employees of the Army who came and went, mainly seasonally. They worked as teamsters, packers or foragers, roles for which Boston was certainly qualified by his past experience.

In a special category among the civilians employed by the US Army in the West were the scouts, men who understood the geography and terrain in which the regiment operated like the metaphorical backs of their hands.

These men were the archetypical loners of the Old West, the mountain men who had devoted themselves to a solitary life in a trackless wilderness, making their way as trappers, professional hunters and as guides for those *wasichu* who still had one foot in the comfortable world of the States. Though he was certainly among the latter sort of *wasichu*, one can see from how quickly Boston might warm to life on the Plains.

In the annals of the scouts who served with the 7th Cavalry, one man stands before others. Charles Alexander "Lonesome Charlie" Reynolds was born in Illinois, but came to the Plains after having served in the Civil War. He had begun scouting for the 7th Cavalry in 1869 and had served in this capacity on the Yellowstone Expedition. He took his nickname for his mountain man's inclination toward spurning the community of the Army post for a solitary life when the regiment was not in the field. It would not be a stretch of the imagination to see Lonesome Charley Reynolds becoming a sort of role model for young Boston.

Boston wrote of occasional visits to Standing Rock, the Indian Agency outpost at the northeastern corner of the Great Sioux Reservation, about 90 trail miles south of Fort Lincoln. This location was one of the centers of distribution for goods that were disbursed under the provisions of the treaties, and a sizable number of Lakota—the so called "Agency Indians" lived in the vicinity of the agency offices and the sutler's store from which goods were sold.

Boston told Emma that he hoped some day to take her to visit Standing Rock "and see all the Indians and how they live. There are about eight thousand in all . . . I went to one dance and the camp was about two miles from the sutler store where I was stopping and just after we reached the dance which was in a large tent it commenced raining so we went in and sat down and I smoked with several Lakota and then left."

CHAPTER 18
THE CUSTER CLAN AND THE BLACK HILLS EXPEDITION

THE PRINCIPAL CONTACT that the men and women of Bismarck and Fort Abraham Lincoln had with the Lakota was what they saw on their occasional, usually uneventful, visits to the agency at Standing Rock about 100 road miles to the south. There was a natural assumption on the part of both Lakota and *wasichu* that a peaceful, albeit arms-length, equilibrium prevailed.

The "Agency Indians" who had signed the Fort Laramie Treaty of 1868, and who lived by their responsibilities under its provisions, assumed that they were secure inside the nearly 45,000 square miles of the Great Sioux Reservation that were off limits to the *wasichu*. However, there was an isolated mountain range inside that reservation, a place called the Black Hills, or Pahá Sapá to the Lakota, which the *wasichu* coveted in the same way that the Lakota had coveted it when they took it away from the Cheyenne a century earlier.

There were rumors, exaggerated but accurate, of gold in the Black Hills. These naturally stirred the fires of greed, which led to demands that the Black Hills be opened to *wasichu* prospectors. By the summer of 1874, this had become a major political issue that reached all the way to halls of power in Washington and New York. Given the economic collapse of the

Panic of 1873 and the fact that global currencies were backed by gold, a substantial new source of gold was enticing to financiers, to the government, and to all who were concerned about the economy. Dreams of a reprise of the spectacular California Gold Rush of 1849 danced in heads around the world.

Conversely, there was strong public opinion, widely expressed in the media in the States, against violating the treaties and the integrity of the reservations. President Ulysses S. Grant was on the horns of a dilemma. As General Grant, he had demanded unconditional surrender from his opponents. As President Grant, he was both celebrated and condemned for his "Peace Policy" toward the Indians in the West.

Grant finally succumbed to pressure to do something. In April 1874, orders went back down the chain of command, reaching the desk of Lieutenant General Phil Sheridan, the commander of the Military Division of the Missouri with responsibility for all the Great Plains, including and especially the Great Sioux Reservation. One of the problems of determining what to do about the Black Hills was that relatively few *wasichu* had ever been there. The idea evolved that a military expedition, not unlike the Yellowstone Expedition of 1873, should enter the Black Hills during the coming summer and conduct a survey.

Controversial at the time, this decision is widely denounced today. In retrospect, using the crystal clear lens of hindsight, many have seen this as unnecessarily provocative, especially in light of the major war with the Lakota and their allies which would flow from the Black Hills Expedition. But that was two years in the future.

The great popular historian Stephen Ambrose even compared the expedition to the 1964 Gulf of Tonkin incident as a pretext for going to war. However, it should be pointed out that there were numerous civilian schemes for an armed incursion into the Black Hills, and these would certainly have resulted in war with or without a government survey. Then, of course, there were already prospectors, alone or in small groups, sneaking surreptitiously into the area.

In any case, an expedition was decided upon, and an expedition it would be. To lead the Black Hills Expedition, Sheridan naturally thought of George Armstrong Custer. It was better to have a media-friendly teetotaler in charge than a man enslaved by the bottle, as had been the case with David Stanley the year before.

Autie would naturally include the Custer clan in this adventure. In the 7th Cavalry command structure for the Black Hills Expedition, James Calhoun served as Autie's adjutant, and Algernon Smith was named quartermaster, while Myles Moylan commanded Company B, Edward Godfrey was second in command at Company K, and Tom Custer rode at the head of Company L. Boston Custer and Fred Calhoun, the youngest brothers of Tom and Jim, were both along as civilian contract employees.

While the 7th accounted for about half the 1,000-man expedition, elements of the 9th Cavalry, as well as the 17th and 20th Infantry Regiments were present. Lieutenant Colonel Fred Grant, the president's son, who had accompanied the Yellowstone Expedition for part of its time in the field in 1873, was included as Autie's "acting aide." Naturally, Lonesome Charley Reynolds was among the scouts, and certainly he was the man upon whom the expedition leader would most rely.

Captain William Ludlow of the Corps of Engineers headed the component that would conduct the actual surveying, and he hired British photographer William Illingworth to undertake the delicate task of documenting the expedition in glass plate negatives. George Bird Grinnell, later one of the towering figures of nineteenth-century natural science and then a Yale graduate student, was brought along under Sheridan's orders as the expedition naturalist. William McKay and Horatio Nelson Ross, described as "miners," also accompanied the expedition to assess the viability of exploiting the mineral resources of the Black Hills.

Libbie fully expected to accompany the Black Hills Expedition, and indeed, her husband had ordered an ambulance wagon to be fitted out for her conveyance. However, as Libbie wrote in *Boots and Saddles*, "At the very last, news came through Indian scouts that the summer might be full of danger, and my heart was almost broken at finding that the General did not dare to take me with him. Whatever peril might be awaiting me on the expedition, nothing could be equal to the suffering of suspense at home."

Nor would Libbie have Maggie's company at Fort Lincoln that summer, for she was away because of ill health. Dr. Lawrence Frost quotes an 1872 letter to Lydia Ann Reed in which Maggie complained of suffering a "siege of headaches with chills and fever," adding that this ailment plagued her for the rest of her life." In a letter to Emma Reed in Monroe, Boston Custer told his niece to "tell Maggie that if she don't hurry up and get well this summer there will be a big fuss and you have her to go out walking with often."

In that same letter, dated July 1, 1874, Boston went on to set the tone for the eve of the expedition's departure from Fort Lincoln.

"The band is playing their farewell serenade," he explained. "I have just been bidding some of the ladies good by and I thought I would write you if only a few lines before going to camp as we leave in the morning at eight o'clock. How I wish you and Maggie were here so I could run in often and see you. Tell Maggie all the officers that the General relieved from duty on the expedition are all going as they finished the case that the General wished them to do and they are all happy as clams."

The Black Hills Expedition departed Fort Lincoln the next morning, a bit more than a year after the Yellowstone Expedition had begun. The cavalry led the way, followed by the infantry, several artillery pieces, a train of more than 100 wagons and a herd of cattle to provide a continuous supply of fresh meat.

As with the previous expedition, the bounty of the cattle herd was supplemented by hunting in a land rich with wild game. In letters home, penned by the Custer boys and others, there were detailed lists of the number of deer and antelope bagged. Autie bragged at one point that "I have killed six antelopes. Bos has killed one."

As might have been predicted, at least part of the big game hunting was for sport. Autie proudly wrote his wife on August 3 that "I have reached the hunter's highest round of fame . . . I have killed my Grizzly." The General and his bear were duly recorded on one of Illingworth's glass plates.

Boston was quickly assimilating to life as part of the 7th Cavalry. In his July 15 letter to Libbie, Autie wrote that "though this is his first expedition, Bos takes to life on the plains as naturally as if bred to it. One of the officers says he thinks it must 'run in the blood.' He has to go through the usual experience that falls to all 'plebs.'"

In Autie's July 15 letter, he gave some insights into the pranking between the Custer boys. He wrote of some rocks which Tom had given to Boston, who soaked them each night in his wash basin. As it was explained, Tom had "assured him that they were sponge stone—a variety that softened by keeping them in water for a certain length of time. After a few nights of faithful practice it dawned upon him that he was again the victim of a practical joke, and he quietly dropped them by the way without saying a word."

Autie added that Libbie "need not trouble yourself to take up arms in his defense, for he gets even with us in the long run."

Later in the expedition, when some of the men took to riding mules in order to spare their horses, Boston was ribbed for doing so. "Tom and Armstrong are always plaguing us especially me," he wrote to Emma Reed on August 15. "Armstrong says I should have a mule that has been in the army for about fifteen years and one that could shoot a rifle ball through the body any place and it would think a fly had bitten it. I would rather ride it than my horse for I can get off it and stand all day in one place without hitching so I can go hunting without taking a man along to hold it."

For his part, Autie wrote that Boston "has been so pleased with his mule from the first, and has praised him to me repeatedly. He is a good animal, for a mule, but endurance, in his constitution, rather triumphs over speed."

In turn, the presence of the slow-moving mule led to another instance in which the older brother "could not resist" playing a trick on Boston.

"Bos rode beside me, and I invented an excuse to go in advance," he wrote of setting up the gag. "I made Vic [Autie's horse] gallop slowly over the divide, and when out of sight on the other side I put spurs to him and dashed through the low ground. When Bos came in sight, I was slowly ambling up the next divide and calling to him to come on. He spurred his mule, shouted to him, and waved his arms and legs to incite him to a faster gait. When he neared me I disappeared over another divide, and giving Vic the rein only slackened speed when it became time for Bos to appear. Then, when I had brought my horse down to a walk I called out, 'Why on earth don't you come on?'"

He kept up the ruse until Boston discovered the joke then matched Vic's steps to those of the exhausted mule.

Gradually, the hazing slacked off, mainly because Boston had not played along. "Every one practices jokes on him," Autie noted. "But he has such a good disposition it does not even ruffle him."

Boston himself told Emma Reed in an August 2 letter that "when we are on the march I always take lunch with Armstrong and he and Tom are always teasing me about eating so much but I eat away and never mind anything that they say . . . they have found out that they can't plague me any so they don't have much to say as they did when we first started out."

On the expedition, the practical jokes extended to other members of the Custer Clan, even in absentia. Autie, who routinely collected small mammals and birds—from badgers to owls—to be sent to zoos in the States, mentioned that he would be bringing home a live rattlesnake for Aggie Bates. Like Libbie, she was mortified of these poisonous vipers.

The collecting naturally interested young George Bird Grinnell. In one of the Custer missives, it was noted that on July 14, he "discovered the remains of an animal of an extinct race, larger than the largest size elephant." It was a group of fossil dinosaur bones.

Other traces of times long ago were observed by the Custer boys in a cave that was shown to them by one of the Arikara scouts. Wrote Autie, "It is about 400 feet long, its walls covered with drawings of animals, and prints of hands and feet. I cannot account for the drawings of ships."

No doubt recalling the conflicts that had occurred on the Yellowstone Expedition—between his bother and brother-in-law, and between Stanley and himself—Autie made some changes in the off-duty entertainment that was permitted. "I am more than ever convinced of the influence a commanding officer exercises for good or ill," he wrote Libbie. "There has not been a single card party, not a single drunken officer, since we left Ft. Lincoln. But I know that if did I play cards and invite the officers to join there would be playing every night."

By July 20, they reached the Belle Fourche River at the threshold of the Black Hills. They had traversed more than 200 miles of the "beautiful and interesting" open spaces, in which, as Autie described, "It always seems as if one could surely see for miles beyond when the top of each divide is reached, and how one can go on all day over the constant rise and fall of the earth, thinking the next divide will reveal a vast stretch of country."

The Black Hills themselves were found to be quite pleasant, at least by comparison to the Plains, hot and dusty under the midsummer sun. The wonders of the place as perceived by the men of the expedition, were perhaps best described by George Armstrong Custer himself in his report to Sheridan, a document that was submitted to Congress by Secretary of War William Belknap in February 1875.

"With regard to the character of the country enclosed by the Black Hills, I can only repeat what I have stated in previous dispatches," Custer wrote. "No portion of the country can boast of richer or better pasturage, natural temperature or purer water, which flows in summer from the earth but twelve degrees above freezing point, and of greater advantages generally to the farmer and stock raiser than are to be found in Black Hills. Building stone of the best quality is to found in abundance, wood for fuel and lumber plenty, rains frequent, with no evidence in the country either of drought or freshet [a flood caused by spring thaws]. The season is perhaps, too short and the nights too cool for corn, but I believe all other grain could be produced here in wonderful abundance."

Such a description, which read like a nineteenth-century real estate brochure, was guaranteed to have the opposite effect of discouraging *wasichu* violations of the forbidden Black Hills. The Lakota had been observed, monitoring the Black Hills Expedition from a distance, but they did not interfere.

The abundant granite in the Black Hills also caught Boston's eye, recalling that their half-sister, Lydia Ann Reed, favored stone construction for houses.

"I wish Mrs. David Reed was out here for she could get all the fine specimens of stone that she wished," he wrote in a letter to Lydia Ann's daughter Emma. "I told Armstrong the other day when we were riding along that if Ann was here that she would have two or three Company's wagons heavily loaded with stone before we could get out of the Black Hills."

Libbie described the return of the expedition to Fort Lincoln on August 30 after having covered nearly 900 miles in their sixty days in the field. As she wrote, "The long wagon-train appeared. Many of the covers had elk horns strapped to them, until they looked like strange bristling animals as they drew near. Some of the antlers were brought to us as presents. Besides them we had skins, specimens of gold and mica, and petrified shells of iridescent colors, snake rattles, pressed flowers, and petrified wood. My husband brought me a keg of the most delicious water from a mountain-stream. It was almost my only look at clear water for years, as most of the streams west of the Missouri are muddy."

On the streets of Bismarck—and on the streets back in the States—the question that had been on everyone's mind was singular. Even before the Black Hills Expedition returned, the world had its answer.

In his message to Sheridan of August 2, carried back to the telegraph office at Fort Lincoln by Arikara scouts, Custer wrote, "I have on my table, forty or fifty small particles of gold in size averaging a small pin head, and most of it obtained from one pan."

He wrote his most thorough assessment of the situation with the gold from Bear Butte on August 15, just as the expedition pulled up stakes for the return march. Most correspondence between the expedition and Fort Lincoln was carried by Arikara scouts, but this one was entrusted to Lonesome Charley Reynolds, who rode south to Fort Laramie, which was a hundred miles closer, albeit by a much less hospitable route. Indeed, Reynolds arrived exhausted, his throat so parched that he couldn't close his mouth. A lesser man would not have made it.

In the dispatch so valiantly delivered, Custer explained to Sheridan that "in a former dispatch I referred to the discovery of gold. Subsequent examinations at numerous points confirm and strengthen the existence of gold in the Black Hills, on some of the water courses gold was found in almost every panful of earth, in small but paying quantities. The miners report that they found the gold in the grass roots and from the surface to the greatest depth reached. It has not required an expert to find gold in the Black Hills, as men without former experience have found it."

By the time that the Black Hills Expedition returned, men in Bismarck were already gearing up for their own expeditions into the Black Hills, and they were going in for neither building stones nor dinosaur bones.

Special Indian Commissioner Christopher C. Cox addressed the subject of the Black Hills in the *Annual Report of the Commissioner of Indian Affairs to the Secretary of the Interior.*

"Certainly, in the light of impending influences soon to be extended over this wild domain, the ideality and characteristics of the savage tribes cannot be much longer maintained," he wrote. "It is due the cause of progress, the Government, and the Indians themselves, that this important question should be settled as speedily as possible. The glowing reports of General Custer (whether true or false) have aroused the frontier, and scores of organizations, more or less extended, are preparing to visit the Black Hills in the coming spring. Already small parties have ventured into the forbidden region . . . The tide of emigration cannot be restrained. The exodus will be effected. It may cost blood, but the ultimate occupation of this unceded territory by the white settler is inevitable."

However, Cox saw all of this as a good thing, adding that "it is a great wrong to the citizens of this Territory that its domain should not be settled by a white enterprising population. Remove the ban which now precludes the location of the white emigrant, and thousands will flock to this region, and thus add greatly to the prosperity of an important region."

Boston Custer's last words on the Black Hills Expedition were an intriguing summary of the summer, and of conversations that had likely taken place in the mess tent of the Custer boys. He reported that "the two miners that the General brought along with him have found gold and a very good quality and have found it in several places so the General expects to come out here next summer."

George Armstrong Custer would not make a personal prospecting trip to the gold fields of the Black Hills in 1875 nor at any other time. The closest that he, or any of the Custer boys, ever came to mining was his earlier investment in a silver mine in the Stevens Lode near Georgetown, Colorado, which he never visited, and which he had written off in August 1874 as a disappointing loss.

In this photograph taken by David F. Barry in his Bismarck studio, Thomas Ward Custer (1845–1876) is in full uniform and wearing his two Medals of Honor. (Little Bighorn Battlefield National Monument)

Maria Ward Custer (1807–1882), the mother of the Custer brothers and Maggie, was born in Pennsylvania but spent most of her early life, and raised her children, in Ohio. (Little Bighorn Battlefield National Monument)

Emanuel Henry Custer (1806–1892), the father of the Custer brothers and Maggie, was a black-smith by trade, but later took up farming. (Little Bighorn Battlefield National Monument)

Boston Custer (1848–1876), the youngest of the Custer boys, was too young to serve in the Civil War, but later worked as a civilian contractor with the 7th Cavalry quartermaster. (Monroe News)

Lydia Ann Kirkpatrick Reed (1825–1906) was the half-sister of the Custer siblings, though they thought of her fondly as being somewhere between a second sister and a second mother. She was the daughter of Maria Ward Custer and her first husband, Israel Kirkpatrick. Her son, Harry Armstrong "Autie" Reed (1858–1876), died alongside his three uncles at the Little Bighorn (Little Bighorn Battlefield National Monument)

Margaret Emma "Maggie" Custer (1852–1910) was just a schoolgirl when her older brothers were achieving heroic status during the Civil War. She longed to emulate her sister-in-law Libbie and be part of the excitement of Army life. In 1872, Maggie married James Calhoun of the 7th Cavalry and went west to join the "Custer Clan." (Little Bighorn Battlefield National Monument)

Lieutenant James Calhoun (1845–1876), who married Maggie Custer, was born into a wealthy and influential Cincinnati family who were displessed when he opted for a life in uniform. (Little Bighorn Battlefield National Monument)

The General, the Old Lady, and the Scamp: Thomas Ward Custer—is seen here standing behind his older brother, George Armstrong Custer, and his sister-in-law, Elizabeth "Libbie" Bacon Custer. This photograph was taken in January 1865. During the Civil War, Tom attained the brevet rank of colonel, while his brother was a brevet major general. After the war, this threesome was together at US Army posts in the West almost continuously. Tom was nearly always posted with his brother, and Libbie insisted on joining her husband on his various assignments. (Library of Congress)

On the steps of the headquarters of the US Army's Department of Texas in Austin in late 1865. From left to right in the foreground are Brevet Colonel Tom Custer, Brevet Major General George Armstrong Custer, Elizabeth Bacon Custer, and Colonel Jacob Green. In the background are Eliza Brown, the Custers' maid, Emanuel Custer (father of Tom and George), and an unidentified man. George Custer was Chief of Cavalry in the Department of Texas at the time. (Little Bighorn Battlefield National Monument)

This .44-caliber Galand & Sommerville revolver was presented to Tom Custer in 1869 by Lord Berkeley-Paget in appreciation for a buffalo hunt he and his brother had arranged near Fort Hayes, Kansas in 1869. It was photographed by the author at Butterfield & Butterfield in San Francisco, just before it was sold to a private collector for $77,000 in 1995. (Bill Yenne photo)

A July 1875 group photo of the "Custer Clan" in Dakota Territory. George Armstrong Custer stands in the center, wearing a large hat and a fringed jacket. Elizabeth Bacon Custer is seated in a chair at his right elbow. Myles Keogh, in a dark hat and shirt, has his hand on her chair. Seated in front of Libbie are Margaret Custer Calhoun and Thomas Weir. James Calhoun is seated at the far left, and Algernon Smith at the far right. Tom Custer is seated next to Smith, wearing a broad-brimmed hat. The man to the left of Smith with the long sideburns is William Cooke. Boston Custer is fourth from the left, seated on the ground in the front row wearing a fringed jacket. (National Archives)

Top: Tom Custer's marker is located slightly forward of that of his brother on Last Stand Hill overlooking the Little Bighorn River in southeastern Montana. These markers approximate the locations where the two men fell on June 25, 1876, and where they were initially buried. In 1877, Tom was reinterred at Fort Leavenworth and his brother's remains were moved to West Point.

Bottom: Markers representing the places where Harry Armstrong "Autie" Reed (erroneously called "Arthur Reed") and Boston Custer were originally buried in 1876. Both were reinterred in Monroe, Michigan in 1878. (Bill Yenne photos, both)

Nevin Johnson Custer (1842–1915) and his wife, Ann North Custer (1843–1922). They were married in Wood County, Ohio but moved to Monroe, Michigan by 1871. Unlike his older brothers, Nevin never served in uniform. A farmer his entire life, he was the only one of the brothers never to visit the West, and not to die at the Little Bighorn. (Little Bighorn Battlefield National Monument)

Margaret Custer Calhoun in 1891 when she had just been appointed as the State Librarian of Michigan. (Public domain image from author's collection)

Nevin Johnson Custer as he appeared in his later years. (George A. Custer IV collection)

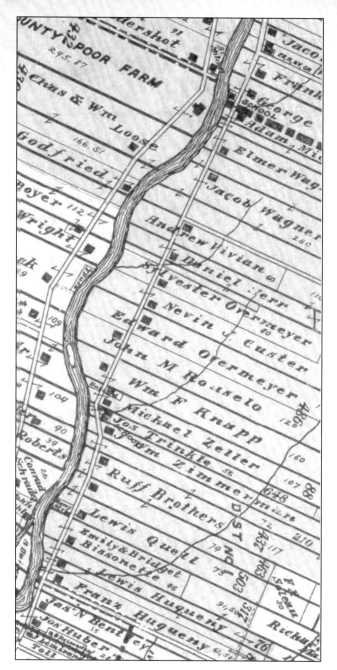

This detail from the Map of Monroe County, Michigan, compiled and engraved by George E. Lang of Carleton, Michigan in 1901 shows the location of the "Custer Farm" in the center, just north (to the right on this map) of the River Raison. Nevin and George jointly purchased this property on what was then called River Road, in 1871. Nevin and Ann would remain here for the rest of their lives and would raise their children here. In 1916, when the road was paved, it was renamed as "General Custer Road," though this was later changed to "North Custer Road." The address of the 1850 house seen here on the property now bears the address of 3048 North Custer Road. A second house, with the address 3029 North Custer Road, was built across the road in 1935 and was occupied by members of the family for many years. (Library of Congress)

CHAPTER 19

THE WINTER OF RAIN-IN-THE-FACE

AUTIE AND LIBBIE had already made plans to travel east in the autumn of 1874—with Aggie Bates in tow—for their occasional visit to their family in Monroe. They also planned a side trip to Chicago to attend the October wedding of young Fred Grant, which afforded an opportunity to press the flesh with everyone from President Grant to Phil Sheridan. Afterward, Libbie returned to Monroe to try to drum up interest in the West among potential future Army brides.

Matchmaking was a favorite cause for her. She was convinced that a good wife was essential for the Army officers in the West. She wrote in *Boots and Saddles* that "I used to dread the arrival of the young officers who came to the regiment from West Point, fearing that the sameness and inactivity of the garrison life would be a test to which their character would succumb." By "succumb" she naturally meant to the temptation of drinking and gambling. Of special concern to her was always "brother" Tom, who never got the better of his taste for drink or for cards.

"Of all our happy days, the happiest had now come to us at Fort Lincoln," she wrote of her satisfaction with the significant matrimonial rate at the post. "I never knew more united married people than those of our regiment . . . The wife had the privilege of becoming the comrade of her husband in that isolated existence, and the officers seemed to feel that every amusement was heightened if shared by the other sex."

As Libbie went to Michigan that autumn, Autie went to New York. *Galaxy* magazine had a continuing interest in his articles from the West, and Sheldon & Company had just published *My Life on the Plains*, a compendium of his previous *Galaxy* articles.

James Calhoun had also planned to go east to retrieve his wife from Monroe, but Autie initially decided that he must remain in Fort Lincoln. As Boston wrote in a September 7 letter to Emma Reed, "Jim is disappointed in not going home for Maggie but it is not best for him and the General to be away at the same time . . . I am so anxious to have Maggie here so I can have someone to tease."

Though Calhoun was not permitted to go home to Monroe, Autie apparently relented to allow him to travel east by train to meet Maggie halfway in St. Paul.

"Tom and I met Jim and Maggie at the train," Boston wrote of their return on September 20. "We came over the river in a yawl boat as the stream ferry was broken in some way and could not run. It seems so good to have her back again and I was so glad to find her looking so much better than when I left home."

Boston had no intention of leaving Dakota Territory himself. As he told Emma, "I would not go if I could—not that I don't care to see you but it would be foolish in me to start back so soon . . . I intended coming home on the last train and spend the winter with you and then come back on the first train as the General wants me to but I think now I will wait one more year."

Boston also mentioned in his September 7 letter that "I am going to be here for some time now the General secured me a place in the Quartermasters Department and I am very glad of it so I can be with Maggie, and if I could only have you here then I would be perfectly satisfied."

He had, as his brother earlier observed, taken to life on the Plains "as naturally as if bred to it." Nevertheless, his letters make frequent mention of Fannie Lewis, a young friend of Emma's in Monroe, who was known to Maggie and Libbie. Illustrative of his having accustomed himself to the Plains—and of his fondness for Ms. Lewis—he sent her a box of stones that he had collected in the Black Hills, and later shipped her an antelope head with which she said she was pleased.

In a later letter, he spoke of taking the hides from wild game they had killed down to Standing Rock to be tanned. In addition to the aid dispensed, the *wasichu* also provided the Lakota with a little commerce.

Emma had expressed an interest in the two bobcats which Boston was keeping as pets. In response, he told her "if you really want one I will send it by mail but you must handle it carefully and let it sleep at the foot of your bed every night." Having apparently not mailed the promised pet, he wrote, "My wild cats are growing nicely. One I call Emma, the other Fannie, so you both can call yourselves fortunate for having a namesake in the far West."

In his letters, he continued to express his fondness for Dakota Territory, though always adding that he yearned for his niece and her friend to join the Custer Clan. "I like it out here so much, but would be better pleased if I could have you with me and I think if all is well one year from this winter will find you enjoying garrison life . . . How I wish I could see you both (young Reed and old Lewis daughter). Now do you know who I mean?"

Despite his affection for and frequent letters to the "old Lewis daughter," Boston found time at Fort Lincoln to enjoy female company. He wrote of "visiting some of the ladies in the post for a few moments," and told of a dance during the first week of November.

"Tom had a little dance party at his house last week and I took a young lady by the name of Miss Slaughter, Mrs. [Captain George] Dandy's sister, and she will be here all winter," Boston recalled. "She is very gay and lively."

Tom and Boston spent a great deal of their leisure time that autumn in one another's company. They often ate together. Officers did not dine with enlisted men, but since Boston was a civilian, it was within the rules.

Occasionally, when they went into nearby Bismarck for entertainment, they found themselves racing in order to get home for dinner time.

"Tom, Capt Algernon Smith and my own littleness went over to Bismarck today," Boston wrote on October 4. "I almost perished for the want of grub, so I don't think I will go very soon again unless I am sure of getting home in time for my meals."

On November 7, as Boston was waltzing Miss Slaughter and as Tom was at the card tables of Bismarck, Autie and Libbie were boarding a Northern Pacific Railway passenger train for their trip back to the home and hearth of the Custer Clan.

About a month later, his brother handed Tom sealed orders detailing a special mission to the Standing Rock Agency. While down at Standing Rock, Lonesome Charley Reynolds had attended a ceremonial dance not unlike those which Boston had mentioned to Emma. As often happened, various participants performed dances which reenacted deeds of bravery and other notable events in their lives.

The demonstration by one of them, a man named Rain-in-the-Face, told of his having ambushed and killed a *wasichu*. He then displayed the large gold pocket watch that had once belonged to Dr. John Honsinger, the 7th Cavalry veterinarian who was killed sixteen months earlier in August 1873 during the Yellowstone Expedition.

Nearing the age of forty, Rain-in-the-Face was no longer a young man for whom bragging about such a surprise attack should be important, but apparently it was for him. He also knew that it was a calculated risk to display the watch as evidence of his deed, but he made the conscious decision to take that risk.

When Reynolds reported the incident to George Armstrong Custer, he reported it up the chain of command, where it was decided that the unarmed Honsinger had not been a casualty of combat, but rather a murder victim, so an arrest warrant was drawn up. It was Tom Custer's job to serve the warrant at Standing Rock and to take Rain-in-the-Face into custody pending a trial.

On December 13, Tom Custer and George Yates rode into snow-swept Standing Rock Agency with Charley Reynolds, backed by about fifty 7th Cavalry troopers. They had picked this date because it was the day that supplies, especially the beef ration, were distributed to the Lakota.

Like Sitting Bull, Rain-in-the-Face was a member of the Hunkpapa Lakota, and like Sitting Bull, he had rejected treaty provisions that confined him to the reservation. Throughout most of the year, Rain-in-the-Face defiantly traveled wherever he wished across Dakota Territory and Montana Territory. In the winter, though, he became an Agency Indian, camping near the Standing Rock Agency to avail himself of *wasichu* largesse.

Little Hair and Charley Reynolds positioned themselves in the sutler's store where the people of Standing Rock came to pick up their treaty goods, and waited. Some hours later, Rain-in-the-Face finally arrived. Reynolds nodded to Custer, indicating that this was the man. He had a blanket over his shoulders and carried his Winchester rifle beneath. When Custer approached from behind, he started to pull out his weapon, but Custer grabbed him and wrestled it away from him. Four other troopers who were also in the room intervened to secure the prisoner.

Rain-in-the-Face was put in chains and taken outside, where Custer manhandled him onto a horse. At some point during this process, Rain-in-the-Face said angrily that he would one day cut out Tom Custer's heart and eat it. Tom and the others reportedly laughed at him.

A large number of Lakota had gathered around the store by this time, angrily demanding the release of Rain-in-the-Face. Reynolds, speaking in Lakota, explained why the prisoner was being taken away and told them that the fifty cavalrymen lined up to surround him would use force to prevent his being freed.

A proposal was then made to substitute two other Lakota men of lesser importance to take the place of Rain-in-the-Face, but Tom Custer rejected this out of hand.

As Libbie Custer wrote in *Boots and Saddles*, her husband interrogated Rain-in-the-Face until at last "he gave a brief account of the murder, and the next day made a full confession before all the officers. He said neither of the white men was armed when attacked. He had shot the old man, but he did not die instantly, riding a short distance before falling from his horse. Rain-in-the-Face then went to him and with his stone mallet beat out the last breath left."

Having admitted to killing Honsinger, Rain-in-the-Face was imprisoned at Fort Lincoln. His own brother, Iron Horse, visited, and according to Libbie Custer, told him "not to attempt to escape, saying, that if he did get back to the reservation he would surely be recaptured. He believed that he would be kindly treated while a captive, and perhaps the white chief would intercede for him to obtain his pardon . . . He thanked the General for his care of his brother, and . . . repeated petitions to ask the Great Father in Washington to spare his life. He then slowly took off his elaborate buckskin shirt and presented it to my husband."

As Rain-in-the-Face was led away in chains, one concern was put to rest for Tom Custer, but at the same time another reached its terrible climax.

On February 16, 1875, at almost exactly the same time, Lulie Burgess, the woman to whom Tom had considered himself betrothed, finally lost the battle with tuberculosis that so horribly consumed the final years of her short life. She passed away in Montclair, New Jersey, four months short of her twenty-seventh birthday.

Tom was 1,600 road miles and a world away, unseen and unmentioned when her family laid her to rest in the family plot in Cooperstown, New York, the town where she had been born. It is unclear when he had last seen her, though it had probably been at the end of May 1874 when he'd had his last extended furlough. In the little book *The Words of Jesus*, which she had given him back in 1868, he wrote poignantly, paraphrasing English hymnist Thomas Gibbons, "For strangers into life we come, and dying is but going home. Going home. Home, Lord, tarry not, but come."

As she was interred, there was no mention of her having had a fiancé. It is apparent that she and Tom had never made it official with a ring, though it has never been apparent why they did not. Nor is it clear why the family ignored a man who had visited Lulie numerous times over a span of eight years—especially a man who had written his will so as to leave half of his estate to their daughter.

It was a singular vexation for Libbie that Tom never found a soulmate to share his life on the Plains. Even if he had married Lulie, her illness would probably have precluded her from ever taking up residence in Dakota Territory. With that in mind, Libbie had attempted to find him a suitable companion from those available.

"Colonel Tom always lived with us, and the brothers played incessant jokes on each other," she wrote in *Boots and Saddles*. "Both of them honored and liked women extremely. Colonel Tom used to pay visits of an unconscionable length to ladies of the garrison, and no amount of teasing on his brother's part would induce him to shorten them. He never knew, when he started to go home from these visits, but that he would find on the young lady's doormat his trunk, portmanteau, and satchel—this as a little hint from the General that he was overtaxing the lady's patience . . . If, in visiting with the young ladies in our parlor, he overstayed the hour he was due at the stables or drill, the General's eye noticed it, and perhaps overlooked others in the room who were erring in the same manner . . . so I learned the bugle-call for stables, and hovering around Colonel Tom, hummed it in his ear, which the voice of the charmer had dulled to the trumpet-call. When the sound penetrated, he would make a plunge for his hat and belt, and tear out of the house, thus escaping reproof."

Among those "ladies of the garrison" were Emma and Nellie Wadsworth, two of the many friends of Libbie's from Monroe who came west to Fort Lincoln for periodic visits. In March, just a month after Lulie's death, Tom and Algernon Smith were seen frequently in the company of the two sisters—though Smith was married.

In a letter to him from New York City in December 1875, Libbie best summarized her feelings about Tom's situation, admonishing him, "Don't spend more money than you can help at the sutler's, drinking and card playing. Don't be influenced by the badness around you. Oh, Tom, if I find that the boy I have loved, and prayed over, has gone downhill. Oh, if only you had a companionable wife."

It was not to be, but there were other, darker clouds on Tom's horizon.

Two months after Lulie died, the Rain-in-the-Face matter, once having seemed to have been settled, reemerged. A prisoner's life was not for him. On April 18, 1875, after four months in custody, Rain-in-the-Face made a break for freedom.

As Libbie explained, he "occupied a part of the guard-house with a citizen who had been caught stealing grain from the storehouse. For several months they had been chained together, and used to walk in front of the little prison for exercise and air. The guard-house was a poorly-built, insecure wooden building. After a time the sentinels became less vigilant."

Two decades later on August 12, 1894, at Coney Island, New York—of all places—Rain-in-the-Face, now working as a "Show Indian" in a theatrical production, crossed paths with reporter W. Kent Thomas and told his side of the story. This was to appear in the December 1896 issue of the Boston-based *Nickell Magazine* and in the March 1903 issue of *Outdoor Life*.

"I was treated like a squaw, not a chief," Rain-in-the-Face complained. "They put me in a room, chained me, gave me only one blanket. The snow blew through the cracks and on to me all winter. It was cold. Once, Little Hair let me out and the long swords told me to run. I knew they wanted to shoot me in the back. I told Little Hair that I would get away sometime. I wasn't ready then. When I did, I would cut his heart out and eat it. I was chained to a white man. One night we got away."

Following Iron Horse's advice, he did not return to the Great Sioux Reservation, but rather he joined Sitting Bull far beyond the western horizon in the rolling hills and mountains of Montana Territory. Word eventually reached Fort Lincoln that he was alive and well, and "awaiting his revenge for his imprisonment."

His threat, often repeated, to cut out and eat Tom Custer's heart, once scoffed at by the Custer Clan, took on a more disturbing dimension now that he was at large. Amid the melancholy of losing Lulie, Tom now had another concern in the back of his mind.

CHAPTER 20

THE WINTER OF DISTRACTION

IN THE SUMMER of 1875, for the second time in as many years, there was Black Hills Expedition supported by the US Army, but it was launched from Fort Laramie in Wyoming Territory and did not involve the 7th Cavalry. Known as the United States Geological Expedition to the Black Hills, it was under the direction of Henry Newton and Walter P. Jenney of the US Geological Survey, with the military escort commanded by Lieutenant Colonel Richard Dodge.

It was packaged as a scientific expedition with the goal of mapping the Black Hills, but the subtext was all about assessing the mineral value alluded to by Custer's report after the 1874 expedition. The presence of gold would be confirmed, and the thin rivulet of prospectors flowing into the once-mysterious hills would become a torrent. This would completely and inexorably upset the delicate balance between native culture and *wasichu* society that existed in Dakota Territory.

A secondary component of the Newton-Jenney Expedition, and of other smaller US Army operations that season was to curb the number of prospectors entering the Black Hills. Under the terms of the Fort Laramie Treaty they were trespassers, and the Lakota demanded action. Enforcing this provision of the treaty was a difficult task that was verging on the impossible. At least, for the 7th Cavalry in the summer of 1875, it was someone else's problem.

Indeed, this summer was the first since the regiment had come to Dakota Territory, that it would *not* be going into the field. Libbie Custer welcomed this turn, and wrote in *Boots and Saddles* that "it is impossible to express the joy I felt that there was to be no summer campaign; and for the first time in many years I saw the grass grow without a shudder."

Neither Libbie nor her husband—nor indeed "brother" Tom—allowed any grass to grow beneath their feet during 1875. Even before the departure of the Newton-Jenney Expedition on May 25, the knowledge that the 7th Cavalry would not be deployed sent the Custers in motion on expeditions of their own—eastward to the States.

Autie left Dakota Territory for New York City by way of Monroe on April 27, while Tom Custer and Lieutenant William Winer Cooke left the following day to spend two weeks in St. Paul, Minnesota. They all came back to Fort Lincoln over the summer, but returned east in September. It is not clear whether Libbie was with her husband on the spring junket, but she was definitely on the train with him in the fall.

As he had in 1874 while Autie and Libbie traveled east, Boston Custer remained at Fort Lincoln, as did Maggie and her husband, although the Calhouns did go east in the fall of 1875.

In a letter to Emma Reed on September 5, he displayed a trace of wistfulness, writing, "I wish you could take dinner with Maggie, Jim and I today. If you conclude to do so dinner will be ready at half past five so don't fail to come. I am going out horseback riding this evening for my health. You may think I am jesting but I am not. I wish you could come back with Libbie this fall. Armstrong, Libbie, Tom and Col Cooke leave for the East next week. I am going to write to Fannie Lewis this evening."

Boston went on to say that, while he was not coming home in 1875, he planned to do so the following year, and he repeated his desire that Emma should make her home at Fort Lincoln as part of the Custer Clan.

"If all is well I intend to call in Monroe sometime next fall [of 1876]," he added. "If you could be here this winter I know you would not get homesick for we had such a pleasant time, last winter and we intend having the same this winter. Tom and I go out hunting now and then at five o'clock in the morning."

On September 23, Boston wrote Emma again to say that "I expect Armstrong and the old lady will take their departure for the East in the morning. I may go with them but only to Bismarck a distance of 5 miles and then return with Mrs. Calhoun, and Jim on the first boat to the bosom of the noted Fort Abraham Lincoln and enjoy the many luxuries of frontier life."

His letter, carried on the same train as Autie and Libbie, reached Monroe at the same time. Here, they visited David and Lydia Ann Reed, who had just moved into a substantial new home on Monroe Street.

Libbie stayed over, while Autie continued on to Albion, New York, to visit one of the Custer boys' cousins on their mother's side, Augusta Ward Frary. He had communicated with her occasionally during his West Point and Civil War years, but had been out of touch for some time when a letter from her reached him at Fort Lincoln in August. Indeed, he had not communicated with her since before he married Libbie in 1864, and he took the opportunity of his reply letter to mention the fact that her father was from Onondaga County, not far from where Augusta lived.

"I have passed and repassed within a few miles of your home quite often of late years and would have been glad to stop and see you had I only known where to find you," he had written in his swift reply. "I spent about a month in New York City in April and May of this year passing over the route from Buffalo to Rochester in going and coming. If I am permitted to carry out my present plans I will probably spend a month or two in New York City between now and December. If so I trust I may have the pleasure of seeing 'Cousin Augusta' again."

He then brought her up to date on the other Custer boys and Maggie, writing that "Maggie is married to a very fine young staff officer of mine and lives next door to us. She has been married three years. I also have two younger brothers with me. One of them, Tom is an officer in my command, the other [Boston], the youngest of the boys is here also in the employ of the government so that we can muster quite an extensive family circle. Both of my brothers are unmarried. Maggie's husband's name is Calhoun and we all like him very much. She became engaged to him while she was visiting us in Kansas. Father and Mother reside in Monroe Michigan, Mother has been in feeble health for several years, so feeble as to prevent her from visiting us in this remote corner of the globe. I presume we must seem almost out of the world to persons living so far east as you do."

While Autie traveled to New York, Libbie went up to Grand Rapids to visit her cousin, Rebecca Richmond, and her family, before continuing on to meet her husband in New York City.

Tom Custer had left a week earlier, on September 13, for a thirty-day furlough accompanied by Cooke and Lieutenant Winfield Scott Edgerly. They stopped in Chicago on their way to Monroe, then turned north to Hamilton, Ontario, where Cooke had family.

By October, with their furloughs extended to mid-November, they had rendezvoused with Autie in New York at the Hotel Brunswick on Fifth Avenue near East 27th Street. Soon after, Libbie arrived, she and Autie planning to remain through the winter after Tom and Cooke returned to Dakota Territory.

"Colonel Tom and one of the oldest friends we had in the 7th [Cooke] were with us part of the time, and we had many enjoyable hours together," Libbie recalled. "The theatre was our unfailing delight. They were all desirous that I should see the military play of 'Ours,' which was then so admirably put on the stage at Wallack's, but dreaded the effect it would have on me. At last one of them said that it was too finely represented for me to miss, and I heard them say to each other, 'We must take the old lady, though it will break her heart and she will cry.' It ended in my going. When we reached the part in the play where the farewell comes, and the sword is buckled on the warrior by the trembling hands of the wife, I could not endure it. Too often had the reality of such suffering been my own. The three men were crying like children, and only too willing to take me out into the fresh air."

She and her husband moved to a small, quieter apartment near the Brunswick, but apparently the younger officers stayed on at the hotel until their application for a further furlough extension was denied. Tom Custer and William Cooke reached Bismarck on November 27 and crossed the icy Missouri to Fort Lincoln the following day.

Though he returned from leave technically two weeks tardy, Tom received some good news from the War Department on December 2. A brevet lieutenant colonel as the Civil War ended, he had reverted back to a regular army first lieutenant's commission in 1866, but now, after nearly a decade, he was officially promoted to captain. On December 17, he took command of the 7th Cavalry's Company C.

In a letter to Emma Reed that evening, Tom waxed despondently about the boredom of the Dakota prairie in winter, especially after the excitement of New York City.

He also candidly shared his exasperation with his sister Maggie and her husband, James Calhoun. Compared to Libbie and Autie, he found them boring and humorless. Of course with Jim, the sourness may have flowed from the fact that his craving for the card table frequently ended so badly in the face of Tom's own adroit playing—rooted either in skill, in luck, or in some combination of the two. In his letter, Tom mentioned luring them to Algernon Smith's home with the promise of a nonexistent dessert, which infuriated the Calhouns. Another prank by a Custer boy gone awry.

A letter to Emma Reed written by Boston on December 28 provides a further insight into the temperament of sister Maggie. He wrote of spending Christmas with the Calhouns, and the gifts exchanged and, adding that "I won't tell you what Maggie got. If I did, there would be no living in the garrison with her. She is about spoiled now and the only way that Jim and I can stay in the house is to humor her in every little trivial thing . . . You would think sometimes to hear her talk to Jim that we were helpless little children, but I think mother spoils her more or less every time she goes home and I think about three more trips home and I will be obliged to change my boarding house. She makes Jim and I drink our coffee sometimes when we don't wish any and many things of this kind which I won't mention."

Boston interpreted Maggie's stern efforts toward discipline as reminiscent of the punishment wrought during their childhood by Maria. In a later letter to their mother, Boston wrote that Maggie "pretends that she is acting like you and will cuff my ears just as though I were a little child and will say that if you did it when I was small that it is perfectly right for her but sometimes she will start in on Jim, Tom and I and give each several good thumps with her fist."

In retrospect, it could have been that Maggie felt generally overwhelmed by her circumstances and was just lashing out. Though she had aspired to emulate Libbie by marrying a soldier and following him into the West, perhaps Maggie had bitten off more than she was willing to chew. Perhaps she was not cut out for the frontier lifestyle after all.

The grass is always greener—or in December, the driven snow whiter— on the opposite side of the continent. In late December, as Tom griped, Libbie wrote to Tom from New York, complaining that "the holidays have been rainy, gloomy. I did not have half the fun I had anticipated, looking in at the shop windows. On Christmas morning I went to church, but came back, weary, disgruntled. Episcopal, but the extreme of ritual-intoned prayers, chanting and processions. Autie always finds the day somewhat of a bore and is glad when it is over. I missed the home atmosphere, all of you."

Of course, Autie was the toast of the town since the success of his book *My Life on the Plains*, published a year earlier, and the publisher had commissioned a second book. He also took time to resume his work with *Galaxy* magazine, penning an article on the Yellowstone Expedition of 1874. Meanwhile, the Redpath Agency in Boston had proposed a lecture tour the next time he came east. They offered him $200 a night for five nights a week, for up to five months, which translates into roughly $450,000 in today's valuation. He declined for the near term, though his interest was certainly aroused. The prominence of the eldest Custer boy on the media stage was well established and burning brightly.

In February, against this glittering backdrop, the Custers prepared for their journey home, after spending half a year outside the bosom of the Custer Clan. "In army life it is perfectly natural to speak of one's financial condition, and it did not occur to us that civilians do not do the same," Libbie recalled. "I do not wonder now that they opened their eyes with well-bred astonishment when we said we were obliged to go because we had used all the money we had saved for leave of absence."

When they reached St. Paul, they learned that the Northern Pacific's trains across Dakota Territory were not scheduled to begin running until April at the earliest. However, as Libbie explained, "The railroad officials, mindful of what the General had done for them in protecting their advance workers in the building of the road, came and offered to open the route. Sending us through on a special train was a great undertaking . . . There were two snow-ploughs and three enormous engines; freight-cars with coal supplies and baggage; several cattle-cars, with stock belonging to the Black Hills miners who filled the passenger-coaches."

That a previously unannounced special train would be quickly filled with "Black Hills miners" in *February* when the land was drifted over with snow, was quite illustrative of how serious the gold fever was being perceived in the States, and of how serious the threat of war with the Lakota *should have been* perceived.

In the near term, though, the adversary was the winter. As Libbie described in *Boots and Saddles*, the snow drifts were so deep that, about halfway between Fargo and Bismarck, "the ploughs and one engine were so deeply embedded that they could not be withdrawn. The Northern Pacific employees dug and shoveled until they were exhausted. The Black Hills miners relieved them as long as they could endure it; then the officers and recruits worked until they could do no more. The impenetrable bank of snow was the accumulation of the whole winter, first snowing, then freezing, until there were successive layers of ice and snow. It was the most dispiriting and forlorn situation."

Finally, a battery and a pocket relay were located. Wires were run and tapped into the telegraph wires that paralleled the tracks. The railroad was able to contact Fargo, and Autie was able to get a message through to Fort Lincoln.

It was his own brother who replied.

"Shall I come out for you?" Tom Custer asked. "You say nothing about the old lady; is she with you?"

"I emphatically forbade him to come," Libbie recalled. "On this occasion I dared to assume a show of authority. The stories of the risk and suffering of our mail-carriers during the two previous winters were too fresh in my memory for me to consent that Colonel Tom should encounter so much for our sake . . . We only succeeded in suppressing our headlong brother temporarily. Against our direct refusal he made all his preparations and only telegraphed when it was too late to receive an answer that he was leaving garrison."

Paying her no mind, Tom Custer had hired the best stage driver in Bismarck, and perhaps in all of Dakota Territory, and together they set out by sleigh, making use of relay mules that had been prepositioned at stables along the way for the use of the mail sleigh.

"At last a great whoop and yell, such as was peculiar to the Custers, was answered by the General," wrote Libbie, "and made me aware for the first time that Colonel Tom was outside. I scolded him for coming before I thanked him, but be made light of the danger and hurried us to get ready, fearing a coming blizzard. His arms were full of wraps, and his pockets crowded with mufflers and wraps the ladies had sent out to me."

CHAPTER 21

LIVELY WORK BEFORE US

"I EXPECT TO be in the field in the summer, with the 7th, and think there will be lively work before us," George Armstrong Custer wrote his brother Tom from New York in January 1876. "I think the 7th Cavalry may have its greatest campaign ahead."

While the Custer boys were enjoying their New York furloughs in the autumn of 1875, there had been some lively work in progress in Washington, DC. The metaphorical dominos that had been set in motion by the Black Hills Expedition of 1874, and by the *wasichu* reaction to the gold in those hills, continued to topple. Each one that fell brought the Black Hills, the Great Sioux Reservation, and an area twice as large in southeastern Montana Territory closer to the brink of war. Washington was afire with discussions of how to prevent this.

The issues were twofold. Simply put, there was the problem of *wasichu* streaming *into* the Great Sioux Reservation, specifically the Black Hills. Then there was the problem of Lakota streaming *out*.

As to the first problem, it had been clear by the spring of 1875 that the prospectors coming into the Black Hills could not, and would not, be stopped.

Red Cloud and Spotted Tail came to Washington in May 1875 to meet with President Grant, as well as with Secretary of the Interior Columbus Delano and Commissioner of Indian Affairs Edward Parmelee Smith.

Sitting Bull and Crazy Horse were invited, but declined. The idea was to negotiate a settlement of the Black Hills issue, but the process was complicated by the fact that all three of these *wasichu* were in the midst of a corruption scandal that was sweeping the Grant Administration like a prairie fire. By the autumn, both Smith and Delano had resigned.

The *wasichu* had offered to buy their way out of the problem. Congress had agreed to appropriate $25,000 and other land elsewhere as compensation for hunting rights to the Black Hills. "I am no dog," Red Cloud told Smith. "I am a man. This is my ground and I'm sitting on it."

In September, the *wasichu* tried again. A delegation headed by Major General Alfred Howe Terry, commander of the Military Department of Dakota (who answered to Phil Sheridan as the commander of the Military Division of the Missouri), and Senator William Boyd Allison of Iowa traveled west to meet Red Cloud on the Great Sioux Reservation. The deal had been sweetened considerably, with the *wasichu* offering to lease the Black Hills for $400,000 a year, or purchase it outright for $6 million—the latter being worth around $150 million today. Again, the answer was no.

The second problem involving the Great Sioux Reservation as summer turned to autumn in 1875 was that of the growing number of Lakota who had gone off the reservation. As the Fort Laramie Treaty provided that *wasichu* would stay *out* of the Great Sioux Reservation, it stipulated that the Lakota would conduct their affairs within it.

Large numbers of Lakota, especially the Oglala who followed Crazy Horse and the Hunkpapa who followed Sitting Bull, had left the reservation in defiance of the government's insistence that they remain there, relocating to areas farther west such as the Powder River Country of Montana Territory. This vast, 25,000-square-mile *terra incognita* included the valley of the Yellowstone River where the 7th Cavalry had tangled with the Lakota in the summer of 1873, as well as the valleys south of the Yellowstone that were drained by a series of roughly parallel Yellowstone tributaries. These included, from east to west, the Powder, the Tongue, the

Rosebud, and the Bighorn, as well as the Little Bighorn (aka Little Horn), a tributary of the Bighorn.

Many of the Lakota, as well as a large number of Northern Cheyenne and other tribes, had been roaming this land during the summers since the creation of the Great Sioux Reservation, but many were now off the reservation permanently and living there year-round.

The Grant Administration, both applauded and ridiculed for its past peace policy, had decided to get tough. In a round of lively work at the White House in November 1875, President Grant set out a military plan for the resolution of the second problem involving the Great Sioux Reservation. He brought in Secretary of War William Belknap and his new Secretary of the Interior, Zachariah Chandler, as well as the new Commissioner of Indian Affairs, Edward Smith.

Getting tough, they decided, would involve demanding that the Lakota and their Cheyenne allies return to the reservation—and if they did not, to send in the US Army.

Lieutenant General Phil Sheridan, commander of the Division of the Missouri, arrived at the White House from Chicago. He was joined by his subordinate, Major General George Crook, the hero of the Apache Wars, who now commanded the Department of the Platte with headquarters in Omaha. They planned a comprehensive and aggressive campaign.

Sheridan's strategic plan for this massive military campaign, the largest in the West for years, was for large US Army contingents to converge upon southeastern Montana Territory from three points of the compass.

Crook himself would lead one from the south out of Fort Laramie, staging through Fort Fetterman in Wyoming Territory. The other two would converge from east and west, traveling through the valley of the Yellowstone. Sheridan intended that the western of these contingents would be led by Colonel John Gibbon out of Fort Ellis near Bozeman in Montana Territory, and the eastern prong to be led by Lieutenant Colonel George Armstrong Custer from Fort Lincoln. In overall command of the

Yellowstone River operations would be General Alfred Terry, the commander of the Military Department of Dakota, which was a subsidiary of Sheridan's Division of the Missouri.

Colonel Samuel Sturgis, who was still *officially* the commander of the 7th Cavalry, remained on detached duty in St. Louis—where he had sat out the Yellowstone and Black Hills Expeditions of 1873 and 1874—and there seems to have been no mention of him actually leading his regiment in the field in 1876.

On December 2, 1875, as Tom Custer was pinning on his captain's bars, as Boston was incurring the wrath of his uncompromising sister, and as Autie was lounging backstage at Edwin Booth's Theater in New York, the new Secretary of the Interior laid down a gauntlet that would set a new line of dominoes toppling. Zachariah Chandler formally announced that all of the Lakota who were outside its boundaries, the so-called the "winter roamers," should go back inside the Great Sioux Reservation by the end of January 1876 or they would be deemed "hostile" and forced back.

However, a winter sufficiently severe to trap multiple locomotives preceded by a line of snowplows until the spring thaw obviously presented logistical challenges to communications and travel on the Plains.

First, it would be virtually impossible to find and convey the message to all the winter roamers spread across more than a half million square miles inside of sixty days. Naturally, the far flung nomadic encampments had no telegraph connection.

Second, it would be difficult for these people to travel hundreds of miles to the Great Sioux Reservation—even if they were inclined to do so, which they were not.

Third, military operations under such conditions to enforce the order would be incredibly arduous.

The original idea was that the big three-pronged campaign would be undertaken in February as a winter offensive, much like the one in 1868 that had culminated in the 7th Cavalry battle attack on Black Kettle and the Cheyenne on the Washita River.

To say that it got off to a bad start would be only partially true. Two of the prongs didn't get off to a start at all. The commands under Gibbon and Custer were snowed in and unable to move into the field.

Crook marched north through the heavy snow, passing through Fort Fetterman. On March 17, Colonel Joseph Reynolds, with six companies from the 2nd and 3rd Cavalry Regiments—about a third of Crook's total force—located and attacked a mixed Cheyenne/Lakota village on the Powder River. They captured it and were in the midst of burning it when a counterattack forced them to retreat, leaving behind their dead and wounded. For the latter and other charges, Reynolds was courtmartialed.

The winter offensive had ended in failure, but the original plan was retained and it would be reorganized as a summer offensive.

No sooner had the winter offensive fizzled to an inglorious halt than George Armstrong Custer received his next set of marching orders. They were not in connection with the Army nor the upcoming campaign, but instead, his presence was demanded in Washington to testify before Congress.

His departure, four days after the Reynolds debacle, left the 7th Cavalry without its combat-experienced commander. The senior officer in charge was Major Marcus Reno, who had joined the 7th in 1871, but after serving as commander of the contingent based at Spartanburg, South Carolina, he had parted company with the regiment to take command of the military escort for the Northern Boundary Survey Commission on the Canadian border in northern Dakota Territory. He had missed the Yellowstone and Black Hills Expeditions and had not been in battle in the more than a decade that had passed since the Civil War. He had only just returned to the regiment at the end of the October 1875 after an extended leave and had filled in as commander while Custer was in New York.

Reno's personal life had recently been visited by tragedy with the death of his wife in July 1874. As his biographer, Ronald H. Nichols wrote, "The emotional impact of losing his wife would have a profound effect on Reno and his Army career. Mary Hannah had been outgoing, warm and entertaining which, during their eleven years of marriage, had a soothing effect on Reno's cold and harsh personality."

The loss of his wife had been compounded by his inability to return to Pennsylvania for her funeral because he was with the Survey Commission, stranded far upriver on the Missouri at Fort Benton in Montana Territory, and could not make passage. When he finally did return, two months later, his wife's family refused to forgive him for not coming sooner to comfort their eight-year-old son, Robert. The boy grew up never having reconciled with his father.

The gloomy and introverted Reno was the antithesis of George Armstrong Custer, and during his months as acting commander at Fort Lincoln, his despondency had to have been exacerbated by his being outside the clamorous world of the Custer Clan, which was the center of social life at the post.

As Reno sulked, the Clan indulged in their usual tomfoolery. Of the Custer boys and their "sisters," Boston told Emma Reed on April 2 that "Tom and I go over to Libbie's every evening after dinner and play billiards and Mrs. Capt. Smith comes up so we play partners and Tom and I jokingly pretend that we want Mrs. Smith for a partner instead of Libbie so Tom or I will say well you take her tonight—meaning Libbie—and I will tomorrow night."

For the family, at least, life without the "General" was an intimate affair. As Boston confided to Emma, "Libbie goes over to Maggie's house every night to sleep and I am always there and sometimes Tom. When they wish to retire and they cant get us out of the room so they both get behind us and commence to undress and especially Libbie reminds me of ducks playing in the water. She told me last night that I had to undress her tonight but I told her I would not do it for any man's twenty dollar bill."

Libbie was always less inhibited by Victorian etiquette than her sister-in-law. It is hard to imagine straight-laced Maggie ever toying with her brother-in-law, Frederic Calhoun, by asking him to undress her.

Even as he was being teased by his brother's wife, Boston was growing impatient for the 7th Cavalry to take to the field on its next adventure. He told Emma, "I am feeling better now than I have felt for months. My buckskin suit will be done this week. I am going out riding every nice day until the expedition leaves."

Back in the States, Autie had found the capital in turmoil. Though the president himself was not personally involved, the Grant Administration had been rocked by a series of nefarious scandals that seemed to go on and on, one after another. Secretary of the Interior Delano had been forced out of office by a far-reaching bribery scandal that filled not only his pockets, but those of the president's own brother, Orvil Grant. Meanwhile, an endemic tax evasion epidemic was discovered to have prevailed throughout the whiskey industry for years. These were just two of the predicaments that consumed the administration and the national headlines in 1875 and cast their shadow into the Centennial year.

A third of the many ignominious affairs was the Trading Post Scandal. Congress was investigating bribery and extortion at the trading posts that surrounded the agencies on Indian Reservations, and it had just been learned in February that Secretary of War William Belknap—a close friend and ally of the president—and his two wives had been taking kickbacks from traders in exchange for appointments and from the sale of government aid intended for the residents of the reservations. This extensive intrigue went back to before the death of Carita Belknap in 1870, and continued after Belknap married her sister, Amanda, three years later. Belknap resigned on March 2, in 1873, but the Congressional investigation, led by Pennsylvania Democrat Heister Clymer and New York Republican Lyman Bass, continued.

George Armstrong Custer was well aware of the corruption on the Indian Reservations, and had even written op-ed articles published in the *New York Herald*—a pro-Custer, though anti-Grant paper—though not under his own name. Perhaps inevitably, he was summoned to testify before Congress, which he did on March 29 and April 4.

In his testimony, he explained that the practice of extortion was widespread and well known, pointing a finger at Belknap, and detailing specific instances of kickbacks that he had witnessed. Because Custer was an outspoken Democrat, and Belknap, like the president, was a Republican, many observers saw a political dimension to the testimony. Perhaps most damning was Custer's assertion of a systematic cover-up, which was widely reported in the media on April 5.

The Times of Philadelphia, the Cincinnati *Inquirer*, and the *Pittsburgh Commercial*, among others, reported that he had been asked why he and other army officers had not previously "given information of these abuses on the frontier."

To this he read an order dated March 15, 1873, stating that "no officer, active or retired, shall directly or indirectly, without being called upon by proper authority, solicit, suggest or recommend action by members of Congress for or against military affairs."

The order also stipulated that if an officer went to Washington to testify before Congress, he must "register his name at the Adjutant General's office stating the authority under which he is absent from his command or station."

Custer added that "this order closed the mouths of all army officers with regard to abuses that existed on the frontier; that the officers knew if the recent complaints were sent to Congressmen through the Secretary of War they would be pigeon-holed, and the officers would probably be pigeon-holed too, causing the officer to lose his commission."

He concluded by saying that "the object of the order was to cover up the doings of the Secretary of War."

The New York Times, which had endorsed Grant for president twice, complained that Democrat Custer carried a grudge against Republican Grant. At the *New York Herald*, where publisher James Gordon Bennett, Jr. idolized Custer, it was an opposite tack. The paper had begun celebrating Custer during the Civil War, when Bennett's father had made the "Boy General" a household name.

Assuming that he was through with his Washington testifying, Autie began his return to Dakota Territory on April 20, stopping in Philadelphia to attend the Centennial International Exposition, a grand precursor of future world's fairs. He then traveled on to New York City, where he was abruptly called back to the nation's capital. In the Senate, an impeachment trial against Belknap was being prepared—despite the fact that the Secretary of War had resigned—and Custer was sought as a witness.

Ulysses S. Grant, meanwhile, was furious with Custer. He was especially angry about the embarrassment heaped upon his administration by a man in uniform. On April 28, he wired General of the Army William Tecumseh Sherman, ordering him to order Sheridan to remove Custer from command of the eastern wing of the three-pronged summer offensive in the West and of the 7th Cavalry during the operation. Sheridan, though a longtime supporter and mentor of Custer's, agreed to place the 7th Cavalry under General Terry's direct command while Custer remained sidelined.

Having allowed himself to be swept into the political quagmire, Autie was feeling its full wrath. He then hastened back to Washington to plead his case to Sherman personally. Sherman, who was on his way out of town, told Custer to take it up with Grant. On May 1, he spent five hours cooling his heels in a White House waiting room before being told that the president couldn't see him. He took it to mean that Grant *wouldn't* see him and he left town. On May 4, as he was passing westward through Chicago, Custer was told that Grant was angry at him for having reported to neither himself nor Sherman before leaving Washington. Being in Chicago, he reported to Sheridan, who berated him for allowing himself to become a political pawn.

The media had a field day. The *New York Herald* headline called it "Grant's Revenge." The *Indiana Democrat* of Indiana, Pennsylvania, asserted that Custer had been "removed to deter other officers from telling what they knew," adding that, "There has never been a President of the United States before who was capable of braving the decent opinion of the country so openly and shamefully as this, for the sake of wreaking such a miserable vengeance."

At last, Grant relented to popular pressure to release his fair-haired problem child to serve on the summer's operation. Too many editorial pages had asserted that Grant was punishing Custer for being a whistle-blower. On May 8, the order confining Autie to Fort Lincoln for the summer was rescinded. Perhaps in part, his decision was thanks to a letter of apology that was signed by Autie, but ghostwritten by Alfred Terry, who had practiced as an attorney before the Civil War and who wanted Custer on the expedition.

Perhaps the wording of the letter gave Grant the soldierly excuse that he needed in order to relent.

"I appeal to you as a soldier," the letter read, "to spare me the humiliation of seeing my regiment march to meet the enemy and I do not share the dangers."

CHAPTER 22

MARCHING TO MEET THE ENEMY

THE MOOD WAS festive as the 7th Cavalry marched forth from Fort Abraham Lincoln on the morning of May 17, 1876. The blackbirds were singing amid the cattails along the Missouri, and the meadowlarks were calling across the golden prairie grasses gently waving in the breeze.

Leading the 7th Cavalry with its twelve companies, comprising more than 750 officers and men, was Lieutenant Colonel George Armstrong Custer, recently and reluctantly rehabilitated through the pragmatism of the commander in chief.

Custer had cut his hair, trimming the golden locks that had earned him the Lakota nickname "Long Hair." Why he did so has never been satisfactorily explained. One of the more common unsubstantiated yarns—even repeated by the auctioneers Butterfield & Butterfield in the catalog of a Custer memorabilia auction in 1995—is that Libbie feared the presence of long hair might cause him to be scalped. She, however, made no mention of this in her memoirs.

The 7th was certainly the tail that wagged the dog of General Alfred Terry's command. The remainder consisted of two companies of the 17th Infantry Regiment and the Gatling gun detachment of the 20th Infantry. Their supplies were carried in 150 wagons and a long string of pack mules that brought up the rear of the two-mile column. The steamboats *Josephine* and *Far West* had also been chartered to provide additional logistical support upriver on the Yellowstone.

Custer had only just returned from the States three days earlier, having made a stop in Monroe to pick up eighteen-year-old Harry Armstrong "Autie" Reed, the youngest child and only son of his half-sister, Lydia Ann Reed.

According to the family narrative, as recalled in Lydia Ann's 1906 obituary, George Armstrong Custer did not "urge" the Reed boy to come, but "as nothing serious was feared, he said: 'If your mother is willing, Autie, come along.'"

The family had decided that it was time for the young man to experience the frontier at the side of his three older uncles. There had been some discussion in family letters that Emma Reed, Autie's twenty-year-old older sister—and the oft-cited correspondent of Tom and Boston Custer—might also come west that summer, but she remained in Monroe.

It was very much a family affair. Autie was flanked not only by his brother Tom and his adjutant, brother-in-law James Calhoun, but also by his wife and sister. As the regimental band struck up "The Girl I Left Behind Me," always their parting tune when the 7th marched out across the Plains, Libbie and Maggie enjoyed a twenty-four-hour reprieve before they would be left behind. The two had joined the expedition for its first day in the field, but would return to Fort Lincoln after camping with their husbands on the first night.

"The General could scarcely restrain his recurring joy at being again with his regiment, from which he had feared he might be separated by being detained on other duty," Libbie recalled in *Boots and Saddles*. "His buoyant spirits at the prospect of the activity and field life that he so loved made him like a boy. He had made every plan to have me join him later on, when they should have reached the Yellowstone." At least this was their intention.

There was also Custer's satisfaction that he would once again be in the limelight that derived from his leading the charge in a campaign on the frontier. He was contributing articles to *Galaxy* magazine again, and he even had one in progress as the expedition was heading west. Equally excited and writing for consumption back in the States while riding with the expedition was Mark Kellogg, a reporter with the *Bismarck Tribune*, whose articles of the imminent Custer triumph were intended to be shared with the *New York Herald*, where publisher James Gordon Bennett was one of the media world's biggest Custer fans. Custer himself would also be sending the occasional letter to the *Herald* during the campaign.

The strategic plan for a more or less simultaneously deployment of the three columns of Sheridan's great summer offensive was wishful thinking. Terry had originally hoped to take the field as early as April 5, but the kerfuffle swirling around Custer had caused a series of delays and postponements.

The western wing, including six companies of the 7th Infantry Regiment and four companies of the 2nd Cavalry, under Colonel John Gibbon, had embarked from Fort Ellis, Montana Territory on March 30. On April 20, as they patrolled the north bank of the Yellowstone, they were across from the mouth of the Bighorn River—the site of the 7th Cavalry's August 1873 battle with Sitting Bull and Crazy Horse. On that day, Custer was in Philadelphia touring the Centennial Exposition.

General George Crook's southern wing, meanwhile, was scheduled to depart Fort Fetterman in Wyoming Territory by May 15, but they were delayed until May 29 because of a lack of scouts. This contingent was the largest of the three columns, comprising more than 1,000 troops organized into ten companies of the 3rd Cavalry, five companies of the 2nd Cavalry, three companies of the 9th Infantry, and two companies of the 4th Infantry.

A significant tactical problem for the US Army was that, while Gibbon and Terry would rendezvous with one another on the river and had a reasonable idea of where the other was before their rendezvous, no communication was possible between them and Crook once he had taken the field, and they didn't know where he was. Nor did Terry and Custer have any idea that Crook was two weeks behind schedule.

As for the people against whom the three prongs were aimed, the enemy against whom they marched, they were thought at the time to be in widely separated encampments spread across the 25,000 square miles of the Powder River Country, though concentrated in the valleys between the Powder River and the Bighorn River, which are roughly 125 miles apart as the crow flies.

In fact, unbeknownst to the three US Army contingents as they deployed, most of the Lakota and Northern Cheyenne would come together that summer to travel and camp in one very large group. They moved as one, leisurely traveling through the Powder River County, hunting the buffalo, which were still abundant in these rolling hills and valleys. They would camp for several days, then pick up and travel to a new location as hunters ranged far and wide. The vast group included the Hunkpapa Lakota bands of Four Horns, Black Moon as well as of Sitting Bull, while the Oglala Lakota followed Crazy Horse and Low Dog.

Gradually, by the middle of June, Terry, Custer, and Gibbon would *begin* to figure out that this great congregation was forming—based on their scouts having discovered abandoned campsites and counting the number of locations where individual lodges, or tipis, had stood. Unfortunately, these sites dated from earlier in the season when the group was still evolving, and this still led to underestimating the number that would be concentrated in one place by the time of contact in the latter half of June.

As they had used Arikara scouts in Dakota Territory, the US Army added Crow scouts to their support staff to help track the Lakota in Montana. It is an interesting irony that the Powder River Country, where the Lakota now roamed, was traditionally the home of the Crow (known as

Absaroka or Apsáalooke in their own tongue), who had been the bitter rivals of the Lakota for as long as anyone in either tribe could remember.

By May 30, the eastern column had reached the Little Missouri River on the threshold of Montana Territory. After entering Montana Territory about 100 miles south of the Yellowstone, they turned north, downstream on the Powder River, conducting a reconnaissance of the area east of the Powder River drainage. The plan was to meet the steamer *Far West* on the Yellowstone at the mouth of the Powder.

A week into the expedition, Tom had been relieved by his older brother from duty at the head of Company C and from the duties of command so that Tom could serve as Autie's aide and therefore ride as part of the command staff. In this role, they were free to ride out in search of the deer and the antelope and to give young Autie Reed a taste for hunting on the Plains.

Shortly after reaching Montana Territory, Terry ordered Custer to depart the main column with a contingent of four companies for several days to search for Lakota camps farther afield.

"Tom, Bos, and I, taking some men, started on a near route across the country, knowing that we would intercept the column later on," the General explained to Libbie, not mentioning that the reconnaissance had been ordered by Terry. "This is the second time I have left the main command, and both times they have lost their way; so you see my 'bump of locality' is of some use out here. We reached this camp about three-quarters of an hour from the time we left the column, but the latter strayed off, and while we were here by nine o'clock, the rest did not reach here until two o'clock. When they found they were lost, the officers all assembled at the head of the column to consult together and try and find the right way."

This was a jab at Terry, who was among these officers. Autie seemed to take perverse delight in how the main column and the General got lost without him. Apparently, Charley Reynolds was with the Custer Clan on this excursion.

At another point about a week later and deeper inside the Powder River Country, Terry admitted to being lost and Autie bragged to Libbie that "I told him I thought I could guide the column. He assented; so Tom, Bos, and I started ahead, with Company D and the scouts as escort, and brought the command to this point, over what seems to be the only practicable route for miles on either side, through the worst kind of Bad Lands. The General did not believe it possible to find a road through. When, after a hard day's work, we arrived at this river by a good, easy road, making thirty-two miles in one day, he was delighted and came to congratulate me."

Knowing his wife's concerns for his safety, he reassured her about his taking leave of the main body of troops, writing, "I have been extremely prudent—sufficiently so to satisfy you. I go nowhere without taking an escort with me. I act as if Indians were near all the time."

In fact, he and his brothers were generally much more relaxed, sensing no danger requiring prudence—at least in the first weeks of the expedition. As in the Powder River Country in 1873, there was time for hunting, and as he told Emma Reed in a letter, Tom Custer was even able to spend some time looking for interesting specimens for her rock collection.

The lack of urgency was such that there was even time for afternoon naps. "When I get into Camp I feel like sleeping," Boston Custer told Emma Reed in his letter on the last day of May. "Three o'clock comes very soon in the morning and breakfast ready about quarter after three."

And of course, the Custer boys always had time for teasing. "Tom stole my gloves today while eating lunch and pulled me down a bank running in to a creek so you can imagine how nicely my brother treats me," Boston complained to Emma in the same letter. "Will try to get my gloves back that your Uncles shamefully stole from me while in the Gen's tent."

Some of the practical jokes were more dangerous than others.

"Worst of all he and the General tried to kill me today by shooting at me," Boston reported. "They fired three shots."

Autie recounted the same incident to Libbie, writing in more detail that "while out with Tom and Bos, we were riding through a part of the country filled with small buttes, in which it was easy to lose one's self. Bos stopped a few moments as we were riding through a ravine, and dismounted to take a pebble from his pony's shoe. I observed it, and said to Tom, 'Let's slip round the hill behind Bos, where he can't find us, and when he starts we'll fire in the air near him.' The moment we passed out of sight our entire party galloped around the hill behind him and concealed ourselves. Tom and I crawled to the top of the hill and peeped through the grass without being seen. Sure enough, Bos thought he was lost, as we could nowhere be seen in the direction he expected to find us.

"Tom and I were watching him, and just as he seemed in a quandary as to where we were, I fired my rifle so that the bullet whizzed over his head. I popped out of sight for a moment, and when I looked again Bos was heading his pony towards the command, miles away. I fired another shot in his direction, and so did Tom, and away Bos flew across the plains, thinking, no doubt, the Sioux were after him. Tom and I mounted our horses and soon overhauled him. He will not hear the last of it for some time."

Nevertheless, the Custer boys got on as well as ever, dining together much of the time. Not usually one to discuss menu items, Autie did mention to his wife in one of his letters that "Tom and I have fried onions at breakfast and dinner, and raw onions for lunch!"

In *Boots and Saddles*, she recalled onions as their favorite vegetable, adding that they "were permitted at our table, but after indulging in them they found themselves severely let alone, and that they did not enjoy." No mention was made of Boston's penchant for onions.

The weather was generally good through the end of May, but on the first of June, when a line of thunderstorms moved in, rain turned to snow, and Terry decided to confine the expedition to camp for several days until the weather improved.

On June 8, couriers running between the column and the Yellowstone made contact with the *Far West*, so Terry decided to take two companies of the 7th Cavalry and to ride downstream 25 miles to make contact with the ship. The intention was to ascertain the location of Gibbon's force. Terry learned that the Montana column was nearby, and the *Far West* was able to deliver Terry to Gibbon the following day.

Gibbon explained that his own reconnaissance had determined that a substantial Lakota and Cheyenne group had been moving through the Powder River Country in the vicinity of the Rosebud, although this information dated back to the third week of May. Terry, being inexperienced with campaigning on the Plains, did not appreciate that the Lakota and Cheyenne did not remain long at any campsite, and that they could now be anywhere within a 100-mile radius.

"The mail will not leave for a day or two but I concluded that I would be in time," Boston Custer wrote on June 8 in his last letter to his mother. "I don't think we will be in Lincoln before September but that will suit me as I would much rather be out here at this time than in garrison. I have not been late to meals but once and that was a morning where I was not awakened . . . I ate much better than I did at Lincoln."

As Terry and Gibbon were conferring, Autie took the time to work on his side job. As he told Libbie in his June 9 letter, "Yesterday I finished a *Galaxy* article, which will go in the next mail; so, you see, I am not entirely idle. Day before yesterday I rode nearly fifty miles, arose yesterday morning, and went to work at my article, determined to finish it before night, which I did, amidst constant interruptions. It is now nearly midnight, and I must go to my bed, for reveille comes at three."

Coincidentally, Terry had ridden into camp about the time Custer retired. He had returned with a plan. He ordered Major Marcus Reno to leave the next day, taking six companies of 7th Cavalry troops south to search the Powder River drainage for any evidence of Lakota villages that might have been overlooked, then to descend the Tongue River, about 40 miles west of the Powder, and rendezvous with Terry on the Yellowstone in six days.

By Terry's strategy, the remainder of the command was to march down the Powder to the Yellowstone from which he had just returned. They would then turn westward on the south bank of the Yellowstone toward the mouth of the Tongue, while Gibbon marched westward on the north bank of the Yellowstone.

Custer, who disagreed with Terry, wrote a letter to the *New York Herald* on June 12 grousing that "it is not believed that Reno will find the Indians, as their presumed abiding place is not believed to be on the Powder, but on the Rosebud."

As Custer and Terry reached the Yellowstone, the *Far West* was busily transporting supplies from the advance supply base at Glendive Creek, about 40 miles to the east, bringing rations and other supplies. Fortunately for the troops, the water in the Yellowstone was high, filled with spring snowmelt from the distant mountains, so even a heavily laden steamboat could reach the mouth of the Powder, or of the Rosebud, with ease.

As planned, Custer turned westward on the Yellowstone toward the mouth of the Tongue, on June 15, with Terry catching up on the steamboat the next day. By now, they had left all their wagons behind, and with them, the nagging need to find passable ground for wheeled vehicles. Relying on pack mules, they were less at the mercy of the terrain.

From the mouth of the Tongue on June 17, Autie wrote his wife that "the officers were ordered to leave their tents behind. They are now lying under tent flies or in shelter tents. When we leave here I shall only take a tent fly . . . We all slept in the open air around the fire, Tom and I under a fly, Bos and Autie Reed on the opposite side. Tom pelted Bos with sticks and clods of earth after we had retired. I don't know what we would do without Bos to tease."

"We are living delightfully," he explained. "This morning we had a splendid dish of fried fish, which Tom, Bos, and I caught a few steps from my tent last evening. The other day, on our march from Powder River, I shot an antelope. That night, while sitting round the camp-fire, and while Hughes was making our coffee, I roasted some of the ribs Indian fashion, and I must say they were delicious."

Young Autie Reed, the understudy to them all, was mentioned only sparingly in the letters from the Custer boys that summer. In a letter to his niece, Emma Reed, Tom said to tell her mother that the young man was well, and Boston did mention him several times. In a letter to his mother on June 21, he wrote that the youngest Reed boy "will stand the trip first-rate. He has done nicely and is enjoying it. The officers all like him very much . . . Tell Ann he is standing the tip nicely and has not been sick a day. Armstrong, Tom and I pulled down an Indian grave the other day. Autie Reed got the bow with six arrows and a nice pair of moccasins which he intended to take home."

Reno and his six companies of 7th Cavalry troopers finally appeared at the mouth of the Tongue on June 19, several days late, having ridden all the way to the Rosebud—about 30 miles west of the Tongue—which Terry explicitly told him *not* to do. He arrived with exhausted men and tired horses—and with no useful information except that he had found the remains of a large Lakota camp with about 400 lodge sites that was several weeks old. Like the similar intelligence that Gibbon gathered, it was stale information about a mobile foe. What it did reveal was that the Lakota and Cheyenne had been on the Rosebud, and not on the Tongue or the Powder.

On June 20, all companies of the 7th Cavalry were reunited under Custer's command, and on the following day, he met with Terry and Gibbon aboard the *Far West* at the mouth of the Rosebud to plan the next phase of the campaign.

Among the things they did not know—and could not have known for lack of communication—was that on June 17, General Crook had met and fought the same congregation of Lakota and Cheyenne warriors. The battle had taken place about 100 trail miles to the south in the distant headwaters of the Rosebud, with Crook's vaunted 1,000-man force being initially overwhelmed by a larger number of warriors—far more than Terry, Custer, and Gibbon imagined from the evidence they had seen or heard about second hand.

Crazy Horse had led them in a marathon six-hour battle that sea-sawed both ways and resulted in several dozen casualties on each side. It was a longer and bloodier battle, against more determined opposition, than the US Army had experienced in years.

Because Crazy Horse withdrew first, Crook claimed victory, but then he too pulled back, withdrawing 50 miles into Wyoming, where he would remain for seven weeks. Therefore, he would be unavailable to add his resources to those of Terry, Custer, and Gibbon in any future battle.

Also known to Crook, but not to the US Army commands on the Yellowstone, were two critical elements of intelligence about the conclave of Indians whom they were about to face in battle—its size and the willingness of the warriors to undertake a sustained battle.

Based on the evidence that Reno, Gibbon, and their scouts had discovered, the great encampment that was being moved across the Powder River Country numbered around 400 lodges. It was estimated that each lodge contained roughly seven people, including two or three warriors, a rule of thumb that was used to estimate the size of an opposing force. In fact, by the second half of June, there were more than twice that number of tipis. Subsequent estimates of the actual size of the Lakota and Cheyenne group do vary widely and have been the subject of numerous calculations and recalculations. However, various estimates that would be made both by Lakota and *wasichu* sources through the years yield an average of around

1,000 lodges, or about 2,500 warriors. While this is an approximation, it gives a rough idea of scale. The Lakota accounted for more than 80 percent of the total.

The second bit of critical intelligence that Crook had learned the hard way, and his colleagues on the Yellowstone did not know, was the tenacity of these warriors in battle. Typical encounters with Plains tribes involved fierce but brief fights, with the Indians withdrawing quickly. The US Army craved a sustained battle in which the enemy could be decisively defeated. Based on the experience in other campaigns, the biggest concern for Terry, Custer, and Gibbon at the time was that the Indians would escape and evade them without a fight. Had they been able to communicate with Crook, they would have known that this summer things were exactly the opposite.

Back aboard the *Far West*, Terry formulated a plan based on what he knew, not what he *should have* known. Because of the intelligence that had come in from Reno's expedition, and from various scouts and other sources, it was determined that the large Lakota and Cheyenne encampment—grossly underestimated as to size—was likely moving up the Rosebud, but no one on the *Far West* knew for sure. Indeed, the Indians *were* on the Rosebud, but much farther away than imagined.

Terry issued written orders, prepared by his adjutant, Captain Edward Smith, for Custer to ascend the Rosebud "in pursuit of the Indians whose trail was discovered by Major Reno a few days hence."

Recognizing that Custer probably knew what he was doing—or would do whatever he thought was correct *anyway*—Terry gave him what might be construed as unlimited freedom of action, adding that, "It is of course impossible to give you any definite instructions in regard to this move-ment, and were it not impossible to do so, the Department Commander [Terry] places too much confidence in your zeal, energy, and ability to wish to impose upon you precise orders, which might hamper your action when nearly in contact with the enemy."

In the memo, mention was made of the Little Bighorn (aka the Little Horn), an upstream tributary of the Bighorn which had rated virtually no mention in previous planning documents.

Smith conveyed to Custer that Terry "thinks that you should proceed up the Rosebud until you ascertain definitely the direction in which the trail above spoken of leads. Should it be found (as it appears almost certain that it will be found) to turn towards the Little Horn, he thinks that you should still proceed southward, perhaps as far as the headwaters of the Tongue, and then turn towards the Little Horn."

He went on to add that "the column of Colonel Gibbon is now in motion for the mouth of the Bighorn. As soon as it reaches that point it will cross the Yellowstone and move up at least as far as the forks of the Big and Little Horns . . . Of course future movements must be controlled by circumstances as they arise, but it is hoped that the Indians, if upon the Little Horn, may be so nearly enclosed by the two columns that their escape will be impossible."

That night, June 21, Autie began his last letter to his wife, writing, "I am now going to take up the trail where the scouting party turned back," he explained. "I fear their failure to follow up the Indians has imperiled our plans by giving the village an intimation of our presence. Think of the valuable time lost! But I feel hopeful of accomplishing great results. I will move directly up the valley of the Rosebud. General Gibbon's command and General Terry, with steamer, will proceed up the Bighorn as far as the boat can go."

Lieutenant Winfield Scott Edgerly, the friend who had accompanied Tom Custer to New York the previous winter and who was now second in command of Company D, recalled that Autie gave a long talk to the officers, telling them that they were "starting on a scout which we all hope will be successful, and I intend to do everything I can to make it both as successful and pleasant as I can for everybody . . . But I want it distinctly understood that I shall allow no grumbling, and shall exact the strictest compliance with orders from everybody—not only with mine, but with any order given by an officer to his subordinate."

Captain Frederick Benteen, Custer's old nemesis asked to whom he meant the remark about grumbling to apply.

"I want the saddle to go just where it fits," Autie replied.

Benteen asked if he ever knew of any criticism or grumbling from him. Custer replied "No, I never have, on this, nor on any other one which I have been with you."

The following morning, Autie hurriedly finished his letter to Libbie, adding that "I have but a few moments to write, as we move at twelve, and I have my hands full of preparations for the scout. Do not be anxious about me. You would be surprised to know how closely I obey your instructions about keeping with the column. I hope to have a good report to send you by the next mail . . . A success will start us all towards Lincoln."

CHAPTER 23
LAST STANDS

THE CUSTER BOYS departed the Yellowstone and headed up the Rosebud on June 22 with all dozen companies of the 7th Cavalry and a pack train carrying supplies for fifteen days. Tom Custer was once again riding in command of Company C, while Boston Custer was with the other civilian muleskinners handling the pack train. Autie Reed rode at the head of the column at the side of his uncle, George Armstrong Custer. James Calhoun was now assigned to Company L, and William Winer Cooke was now Autie's adjutant.

In the Custer column, there were thirty-one officers, 561 enlisted men and around fifty others, including civilian employees as well as both Arikara and Crow scouts. Among his scouts, Autie included Charley Reynolds, of course, and Bloody Knife, the most trusted of the Arikara, and a scout with whom he had worked for years. He also brought Michel "Mitch" Bouyer, a Crow-speaking half Lakota, half French Canadian scout who worked for the Crow Agency.

The Gibbon column, with less ground to cover, would depart from the mouth of the Bighorn on June 24 with a train loaded for about a week in the field. The general plan was for the Gibbon and Custer columns to converge on June 26 on the Bighorn, though both knew that circumstances might intervene to alter that intention. They had supplies enough to meet reasonable contingencies.

Winfield Scott Edgerly observed that "everybody was in excellent spirits, and we all felt that the worst that could happen would be the getting away of the Indians."

Indeed, all of the ensuing actions taken by George Armstrong Custer were motivated by this concern. He wanted to press the foe into a decisive battle before they had a chance to pull up stakes and elude his 7th Cavalry. In retrospect, we know that this is the last thing which should have concerned them.

According to Gibbon in his memoirs, he shook hands with Custer as he departed and "made some pleasant remark, warning him against being greedy" by defeating the enemy before Gibbon got into the fight. Autie's last words to Gibbon were a conciliatory "No. I will not."

Autie had announced plans for marches of at least 25–30 miles a day, which was strenuous, though not unrealistic given that they were not slowed down by the wheeled vehicles—either supply wagons or the Gatling gun carriages. By the evening of June 23, they had covered 45 miles in a day and a half on the trail, despite having to spend time to cross and recross the Rosebud several times.

The following day, they made an ominous discovery on the Plains near the present location of Lame Deer, Montana. It was the site of an enormous encampment and the site of the annual sun dance ritual that had been celebrated by the Lakota and Cheyenne around June 14. It was at this sun dance that Sitting Bull had a vision that would be remembered by all the Lakota present for the rest of their lives, and widely repeated through the years. He had seen many soldiers falling into the Indian camp like grasshoppers. Because they were upside down in the vision, he knew that the soldiers would die.

Though no one who traveled with the 7th Cavalry that day could know about Sitting Bull's sun dance vision, they could certainly now see that the size of the group that celebrated here was more than twice as large as the 400-lodge estimate. Despite this, the concern was more that the Indians would scatter than that they would remain is a single massive force.

The 7th Cavalry camped for the night on June 24 at 7:45 p.m., later than usual, having made 28 miles that day. The Arikara scouts who had ridden out ahead returned to report that they followed the Lakota and Cheyenne trail and had seen their encampment on the Little Bighorn River from an outcropping of high ground that they called the "Crow's Nest."

Autie made the decision to strike as soon as possible, and ordered his officers to awaken their men for a 1:00 a.m. departure and a nighttime march.

At this point, there was a strange interaction involving Tom Custer. A Crow Scout named Red Star, who was there, later related the tale to Orin Grant Libby, who quoted it in his book *The Arikara Narrative of Custer's Campaign and the Battle of the Little Bighorn*, originally published in 1920. Nodding toward Tom, Autie told Bloody Knife in sign language that his brother "is frightened, his heart flutters with fear, his eyes are rolling from fright at this news of the Sioux. When we have whipped them, he will be a man." Lieutenant Edward Godfrey of Company K also recorded this incident in his diary.

Mitch Bouyer, who had observed the encampment from the Crow's Nest, said it was the largest he had ever seen, but when Autie and Tom went up at daybreak on June 25, 1876, to look for themselves, visibility was poor and they could make out few details at the distant camp through the haze created by campfires.

What the observers were able to see, however, were a small number of Lakota riders, probably hunters, passing through the hills around the Crow's Nest. There presence elicited concerns that the 7th Cavalry column had been detected. Assuming that it was no longer possible to launch a surprise attack, Autie decided to attack as soon as possible.

As there were still more than a dozen miles to cover, the column did not complete the passage over the ridge into the valley of the Little Bighorn until past noon. The official pocket watch was set to Chicago time (today's Central Time) as time zones did not yet officially exist, so it was about an hour earlier by contemporary reckoning of the Mountain Time Zone.

Because of the haze, it was still hard to make out the size and extent of the camp. As they rode closer, they descended to the valley floor and the village fell out of sight beyond the cottonwood groves along the river.

As he had done at the Washita eight years earlier, George Armstrong Custer planned on an enveloping assault, though with just three attacking forces, or combat battalions. To command these, he picked his most senior officers. Captain Frederick Benteen, with three companies (D, H, and K), would go to the left, while Major Marcus Reno, also with three companies (A, G, and M), would attack in the center. Custer himself would take five companies (C, E, F, I, and L) and go wide to the right. Company B under Captain Thomas McDougall was designated to guard the pack train in the rear.

Though he retained direct command, Custer later further subdivided his own contingent into two battalions. These were led by Captain George Yates, the Custer Clansman from Monroe who commanded Company F, while the other was led by Captain Myles Keogh, the Ireland-born one-time papal guard, who commanded Company I. Because it was a verbal order, and most of those aware of it died a few hours later, it is not known for certain which companies were assigned to which battalion commander, though it is likely that Yates led E and F, and Keogh the others.

Reno would strike first, following the Little Bighorn northward to attack the southern end of the long narrow encampment that ran along the river. Custer would lead his command up onto the ridge which rose on the eastern side of the river—and then descend to strike at the heart of the camp. Benteen's mission was to intercept those of the enemy who attempted to escape, but be ready to back up Custer's attack.

As the Reno and Custer contingents passed a lone tipi, about 4 miles south of the camp, a cloud of dust arising from the camp ahead made it seem that some of their quarry had mounted up to escape, so Autie accelerated the schedule.

Because Custer's five companies had to climb the hills and ride parallel to the encampment before turning to attack, Reno's three companies made the first contact.

From the hills above, Autie, Tom, and their young nephew probably saw Reno engaged with the enemy, but they would never know that his attack foundered, or that his men would later take horribly heavy casualties as they scrambled toward the hills to save themselves.

As they reached the ridge, the men of the Custer contingent would have beheld below them, just a mile away, the sobering sight of the vast Cheyenne and Lakota encampment of 1,000 lodges, more than twice the size they had expected.

At about 3:15 Chicago time, Autie dispatched Sergeant John Kanipe to get the pack train and bring it to him on the ridge.

Approximately one mile past where they first beheld the scale of the camp, and at approximately 3:30, Custer's command reached the head of Cedar Coulee, which leads into a broad valley known as Medicine Tail Coulee. This in turn leads in a northwesterly direction off the ridge and down toward the river, a distance of about one mile.

Wondering what had happened to Benteen, he had William Cooke, his adjutant, scribble a message asking him to deliver additional ammunition. They gave this to a regimental band trumpeter to deliver. John Martin, an Italian immigrant who had recently anglicized his name from Giovanni Martini, then delivered Custer's last written order. It read, "Benteen. Come on. Big village. Be quick. Bring packs. W.W. Cooke. P.S. Bring pacs."

According to Martin, he left the regimental commander in a buoyant mood, excitedly using phrases such as "We've caught them napping."

Kanipe recalled him saying that "there are plenty of them down there for all of us."

As he was riding to the rear to look for Benteen, Martin passed Boston Custer. The younger brother had been with the pack train, but at the sound of battle, he rode hard to find his brothers. As Martin explained to Boston where to find them, the younger Custer mentioned that Martin's horse had been nicked by a bullet. Boston then galloped north toward the gathering storm of battle.

Except at a distance of several miles, no one from the 7th Cavalry would ever again see anyone in the Custer contingent alive. This group numbered thirteen officers, 193 enlisted men, and four civilians—Boston Custer, Autie Reed, Mark Kellogg, and Mitch Bouyer. A Crow scout named Ashishishe, and known as "Curley," was also with them, but he left the command at some point after riding with Bouyer to ascertain Reno's status and reporting this to Custer.

It is known that the Custer contingent continued north along the ridge, paralleling the river and the encampment, with *part* of the command descending Medicine Tail Coulee. It was a natural route of attack and the soldiers took it. Because it reached the river in the vicinity of a shallow ford directly across the river from the northern encampment, it was also a natural route of *counterattack* and the Lakota took *this*.

At about the same time as the Medicine Tail Coulee attack and counterattack, Reno's command was making its desperate retreat across the Little Bighorn and their ascent of the ridge in search of a defensive position. By around 4:10, they had congregated atop what is now known as Reno Hill, where they dug in for a siege.

Benteen, coming forward in accordance with Custer's orders, joined them shortly thereafter, and the pack train reached Reno Hill about an hour after that. Throughout this time, they heard a continuous fusillade of gunfire farther to the north in the direction that Custer's command had taken, but this area was obscured visually by intervening hills.

Finally, in an effort to reach Custer, Captain Thomas Wier took his Company D forward from Reno Hill shortly before 5:00. They made it only about a mile. Before they were forced back to the relative safety of Reno Hill, they observed a huge number of Lakota or Cheyenne on horseback circling a position at the crest of the ridge about 4 miles north of Reno Hill. This, they correctly deduced, was the position of the Custer command.

What they saw, obscured by dust and distance, was the last stand for three of the four Custer boys and 207 others.

It is not known exactly how the brothers and the others reached this area—which peaks at the place known alternately as Custer Hill or Last Stand Hill—nor exactly what happened on the way. This has been investigated, examined, discussed, and debated by countless scholars and history buffs for decades.

Through the years, serious estimates have placed the number of Lakota and Cheyenne warriors on the hill as high as 12,000. John S. Gray, who has researched the battle and related demographics in such minute detail as to be considered the benchmark for such data, placed the number at 2,000. This would mean that the 7th Cavalry troops on the hill were outnumbered ten to one.

Based on what Curley said he saw, though his recollections beg as many questions as they answer, it is possible that Captain Yates led Companies E and F through Medicine Tail Coulee to the river before withdrawing north and east to rejoin the rest of the command on the ridge.

United on Reno Hill, the Reno and Benteen detachments continued to take fire through the night, and at daybreak on June 26, the Lakota and Cheyenne attacked in force. Throughout the attacks and the blistering summer heat, valiant attempts, not always successful, were made to reach the river to fill canteens. It is indicative of the desperate lack of water that most of the 7th Cavalry troopers who were awarded the Medal of Honor at the Battle of the Little Bighorn received it for carrying water from the river—under what many of their citations referred to as "a most galling fire."

Late on the afternoon of June 26, the Cheyenne and Lakota began to break camp, and at sundown, they were streaming out of the valley of the Little Bighorn, heading back to the valley of the Rosebud. The next morning, there was not a single Cheyenne or Lakota to be seen anywhere on the battlefield. Reno and Benteen spent the day tending to their casualties and did not ride north to investigate what had happened on Custer Hill.

Terry and Gibbon had begun moving upstream on the Bighorn River on June 25, and the following day, their advance guard met three Crow scouts who had seen the battle and told a story that seemed like a wild exaggeration. The story of Custer's annihilation was too far fetched for Terry to believe, so he sent two scouts to rendezvous with Custer and find out what had *really* happened. They arrived on June 26 as the battle on Reno Hill was still going strong and turned tail.

Curley, the last witness, had actually ridden north looking for Terry, but he did not locate the *Far West* until June 28, by which time Terry was already at the battlefield.

The lead elements of Terry's column, who arrived on the scene early on the morning of June 27, were the first US Army troops to ride up to Custer Hill since the battle nearly forty-eight hours before. Reno and Benteen were still licking their wounds at a new camp near the river at the base of Reno Hill. They got the news of Custer's demise from Terry.

The realization emerged of a monumental defeat, unlike anything that could have been imagined when they started out on May 17. Including losses suffered by the Reno and Benteen contingents, the 7th Cavalry had lost 263 soldiers and civilians killed, and there were fifty-nine seriously wounded.

As Terry and the others surveyed the battlefield on Custer Hill, they tried to piece together what had happened in the roughly ninety minutes between John Martin's last conversation with Boston Custer and when the intensity of the gunfire heard from Custer Hill finally waned.

The burial details moved in, working quickly in the relentless heat, overpowering stench, and huge black clouds of flies. They scratched at the ground with what few shovels they had to bury the mutilated and rapidly decomposing remains while keeping one eye open for a return of the warriors who had won this battle a few days before.

For Terry, the places where the bodies were found were the only indication of the sequence of events. While bodies were found in Medicine Tail Coulee from the banks of the river to the far side of the ridge, most of the deceased were grouped into clusters across a roughly three-quarter-mile arc on the westward facing side of the ridge side near its crest.

Following the route taken by the troops, the first cluster, a narrow skirmish line containing about an eighth of the dead, was located on what is now called Calhoun Ridge because James Calhoun and many Company L troops were found here. So too were the remains of many from Tom Custer's Company C, and those of Lieutenant John Jordan Crittenden III of the 20th Infantry Regiment—son of General Thomas Leonidas Crittenden—who was on temporary assignment with the 7th Cavalry.

Tom Custer's friend, Winfield Scott Edgerly of Company D was part of the burial detail. In an article published in the *Leavenworth Times* on August 14, 1881, he explained that "the first dead soldiers we came to were Lieuts. Calhoun, Crittenden, and enlisted men of L troop. The bodies of these officers were lying a short distance in rear of their men, in the very place where they belonged, and the bodies of their men forming a very regular skirmish line. Crittenden's body was shot full of arrows."

Moving north, the largest concentration contained about a third of the bodies, including that of Myles Keogh. Adjacent to it was a smaller scattering of bodies, including that of Mark Kellogg, found on what is now called Custer Ridge. Edgerly noted that Keogh's I Company had "evidently been falling back."

The exact numbers in each location are not known because, while attempts were made to place markers where each man was found, more than 210 markers were found when the battlefield was revisited a year later for a more formal burial. This is due, no doubt, to the conditions under which the initial interment was done and a desire to mark each location where artifacts were found. The reckoning of the number of bodies buried on and near Custer Hill also varied from 204 recorded on the site by Reno, and 212 noted by Edward Godfrey in his diary. Through June 29, the final tally, including those at or around Reno Hill, was 261, only two short of the 263 who are known to have perished.

Downhill from Custer Ridge, there is the terrain feature known descriptively as Deep Ravine. Some deceased were found scattered along the southwest shoulder of the ravine, and about a fifth of the total number of the bodies were on the north side in what was obviously a skirmish line.

The northernmost cluster, indicating the group that had ridden the farthest, was the tightest grouping. A fifth of the total dead, they were found on Custer Hill, the knoll uphill from Deep Ravine. In this group were Autie, Tom, Boston, and Autie Reed.

Edgerly reported that "we found the bodies of General Custer, Colonel Cooke, his adjutant, Colonel Tom Custer, several enlisted men and several horses, while lower down, just at the base of the knoll were Lieutenant Riley, Captain Yates, and a great many enlisted men and horses. General Custer's brother, Boston, and his nephew, Reed, were about a hundred yards from the General's body."

They were moved uphill, and buried about fifty yards from Autie and Tom, who were just a few feet apart.

Captain Francis Gibson, who had been with Benteen, wrote his wife on July 4, telling her that his men had personally buried "Custer and Tom and their young schoolboy brother." He was probably referring to Autie Reed, as Boston was obviously not a schoolboy.

The bodies of the officers were marked by a stake with their names inserted into a cartridge case that was pounded into the stake. Lieutenant Edward Maguire, Terry's engineering officer, later sketched at least eight detailed maps of the battlefield. In his first one, he located and named the places where Boston Custer and Autie Reed, as well as nine of the officers, were buried.

Edgerly went on to say that "the only bodies of officers that I saw mutilated were Colonel Tom Custer and Colonel Cooke. All the bodies were stripped of their uniforms. The great majority of the men were stark naked, but in a good many cases they left the undershirt, socks and drawers on the bodies." In the case of Cooke, both his scalp and his prominent sideburns had been stripped from his corpse.

Other reports mention that James Calhoun was scalped, so perhaps Edgerly was speaking of more extensive mutilations. In a December 21, 1876, letter to Maggie Custer Calhoun, Myles Moylan confirmed that her husband had been scalped, but his "face was not disfigured nor were his limbs mutilated."

However, in a letter to Fred Calhoun on July 6, Myles Moylan had written that "the officers and men, all over the field, were badly cut up and their heads knocked in."

By all accounts, George Armstrong Custer was not seriously mutilated. He was stripped and shot twice, once in the chest below his heart, and once in the left temple. Edward Godfrey later said that he had been shot by an arrow in his private parts, but this was not made public out of deference to his wife. Other stories have his fingertip cut off and his eardrums punctured. There are no stories of his being scalped.

Tom Custer, however, was extensively disfigured. His pistol had been taken from him and used to shoot him in the head at close range, causing a massive wound. Somebody else had attempted to scalp him, had a great deal of trouble removing it, and wound up severing his head at the neck before completing the grisly, and clumsy, task. His skull had then been smashed with a blunt object.

His body was reportedly identified only because someone—either Edward Godfrey, Private Charles Windolph of Company L, or both—recognized the tattoos on his arms. These included Lady Liberty, the Stars and Stripes, and his initials, "T.W.C." The scar on his cheek that he had carried since Sailor's Creek in 1865, would have been obscured when his skull was crushed. His abdomen had been cut open, but it is not definitive that his heart had been removed as Rain-in-the-Face had threatened.

Libbie Custer, repeating what had been supposed, wrote in her essay in Theophilus Rodenbough's 1891 anthology about Civil War heroes, that "the vengeance of that incarnate fiend was concentrated upon the man who had effected his capture. It was found on the battlefield that Rain-in-the-Face had cut out the brave heart of that gallant, loyal and lovable man, our brother Tom!"

The threat made by Rain-in-the-Face to cut out Tom Custer's heart was certainly well known, and when it was learned that Rain-in-the-Face had, in fact, been present at the Little Bighorn, the natural assumption was that he had made good on the promise. This quickly became part of nineteenth-century popular culture. Indeed, two years later, no less a figure than the great poet Henry Wadsworth Longfellow immortalized the myth in the words of his poem "The Revenge of Rain-in-the-Face":

> *Into the fatal snare*
> *The White Chief with yellow hair*

And his three hundred men
Dashed headlong, sword in hand;
But of that gallant band
Not one returned again.

The sudden darkness of death
Overwhelmed them like the breath
And smoke of a furnace fire:
By the river's bank, and between
The rocks of the ravine,
They lay in their bloody attire.

But the foemen fled in the night,
And Rain-in-the-Face, in his flight,
Uplifted high in air
As a ghastly trophy, bore
The brave heart, that beat no more,
Of the White Chief with yellow hair.

Unfortunately, the poet took considerable license with the facts, insinuating that the "heart that beat no more" belonged to "the White Chief with yellow hair," and not to his brother Tom.

Through the years, Rain-in-the-Face himself both confirmed and denied the story numerous times. In his 1894 interview with W. Kent Thomas at Coney Island, Rain-in-the-Face recalled that after he had escaped custody at Fort Lincoln, he "sent Little Hair [Tom Custer] a picture, on a piece of buffalo skin, of a bloody heart. He knew I didn't forget my vow. The next time I saw Little Hair, ugh! I got his heart. I have said all."

In 1905, about two months before Rain-in-the-Face died, he was interviewed by Santee Lakota author and lecturer Dr. Charles Eastman for an article that appeared in the October 27, 1906, issue of *The Outlook* magazine. Eastman asked him specifically whether the tale of Tom's heart was a true story.

"Many lies have been told of me," he told Eastman. "Some say that I killed the Chief [George Armstrong Custer], and others that I cut out the heart of his brother [Tom Custer], because he had caused me to be imprisoned. Why, in that fight the excitement was so great that we scarcely recognized our nearest friends! Everything was done like lightning. After the battle we young men were chasing horses all over the prairie, while the old men and women plundered the bodies; and if any mutilating was done, it was by the old men."

Then, in 1908, George Bird Grinnell interviewed Little Horse at the Northern Cheyenne Indian Reservation in Montana. His admission to having killed Tom Custer adds another level of complexity to the mystery. Like so many things that happened on that hillside on June 25, 1876, we will never know for sure.

As the 7th Cavalry was burying its dead, Captain Grant Marsh of the *Far West* was under Terry's orders to bring his vessel up the Bighorn River as far as possible in order to retrieve the wounded. By June 29, four days after the battle, this had been accomplished, albeit with great difficulty. This river, with its twists and turns, had never before been navigated by a steamboat. In the meantime, the injured men had been brought down from the battlefield and they were loaded aboard for the 700-mile journey to Fort Abraham Lincoln.

The outside world had yet to learn of the debacle on the Little Bighorn.

CHAPTER 24
AFTERMATH

IN AN "EXTRA" edition published on July 3, 1876, the *Bozeman Times* in Bozeman, Montana, 200 miles upstream on the Yellowstone River, was the first media outlet to convey the news to their readers, but this information would not reach the States for two more days.

H.M. "Muggins" Taylor, a scout with the Colonel John Gibbons's Montana column had raced back to Fort Ellis at Bozeman from the mouth of the Bighorn River to carry the news. Captain Daniel W. Benham then dashed to the telegraph office to wire General Phil Sheridan's headquarters in Chicago. However, in a comedy of errors, the message was *mailed* instead of wired, and the telegraph office was closed the following day because of the July 4 holiday. Meanwhile, the news reached Helena, the territorial capital, on Independence Day, where Andrew Fisk, editor of the *Helena Herald*, quickly published an "Extra." From here, the news reached the outside world via the Associated Press wire in Salt Lake City on July 5.

"Custer took five companies and charged the thickest portion of the camp," read the reasonably accurate report. "Nothing is known of the operations of this detachment, only as they trace it by the dead . . . The Indians poured in a murderous fire from all directions. Besides the greater portion fought on horseback. Custer, his two brothers, a nephew and a brother-in-law were *All Killed* and not one of his detachment escaped. 207 men were buried in one place and the killed are estimated at 300 [the *Bozeman Times* said 315] with only thirty-one wounded."

The first dispatch acknowledged, albeit not by name, that three Custer brothers and their nephew were among the battle deaths. On July 6, as the first items began to appear in the East Coast papers, the *Bismarck Tribune* was the first to publish a list of the names, which numbered 260 in this edition, although Autie Reed was misidentified as "Arthur" Reed. The *New York Herald* and *New York Times*, named both Tom and Boston, as well as James Calhoun, in the bodies of their articles.

Coming on top of the gala celebrations of Independence Day and the 1776–1876 Centennial, the news that five companies of the 7th Cavalry had been eradicated to the last man in a single bloody afternoon came as a numbing jolt. The fact that the colorful George Armstrong Custer, the "boy general" turned "Indian fighter," who was well known and well covered in the media, added a special dimension to the story.

Just as the battle is still the most remembered of post-Civil War, nineteenth-century America, it gripped headlines and imaginations through 1876 with a firm hand like no similar story in recent memory. The term "Thermopylae of the Plains" was coined, a reference to the epic loss of the 300 Spartans at Thermopylae in Greece in 480 BC. Towns across the country were renamed "Custer" and there was talk of erecting monuments.

At Fort Abraham Lincoln, however, it was personal.

Coming downstream with the casualty-laden *Far West*, Captain Grant Marsh had set a steamboat speed record, traveling 710 miles in fifty-four hours. When the vessel pulled into Bismarck at 11:00 p.m. on July 5, few people in Bismarck had officially heard the news, but there had been whispers among the Lakota who camped near Fort Lincoln about a big battle somewhere in Montana Territory.

In *Boots and Saddles*, Elizabeth Custer would write, "With my husband's departure on May 17, my last happy days in garrison were ended, as a premonition of disaster that I had never known before weighed me down. I could not shake off the baleful influence of depressing thoughts." She also recalled, suggesting a premonition, that on June 25, the day of the battle, the wives of the officers on the expedition, "borne down with one common weight of anxiety, sought solace in gathering together in our house."

The reporting of such omens may or may not have been literary license. Though she did not mention it, plans had actually been in motion for the wives to later travel to Montana Territory aboard the steamer *Josephine* to meet their husbands in the field. The assumption was that there would be no serious fighting.

Captain Marsh delivered General Terry's official dispatch to Captain William McCaskey of the 20th Infantry, Fort Lincoln's post commander. McCaskey called on post surgeon Dr. J.V.D. Middleton at 2:00 a.m. on July 6, and they started knocking on doors.

Beginning with Libbie Custer, they worked their way through the thresholds of the Custer Clan homes. Nettie Bowen Smith, wife of Captain Algernon Emory Smith heard a rapping upon her door, and so too did Annie Gibson Yates, wife of Captain George Yates. Annie woke her four-year-old son George and clutched her seven-month-old baby, Milnor.

When it hit Margaret Custer Calhoun that not only her husband, but her three brothers, were never coming back, she felt the sudden void and shrieked, "Is there no message for me?" She longed for a final missive from the field that never came.

Nevin Johnson Custer, who would for the next four decades bear the burden of being the "only surviving" Custer boy, received the news in Hastings, Ohio, where he had stopped for the night after being "down in Ohio to see about some land."

"I didn't believe it at first, but I drove on home [120 miles] as fast as the team could travel and there I found Monroe all draped in mourning."

At 4:00 on the afternoon of July 7, bells across Monroe were rung and businesses closed. A band marched, playing a dirge, to the city's court house, where Mayor George Spaulding, backed by a portrait of George Armstrong Custer draped in black, called a throng of citizens to order in a public meeting and read messages of condolence.

Almost immediately, Monroe formed a Custer National Monument Association, and presumptuously named Phil Sheridan as their president. He was in absentia for the public meeting, possibly not yet knowing of his election. The association's vice president, former Michigan senator Thomas White Ferry, sent a message from Washington for Spaulding to read in which he declared that he shared in the grief of those assembled. Among the clergymen who spoke was Reverend Erasmus Boyd, the headmaster of the Boyd Seminary, the alma mater of both Maggie Custer Calhoun and Libbie Bacon Custer.

Judge Rufus E. Phinney of the association read a resolution stating that "we friends and acquaintances of those who have so ruthlessly been taken from us, find most grateful comfort in the memories they have left us of their chivalric spirits and noble achievements."

Nevin Custer might have been at this meeting. The parents of the Custer boys, Emanuel and Maria may have been there as well, but Maria was in poor health and the death of three sons would probably have laid her low and rendered her housebound. Nevin was not mentioned in an article about the meeting in the *Monroe Commercial*, but the reporter did acknowledge that Emanuel and Maria, the "aged parents," had shared one of Boston's last letters with him.

David Reed, the husband of the Custer boys' half sister Lydia Ann Reed and the father of Autie Reed, was *not* there. He had departed for Dakota Territory that same morning to share his grief, and a shoulder upon which to cry, with Maggie and Libbie. He reached Fort Lincoln on July 13. In her obituary three decades later, it was written that Lydia Ann had taken it very hard, commenting that "the human mind cannot picture the soul agony and shock dealt Mrs. Reed."

There are conflicting stories as to whether their daughter, twenty-year-old Emma Reed, the frequent correspondent of Tom and Boston Custer, went west with her father, though she probably did not.

Mention was made in the *Monroe Commercial* of Maggie and Libbie, "both bereft of their companions and left alone afar on the frontier." They, along with Nettie Smith and Annie Yates, left Fort Abraham Lincoln and the "afar frontier" for Monroe for the last time on July 30. The four women were widows before their time. Maggie was but twenty-four, Annie was twenty-seven, and Nettie was thirty-three. Libbie, at thirty-four, being the oldest, took on a motherly role, calling the others "my widows." The "Old Lady," who had borne that title for a decade, now bore it without the company of the "General" and the "Scamp."

On a special train arranged by the Northern Pacific, the widows were accompanied by David Reed, as well as by Annie's young children. They were also escorted by Reverend Richard Wainwright, an Episcopal minister who had become sort of a fixture at Fort Lincoln, and who was along to offer them spiritual solace.

The arrival of the entourage in Chicago on August 3 was reported in numerous newspapers, though they stayed for just a few hours—as guests of the Potter Palmer at the popular Palmer House Hotel. Phil Sheridan did not meet them, but sent a member of his staff. As had the Northern Pacific, the Michigan Central Railroad put on a special car to whisk them onward overnight.

Reaching Monroe, in familiar surroundings but entirely unaccustomed to life "bereft of their companions," they were greeted by Reverend Boyd. In addition to having been a schoolmaster to two of the widows as young women, he was the man who had officiated at Libbie's wedding. A reporter from the Toledo *Journal* who was among the throng of well-wishers and curiosity-seekers who greeted them reported on August 5 that Libbie "fell fainting in Mr. Boyd's arms with a cry that was almost a shriek of anguish."

As Nettie Smith continued onward to her parents' home in upstate New York, the others took up temporary residence in the house on the northwest corner of Monroe and Second where Libbie had been born and raised.

With the mortal remains of those who died still languishing in shallow graves 1,500 trail miles away on a hot and dusty Montana hillside, there could be no funeral, but a memorial service was held at the Methodist Church on August 13. Though George Armstrong Custer was the focus of commemoration in the proceedings of the Custer National Monument Association, Tom, Boston, young Autie Reed, James Calhoun, and George Yates, were each remembered with attention equal to this man who occupied the national headlines. Hymns were sung, widows wept, and when he mentioned each man and recalled his date and place of birth, the pastor told the congregation "these names that we come to commemorate today no longer belong to private homes, they are the heritage of the nation."

On July 15, the *New York Herald* editorialized that the money being collected for a monument to the elder of the Custer boys should instead be collected by itself to be used for a "Widow's Fund." When this idea fell on deaf ears, the *Army and Navy Journal* took up the cause. The founders of this publication, William Conant Church and his brother, Francis Pharcellus Church, were no strangers to the Custer mystique, as they had also founded *Galaxy* magazine, which had published Autie's dispatches from the frontier. With General Winfield Scott Hancock and himself as trustees, William Church went to work.

When retired Colonel Theophilus Rodenbough of the *Army and Navy Journal* contacted Libbie for a list of potential beneficiaries, she wrote a confidential letter on October 8, telling him that Maggie Calhoun and Annie Yates were both in need, and that the widows and children of the enlisted men should also be remembered.

She added that since the Fund "exceeds so far all their ideas of what was expected to be raised . . . they would gladly accept the help and not feel others were being robbed of what they needed." She closed by praising "the generosity of our army . . . showing that noblest phase of generosity, that deprives itself to benefit others."

In a November 15, 1876, letter that was later in the possession of Dr. Lawrence Frost, Church told Libbie Custer that $10,270 (around a quarter of a million in today's dollars) had already been collected from nearly 2,000 individuals. Among the disbursements, Libbie received a check for $900, while Maggie Calhoun, Nettie Smith, and most of the other widows without children received $510. Annie Yates and her children were paid $1,050.

According to the *Congressional Record*, Michigan Congressman Alpheus S. Wilson introduced a series of bills in July 1876 calling for pensions to be paid to Libbie, as well as to the "aged parents" of the Custer boys who had been deprived of their only means of support. These bills did not pass the 44th Congress.

The wills, which Autie had made out in 1870, and Tom in 1873, passed through the hands of the Monroe County Probate Court, with Tom's $900 estate eventually paid to his mother. He had stipulated that half should go to Lulie Burgess, but she had died in 1875. According to Lawrence Frost, Autie's estate of $1,447.73 was insufficient to pay his bills, so Libbie had to sell one of his horses. Much of his indebtedness involved the fallout from his investment in the failed silver mine in the Stevens Lode in Colorado.

Libbie did receive $4,750 from a $5,000 life insurance policy that her husband had purchased in June 1874. She assumed that the discrepancy was a wartime risk premium. In August 2006, when Ron Karklela of the New York Life Insurance Company presented a replica of the policy for display at the Fort Abraham Lincoln State Park in North Dakota, Tracy Potter of the Fort Abraham Lincoln Foundation said that several 7th Cavalry officers had life insurance policies ranging from $5,000 to $10,000, adding, "Apparently, the officers who took out $10,000 policies didn't have quite as much confidence in Custer as he had in himself . . . The insurance company paid out a lot of money."

The Equitable Assurance Company, meanwhile, informed Libbie that it had not received the June 1876 premium payment on the $3,000 life insurance policy that her husband had taken out with Emanuel and Maria as beneficiaries. Bearing in mind the cost of adverse publicity if they remained recalcitrant, the company finally agreed to make the payout.

Nevin Custer, meanwhile, found himself at a public auction paying $775 to buy his older brother's share in the "Custer Farm" on River Road in Frenchtown, across the River Raisin from downtown Monroe, which they had purchased jointly in 1871.

Through the aftermath of the Little Bighorn, Nevin and his wife Ann North Custer remained on the farm, their hands full with raising six children. When the news of the battle reached Monroe in July 1876, Claribel Custer, the oldest, was 12. George Armstrong Custer, May, Lula, and James Calhoun were between 4 and 11, and little William Bacon Custer— his middle name being Libbie's family name—would turn two on July 29. The youngest, Charles Kendall Custer, was born on February 6, 1879. This growing family would have been a comfort to their grandmother, Maria Custer, through the difficult later years of her life.

While the newspapers duly mentioned Emanuel and Maria as surviving elders of the family, there seems to have been no mention whatsoever of the fact that Emanuel Custer's mother, the 94-year-old grandmother of the Custer boys and Maggie, was still alive!

Catherine Valentine Custer had been living in Cresaptown, Maryland, when she lost her husband, John Fedele Custer, in 1830. In 1842, she had moved permanently to Clarksburg, Virginia (West Virginia after 1863), about 100 road miles west of Cresaptown. Apparently, John and Catherine had lived there previously, because their youngest daughter, Ellen Custer, was born there in 1825.

In the History of Clarksburg and Harrison County from its Earliest Settlement to the Present Time, published by the Clarksburg Telegram in April 1876, Catherine is described as "a woman of remarkable physical constitution and mental vigor." It was acknowledged that she was "the grandmother of George A. Custer of the United States Army." The paragraph about her in this document notes that she was living with her son James, and that another son, Alexander, lived nearby. Both were brothers of Emanuel Henry Custer.

Despite the "physical constitution and mental vigor" that continued to manifest itself in her ninth decade, Catherine apparently had no contact with her son Emanuel and his family while the Custer siblings were growing up in northeastern Ohio. Of course, Clarksburg was more than 300 difficult road miles away in an era when people rarely traveled that far from home. For this reason perhaps, Catherine has been ignored in Custer biographies—until now. Catherine passed away on August 8, 1877, having outlived her three notable grandsons by nearly fourteen months.

Through the winter of 1876–1877, as widows, parents, and grandparents mourned, and as courts and accountants picked the metaphorical bones of those killed in action, the actual bones remained in the drifting snows of a Montana winter, picked at by wolves, coyotes, ravens, and other predators. Naturally, it was assumed that the bodies would be recovered and reburied, and naturally the families were making inquiries. However, much to their surprise, the US Army had no intention of revisiting the hastily prepared gravesites overlooking the Little Bighorn.

As Commanding General of the Department of the Missouri, Phil Sheridan found the lion's share of the inquiries routed to him. Having known many of the deceased personally, he was in sympathy with the goals of the families. He finally endorsed the requests and sent this idea up the chain of command to the War Department, which was in a state of flux. Since Rutherford B. Hayes had succeeded Ulysses S. Grant in the White House on March 4, 1877, a new cabinet was being sworn in and George McCrary was moving into the office vacated by outgoing Secretary of War J. Donald Cameron.

With things thus falling through the cracks on the civilian side, Sheridan wrote in early April to his boss, General of the Army William Tecumseh Sherman, telling him that he had already asked McCrary to authorize the necessary expenses, adding that "the sum required will be small."

Sheridan then proposed that "in case it meets with the approbation of the Secretary and yourself, to bury all the officers' bodies, except General Custer, at Fort Leavenworth. Mrs. Custer wants General Custer buried at West Point, and I recommend that she be gratified in this desire. I can detail an officer to bring the bodies down in suitable boxes to Fort Lincoln and there transfer them to the proper coffins. The satisfaction it will give to the wives, families, and friends of the officers will be very great."

The reply, coming from a member of Sherman's staff, was prompt but disappointing. It read that "the question was submitted, by the General, to the Secretary of War who regrets that your application cannot be granted, for the reason that no appropriation is applicable to the purpose, and the accounting officers do not allow accounts for such expenses."

By the end of the month, though, political pressure derived from the continued prominence of the Little Bighorn in the media, loosened the secretary's purse strings and the funding was found. Sheridan had, in the meantime, commented publicly about rumors of desecration of the graves, not only by wild animals, but by souvenir hunters "in the shape of human coyotes," who were said to be selling bones that they had pilfered.

Thus authorized, Sheridan picked his own brother, Lieutenant Colonel Michael Sheridan, to lead the recovery detail. This coincided with plans by the US Army to build an outpost at the confluence of the Little Bighorn and the Bighorn, about a dozen miles north of the battlefield, that would eventually be named Fort Custer. Guided by Company I of the 7th Cavalry, Michael Sheridan and his men reached the future Fort Custer site in late June. This was barely a week after the arrival of the construction crews, who were escorted by the 11th Infantry Regiment.

Michael Sheridan was on the battlefield by July 2, 1877, with caskets to recover the officers who had been positively identified a year earlier. He was accompanied by some of the 7th Cavalry troopers who had been there, and who had some recollection of the scene. He also carried a detailed rendering of Lieutenant Edward Maguire's original map, sketched onsite one year earlier. This was a place to start.

It was still a daunting task. Some of the graves had been opened, and many of the bodies appeared to have had just a shovelful or two of dirt thrown on them. Human bones were strewn across the hillside and intermingled with the bones of more than 200 horses that had also been killed. There were mass graves that had multiple bodies in them.

On Custer Hill, Maguire's map indicated that Autie and Tom were together, with William Winer Cooke a short distance away. George Yates, Algernon Smith, and Lieutenant William Van Wyck Reily were spread across the hillside slightly above. Boston Custer was a short distance downhill, with Autie Reed farther down. The places indicated for John Crittenden, Myles Keogh, and James Calhoun were much farther to the south.

The grave in which Autie and Tom were buried was more than a foot deep, deeper than most others, and a sheet of canvas had been placed over it. When the grave was opened, the burial detail began placing the bones presumed to be Autie's into one of the coffins, but they stopped when they found a corporal's uniform shirt. According to W. Kent King, writing in 1980 in his self-published *Tombstones for Bluecoats: New Insights Into the Custer Mystery*, they stopped loading these bones and moved to another body. Both King and Tony Perrottet, writing in *Smithsonian* magazine in

2005, quote Sergeant Michael Caddle of the burial detail as writing later that "I think we got the right body the second time."

Michael Sheridan and his team did the best they could in the two days that their tight budget permitted. A modern forensic team would have stayed much longer but would have faced some of the same problems given the conditions after a year of neglect. They departed the battlefield with coffins containing the remains of all those whom they were reasonably sure they could identify. Crittenden's father had asked that he be buried where he had fallen, and this was done.

Gradually, efforts were made to clean up the battlefield, with a National Cemetery established on the shoulder of Custer Hill in 1879. The final reburials took place by 1881 as a large stone monument was installed on Custer Hill. In 1890, marble markers were placed at the locations where temporary markers of fallen soldiers had existed through the years.

On Tuesday, August 2, 1877, the remains deemed to belong to Tom Custer, James Calhoun, Algernon Smith, George Yates, and Lieutenant Donald McIntosh of Company G, reached Fort Leavenworth by steamboat. Remains associated with other members of the Custer Clan went elsewhere. William Winer Cooke went to the Hamilton Cemetery in Hamilton, Ontario, and Myles Keogh, by the terms of his will, was taken to Fort Hill Cemetery in Auburn, New York.

On the day following the arrival at Leavenworth, the *Leavenworth Daily Times* summarized the funeral scheduled for Saturday evening, writing that the men who "gloriously fell in conflict with hostile Indians" would be reinterred in the National Cemetery . . . with appropriate military honors . . . The remains will be conducted to the cemetery on artillery caissons, each drawn by two bay horses . . . Following each caisson, will be a horse, caparisoned in mourning, and led by a cavalry soldier, according to the customs of funeral ceremonies for officers in the cavalry service. During the march to the cemetery, guns will be fired, flags lowered to half mast, and all work suspended at the post."

In the post chapel, filled to overflowing to hear the Episcopal services led by Chaplain John Woart, were various dignitaries and unformed personnel. However, Colonel Samuel Sturgis, still the commander of the 7th Cavalry and still in absentia on detached duty, was not mentioned. General of the Army William Tecumseh Sherman sent his wife, Eleanor Boyle "Ellen" Ewing Sherman.

Whatever may have been said by the officers and celebrities present, perhaps the most fitting epitaph for Tom Custer was penned years later by Charles Windolph, who had recognized his body on Custer Hill by his tattoos. Windolph called him "a prince of good fellows and full of the bravery that ever characterized the Custers."

Margaret Custer Calhoun, who had taken ill—feverish nights and dizzy spells—upon her return to Monroe a year earlier, had initially planned not to attend the funeral, and said so in a June 14 letter to Libbie Custer. However, in July, she and some others, including Annie Yates and her children, went up to the small resort town of Petoskey on Little Traverse Bay in northern Michigan. Here, her health improved and on July 24, she told Libbie that she now planned to go to Fort Leavenworth.

No one else from the Custer family is known to have gone to the funeral. The Monroe newspapers reported that Maggie "represented" the family. Annie Yates, as well as Nettie Smith, also made the decision to be on hand when Reverend Woart's benediction laid their husbands to rest.

Consuming much of Maggie's time in the weeks before the funeral was her lobbying to have her brother Boston also buried at the National Cemetery—though he was not a service member. As she told Libbie, Michael Sheridan had promised her that he would be. He was not. Both he and Autie Reed were interred in Woodland Cemetery in Monroe in January 1878. In that same month, Maria Custer and David Reed had each paid $100 to purchase a family plot at the cemetery. Known today as the

Custer-Reed Plot, it contained ninety gravesites, of which twenty-seven had been filled at the time of the family plaque dedication in May 2014.

With regard to her husband, Libbie got her wish. On October 10, 1877, Elizabeth Bacon Custer, in the company of Maggie Custer Calhoun, Emanuel Custer, and a large gathering of dignitaries, watched as the casket containing what were identified as the remains of George Armstrong Custer was lowered into his final resting place at the US Military Academy at West Point.

CHAPTER 25

AND THEIR LIVES WENT ON

THE CUSTER CLAN was no more.

Among the survivors on the field that day, some moved on and some remained in the 7th Cavalry. Edward Settle Godfrey and Myles Moylan—who was married to Charlotte "Lottie" Calhoun, the sister of James and Frederic—stayed with the regiment. For their actions during the campaign against the Nez Perce in 1877, both Godfrey and Moylan were awarded the Medal of Honor. Moylan was still with the 7th at Wounded Knee in 1890, and Godfrey served in Cuba during the Spanish American War and went overseas during the Philippine Insurrection of 1899–1902.

Others were deeply injured by post-traumatic stress. Thomas Weir, who led the failed attempt to reach Custer Hill at the height of the battle, suffered a nervous breakdown. In New York in December 1876 to take charge of a cavalry rendezvous, he locked himself in his room for several days and was found dead. The cause was reported as melancholia.

The widows had scattered. Nettie Smith was in New York, and Annie Yates in Illinois. Neither remarried. It was upon Elizabeth Bacon Custer whom the eyes of the media rested as though she was a symbol for all the widows. This was in part because of the media profile attained by her through her colorful husband, and in part because of her decision to relocate from Monroe to the nation's once and future media center, New York City.

Though she was criticized by those who felt that a woman's place was not in the workforce, she had let it be known that she intended to get a job. In correspondence with her cousin, Rebecca Richmond, in March 1877, Libbie said that she wanted to work to keep her mind busy—*and* that she needed the money. She traveled east expecting to seek employment at a hospital or rehabilitation facility, but a friend recommended an alternative. In May 1878, she became the secretary for the newly formed Society of Decorative Arts. Founded by the wealthy and socially connected Candace Thurber Wheeler, the so-called mother of interior design, the organization encouraged and assisted the careers of women who were skilled in arts and crafts.

In the coming decades, however, Libbie's principal occupation, and one at which she worked tirelessly and successfully, was to be the perpetuation of the memory of her husband as an unquestionably heroic figure. In her campaign, she had many supporters, from the newspapers who had embraced Autie since he was the "Boy General" of the Civil War, to many who rode with him in Montana Territory that summer. Conversely, she also had numerous foils. Indeed, it was they who became the *raison d'être* for her crusade. There were many throughout the military establishment who questioned her husband's tactical judgment at the Little Bighorn. They ranged from Frederick Benteen—no friend of George Armstrong Custer in life, who spoke freely in condemning him for his mistakes of judgment at the Little Bighorn—up to and including Ulysses S. Grant, now retired. She was dogged in her determination to set the record the way that she and Autie's media supporters saw it.

Turning to writing, Libbie began with essays and poetry and eventually published three memoirs, *Boots and Saddles* in 1885, followed by *Tenting on the Plains* in 1887, and *Following the Guidon* in 1890.

Margaret Custer Calhoun, who lost not only her husband, but three brothers and a nephew, at the Little Bighorn, was an occasional visitor of Libbie's in New York, though she perceived that her principal duty in life was to her parents, especially her sickly mother. She had moved back into her girlhood home at Third and Cass Streets in Monroe, and it was here that she was found when the census takers of 1880 came knocking.

Both Emanuel and Maria Custer were sixty-nine when the staggering news reached Monroe from the Little Bighorn. No parent expects to experience the death of a child. To learn of the violent death of *three*, and to be reminded of it by an obsessive media, is torture of the cruelest nature. Maria, already infirm, survived an emotionally painful six years, until, in the darkness of winter on January 14, 1882, she died. She was laid to rest near her youngest son in Woodland Cemetery.

"Though possessed of a remarkably strong constitution, Mrs. Custer has been a sufferer for a number of years," observed the obituary writer at the *Monroe Democrat* on January 19. "Since the breaking out of the war twenty-one years ago when her sons entered the army, her's has been a life of constant anxiety and sorrow. Her health was seriously impaired previous to the death of her three sons, son-in-law, and grandson . . . her remarkable fortitude and heroic spirit enabled her to survive the shock for a time, but bereavement was too great; she never fully recovered from it. The mother's heart was broken and she died gradually."

Emma Reed was, it might be said, the last orphan of the Custer Clan. Less than a month from turning twenty when she received the news of the Little Bighorn, she had barely missed the opportunity to join that unique circle of family and friends. As Maggie had with Maria, Emma remained for a time as caregiver to her own mother. Lydia Ann Reed, Maria's eldest daughter was just fifty, and despite the loss of her son and three half-brothers whom she had treated as brothers or stepsons all their lives, she eventually recovered from—or came to manage—her post traumatic shock.

Emma, the tireless correspondent with Tom and Boston, had become a pen pal of James Calhoun's brother, Lieutenant Frederic Sanxay Calhoun of the 14th Infantry Regiment, and eventually they became engaged. In their respective losses, they had much in common. On February 24, 1879, they were married in Monroe, and following in the footsteps of Libbie and Maggie, Emma joined her soldier husband in the West. Here, they experienced the garrison life, albeit under quieter circumstances, reminiscent of that of the Custer Clan. The Calhouns were initially posted to Fort Douglas in Utah, but their only child, Emma May Calhoun, was born in Monroe in 1882. Three years later, they were at Vancouver Barracks in Wyoming Territory (not to be confused with Vancouver Barracks, Washington). After his retirement in 1890, they moved to Massachusetts.

Following Maria's death in 1882, Maggie Calhoun rejoined the world, moving to New York City, where she took up residence with her sister-in-law. Libbie now lived at the fashionable Stuyvesant Apartments at 142 East 18th Street, near Gramercy Park. The women also summered at Onteora in the Catskills, where Candace Thurber Wheeler had property that was gradually evolving into an artists' and writers' colony.

On September 7, 1884, there was a major fire in the air shaft at the Stuyvesant. An article in the *Monroe Democrat* of September 11, speaks of Maggie and Libbie escaping the burning building in the middle of the night, and of Libbie being prevented by the police from returning to the building to check on a safe containing the correspondence with her husband. However, the police were unable to prevent the theft, during the ruckus, of Libbie's purse and Tom Custer's watch, which he had given to Maggie as he departed for the Little Bighorn. Luckily, the manuscript in progress of *Boots and Saddles* survived.

A year later, as Libbie's book was being published, Maggie was out west on an extended visit with her niece and sister-in-law, Emma Reed Calhoun and her husband in Wyoming.

Maggie, like Libbie a decade earlier, had been growing restless and had decided that she too wanted to be somehow gainfully employed. Recalling that she had taken an interest in drama while she had been at the Boyd Seminary two decades earlier, she decided to brush up on her dramatic elocution and go on the stage. She traveled up to Detroit to study under Edna Chaffe-Noble at the Detroit Training School of Elocution, an institution whose alumni would remain prominent in the field through the middle of the next century.

A short item appearing in the *Isabella County* [Michigan] *Enterprise* on January 17, 1890, reported that "Mrs. Margaret Custer Calhoun, a sister of the late Gen. Custer, is gaining quite a reputation in New York as parlor elocutionist."

In a biographical sketch of Maggie appearing in *Portrait and Biographical Album of Ingham and Livingston counties, Michigan*, it was noted that she went on to "great success as an elocutionist. She has much of the dash and enthusiasm of her distinguished brother, and personally is gifted with great ease, grace, power and magnetism. The press notices that have been given her throughout the country show her to be an elocutionist of the highest order, and one who does not ape the style or mannerisms of someone else, but whose impersonations show a genius in their originality of conception. She is possessed of a very sweet and clear voice and her readings are given with such power of expression that one loses his identity in listening to her. She has not worked for herself alone but has given various benevolent institutions the advantage of her splendid talent."

This vignette in the form of a glowing review went on to say that she had gone on the road with "her attention to this branch of art and has given readings throughout different parts of the country."

In the meantime, Libbie had been suggested as a potential agent for the US Bureau of Pensions office in Detroit. She did not want to move back to Michigan, but decided the job would be perfect for Maggie. According to letters in the Department of Special Collections in the library at the University of California, Santa Barbara, Libbie was in communication with Farnham Lyon, a Civil War acquaintance of her husband's who was now a well-connected hotel proprietor in Saginaw, Michigan. He was a friend of President Grover Cleveland's personal secretary, Daniel S. Lamont and David M. Benjamin, a Grand Rapids businessman and a stalwart Cleveland backer. With all of these elements in place, Libbie headed to Washington to see Cleveland. However, the president snubbed her, and as she wrote in a cynical op-ed in the Chicago *Inter Ocean* for November 14, 1885, "the Commissioner of Pensions was so busy he asked to be excused when I called upon him."

Though this exercise ended in disappointment, the Michigan contacts that had been made led to Maggie's being offered the post of Michigan's State Librarian in 1891. She succeeded Harriet Tenney, who had served for eleven consecutive terms under seven governors. She or her husband, Eugene Tenney, who was appointed to the post in 1859, had served more than three decades.

"Although Calhoun never had the influence of a Harriet Tenney, she actually had several significant accomplishments," observed Jim Schultz of the Michigan Department of History, Arts and Libraries. "She persuaded the Legislature to increase the appropriation Harriet Tenney had recommended by $1,000 and to remove all restrictions on employing clerical help, as she maintained that the State Library's patrons deserved skilled labor . . . Both Harriet Tenney and Margaret Calhoun earned the respect of the male governors and legislators with whom they worked, laying the groundwork for an unbroken succession of female state librarians from 1869 to 1968."

Emanuel Custer passed away on November 27, 1892, about two weeks short of his eighty-sixth birthday. He was buried next to his wife at

Woodland Cemetery where a single granite obelisk now commemorates them both.

After her father's passing, Maggie Calhoun left her post at the Michigan State Library and moved on, spending more time with her sister-in-law in New York and in various travels, such as a visit to the 1893 World's Columbian Exposition, better known as the Chicago World's Fair.

Meanwhile, Libbie and Maggie continued to spend a great deal of time in the Catskills at Onteora. This is where they met educator and playwright Marguerite Merington, who later edited an edition of Libbie's correspondence, and became her confidant. The artists' colony continued to grow, with numerous cottages being added there through the last decade of the century, including Libbie's own, built on property that she bought in 1898.

Meanwhile back in the Midwest, a new generation of Custers was coming of age as the twentieth century approached. With only one possible exception, they were all Nevin's children. The one lone and questionable anomaly was the son of Rebecca Minerd, whom she named "Thomas C. Custer," claiming that Thomas Ward Custer was his father. Never acknowledged by the Custer family, "Tommy" was raised by Rebecca's parents and is listed as a nine-year-old "grandchild" living with them at the time of the 1880 Census. Little is known of Tommy Custer other than his membership in an organization of sons of veterans, his marriage in February 1892 to Addie Viola Benn, and his death from typhoid fever in Tontogany in August 1896. His obituary in the *Wood County Sentinel* listed him as being the son of Thomas Custer and the nephew of "Gen. Custer." He had a funeral, but there is no gravestone. He left no heirs, but rather an enduring mystery that remains as a footnote to the Tom Custer folklore.

As detailed in Appendix 6, Nevin's seven children had all been born between 1863 and 1880, and they all reached adulthood before the turn of the century. Two were married by that time, one had given Nevin and Ann their first grandchild, and one was dead.

On Friday, September 1, 1899, with four months left before the calendar turned to a new century, twenty-one-year-old Charles Kendall Custer, the youngest of the siblings went to the home of a neighbor to show off a new revolver that he had just purchased. Contemporary accounts indicated that this took place in John Rousselo's yard, though later accounts state that it was in Charles' home. In any case, as they examined the weapon, Custer explained that he had loaded and fired the gun, but that the cylinder was now empty. It wasn't.

In a description of the incident in the *Monroe Democrat* that was reprinted in the *Petersburg Sun*, it was about thirty seconds after the bullet entered below his heart that Charles Custer gasped that he had been shot. Bleeding profusely, he was taken into Rousselo's home while Dr. Lou Knapp was summoned. It was the physician's opinion that death was imminent and the only thing to be done was to keep the patient comfortable. Without losing consciousness, Custer survived until 5:00 a.m. on Sunday, September 3. His obituary commented that "his cheerful and willing disposition made him a general favorite among his acquaintances."

Happier tidings flowed into the household of Nevin and Ann from the weddings. James Calhoun Custer was the first of their children to wed. In 1894, at the age of twenty-two, James married twenty-year-old Elizabeth Ann Renner. Born shortly thereafter, their daughters were the only members of their Custer generation to be born in the nineteenth century. Margaret Elizabeth was born in 1896, and Miriam Irene in 1897, both in Monroe.

On December 28, 1898, Nevin and Ann's third child, Maria Matilda Custer, known as "May" (sometimes seen as "Mae"), became the second to marry. Her husband, Charles Wesley Elmer had been born in 1872 in West Eaton, New York, about 30 miles southeast of Syracuse, and was five years her junior. His father, D.T. Elmer, had later been a newspaper man in

Monroe. Charles and May lived for a while in Toledo before going east to New York City, where Charles worked as a court reporter, eventually managing his firm. In the 1930s, he turned his avocation as an amateur astronomer into a successful career in the field of precision instruments.

Through the years, Nevin himself assiduously avoided the limelight. A rare mention of him was made in *The Evening News* of Detroit on July 14, 1898. An article shared with me by George A. Custer IV discussed the appearance in Detroit of Buffalo Bill Cody and his Wild West traveling show—which had long contained an homage to George Armstrong Custer. The major thrust of the article was Cody's desire to lead a contingent of troops to fight in the Spanish American War, but mention is made of a visit that Cody had made the previous day to Monroe.

Members of Cody's show, and accompanying him to Monroe, were Red Horn Bull and Black Heart, two men who had been present at the Little Bighorn twenty-two years before. Describing Nevin as a "plain, homely farmer," the article tells of their meeting with the surviving Custer brother.

"A look of stern bitterness crept over the old farmer's face when he found who he was talking to, and several of the Indians involuntarily drew back," wrote the unnamed journalist. "When the old man was introduced to Red Horn Bull, however, a part of whose face is said to have been shot away by [George Armstrong] Custer, the dead hero's brother burst into tears and left the tent."

CHAPTER 26
A NEW CENTURY

THE NEW CENTURY opened with six members of the Custer boys' generation still alive. Of Emanuel and Maria Custer's seven children, listed in
Appendix 5, only Nevin and Maggie survived. Two of their seven had died
as infants and three at the Little Bighorn. However, both of Maria's children by her earlier marriage to Israel Kirkpatrick, and both of Emanuel's
children with Matilda Viers Custer—who survived to adulthood—were
still alive. Within six years, though, these four half-siblings, noted in
Appendices 3 and 4, had passed.

Of Emanuel's sons, Henry C. Custer died in Osceola County, Michigan,
in 1900 at the age of seventy-eight. Brice William Custer, who had served
as sheriff of Franklin County, Ohio, from 1887 to 1891, a prestigious post,
given that the county seat, Columbus, is also the state capital. He died in
that county in 1904, two weeks short of turning seventy-three.

Though Henry C. Custer had served in the 5th Michigan during the Civil
War at a time when George Armstrong Custer commanded the division that
contained this regiment, there seems to have been relatively little contact
between the families. One exception is that Boston lived with Brice and his
family for a while prior to 1874, and Brice's wife and son made an extended
visit to Emanuel and Maria's home around the same time. Given the tone of
Boston's October 14, 1874, letter to Emma Reed, which is quoted in Chapter
Fourteen, there seems to have been bad blood between the families.

While neither Henry C. Custer, Brice Custer, nor David Kirkpatrick had more than passing contact with the Custer boys and Maggie through the years, David's sister was a different story. As we have seen, Lydia Ann Kirkpatrick Reed, known simply as "Ann," had been like a sibling—or a foster mother—to her half-siblings. She was an integral part of their lives, their joys, and the suffering that flowed from their singular tragedy. Her children had grown up knowing them, and her son, Harry Armstrong "Autie" Reed, had died at the sides of three of the Custer boys. She was forty-five when she learned of the death of her son and her three half-siblings, and by all accounts, she never fully recovered emotionally. She passed away at her home in Monroe at the age of eighty on June 27, 1906. Her niece, Nevin's oldest daughter, Claribel Custer Vivian, was with her. They were awaiting the arrival of Claribel's sister, May Custer Elmer, from New York at the time.

Lydia Ann's obituary, which was syndicated in newspapers around the country under the headline "Was Custer's Sister," provided a great deal of information about the later years of her life. It began by reminding readers that three decades and two days had passed since "the disaster that crushed her spirit and undermined her health."

The article went on to say, "Confined to the house for a number of years and gradually, steadily, failing, her death was nevertheless not looked for. Her condition had been about the same as for the past several months and no undue anxiety was felt for her . . . Modest and unassuming as she was, her acts of charity were performed without the knowledge of even her intimate friends. There were several charitable movements that she favored and every year, at regular intervals, she sent generous contributions of money, giving it to a friend and making her promise not to reveal her name. This wish was carried out and until her death removed the need of concealment. It is safe to say that scarce half a dozen people knew of her kindnesses to the poor, and many a family in urgent need has been relieved by her gifts, without having any idea as to the identity of the angel of mercy who was aiding them."

Nevin's daughters had always been close to their father's older stepsister. In a strange comment in the forward to the collection of Libbie Custer's letters that she edited, Marguerite Merington wrote that May Custer "had been adopted by the Reeds." What this meant is unclear. Charmaine Wawrzyniec at the Monroe County Library told me that she could find nothing to show that May was legally adopted. When I asked George A. Custer IV, he said that he had never heard of it. Merington likely was using the term as a metaphor for how close the two women were. In Lydia Ann's obituary, May was described as her "favorite niece."

Another source of confusion may be that May's middle name was "Reed," though Merington had to have known that this did not imply an adoption. Parenthetically, Lydia Ann could be said to have unofficially "adopted" George Armstrong Custer in 1852 when she brought him up to Monroe to attend the Stebbins Academy, and perhaps it was the same idea with May.

On June 30, Lydia Ann was laid to rest at Woodland Cemetery near her son Autie and her daughter Lilla Belle, who had died in 1858 at the age of three. The three brothers of Claribel and May served as pallbearers. Seven years later, in March 1913, she was joined at Woodland by her husband, David Reed, who had been the only member of the extended family to go west to Fort Abraham Lincoln from Monroe in the aftermath of the Little Bighorn.

Ann's precocious daughter, Emma Reed, who had married Frederic Sanxay Calhoun, the younger brother of James Calhoun, lost her husband two years before she lost her mother. As we have noted, Emma had been denied by account of age her aspiration to join the Custer Clan of the 1870s. With Fred's death in March 1904, she found herself a widow at forty-seven. She never remarried; nor did her daughter, Emma May Calhoun, born in 1882, ever marry. They died in 1943 and 1960, respectively, and are both buried, along with Fred Calhoun and other Calhoun family members, at Spring Grove Cemetery in Cincinnati.

Emma's older sister, Marie, who also never married, died in 1931 in Monroe at the age of eighty-two and is buried in the family plot, Woodland Cemetery. The two sisters had done considerable traveling. During the early part of the twentieth century, they had summered with their aunt, Elizabeth Bacon Custer, at her cabin at Onteora in the Catskills, and Emma spent time in Honolulu at a time when Hawaiian holidays were not yet commonplace.

After twenty-seven years as a widow, Margaret Custer Calhoun remarried at the age of fifty-one. The wedding took place on July 2, 1903, at Onteora, with the invitation cards being prepared and posted by Libbie Custer. Based on correspondence from the time, Dr. Lawrence Frost concluded that Maggie had been "swept off her feet" by John Halbert Maugham.

The wedding announcement noted that after the wedding, the couple would reside at the fashionable Hotel Iturbide in Mexico City. Not mentioned was that the groom had business interests in Mexico.

Maugham had led a very complicated life. Born in England in 1846, he immigrated to the United States in 1861, apparently without his parents, and made his way to Iowa. He had a son named Charles with a woman named Martha "Mattie" Stout, who was married to someone else. John and Mattie were finally married in 1874, and by the 1880 Census, they were living in Colorado with Charles and his younger brother, Ralph. In 1894, though, John was living alone in a rooming house in New York City.

By the turn of the century, he was pursuing a career as a banker. In 1902, Maugham was listed as a director and later vice president of the newly formed International Bank and Trust Company of America, which had been created through a merger involving a Mexican bank, with the idea of establishing branches in Havana, Rio de Janeiro, and other Latin American cities.

Unfortunately, the International Bank and Trust Company got into trouble rather quickly. Under investigation by the New York District

Attorney's office, it failed in October, 1903, only three months after John and Maggie Maugham had gone south to Mexico. The bank bounced back, but apparently John did not bounce with it. However, he did reemerge as vice president of the Ferguson Contracting Company, a large railway construction firm.

Not long after her wedding, Maggie Custer Calhoun was diagnosed with what the *New York Times* called stomach cancer. Other sources say it was liver cancer, and the Monroe *Record-Commercial* reported that she suffered from "heart trouble and a general breakdown." Doctors recommended surgery for the cancer, but she had embraced Christian Science as a faith, and shunned traditional remedies. Lawrence Frost wrote in his biography of Libbie that it was "a steadfast fear of ether" that caused Maggie to embrace the faith. In her *New York Times* obituary, it was written that under Christian Science "ministrations her spirits improved considerably, though at times, she still suffered great pains."

Her final days, at the apartment in the Hotel Glendening at 202 West 103rd Street that she shared with her husband, were excruciating. At last, on March 22, 1910, the suffering stopped. Her niece, Nevin's daughter May Custer Elmer, who also lived in New York, told the *New York Times* that she had "repeatedly tried to visit her aunt's room, but had been barred by the [Christian Science] healers on each occasion."

According to the paper, even John Maugham had been refused entry toward the last, and "when he learned of his wife's death, became nearly frantic with grief and fairly pushed the healers from his rooms. He wanted to assault Wentworth Byron Winslow, the healer. Friends declared that he was greatly incensed at the faith he formerly professed."

Various newspapers, from the *Sacramento Union* to the *Evening Chronicle* of Charlotte, North Carolina, carried a syndicated report, datelined New York, explaining that Maggie had "been treated for some time by faith healers, and would not allow physicians to attend her. Mrs. Maugham's first husband, Lieutenant James Calhoun, lost his life in the same battle in which General Custer died, as did also her two brothers, Lieutenant [sic] Boston Custer and Captain Thomas Custer, and a nephew, Autie Reed." Though Autie still commanded headlines, the others were not forgotten.

Maggie joined Boston and their parents at the family plot at Woodland Cemetery in Monroe. Claiming that he was too distraught to make the trip, her husband did not attend Maggie's funeral.

John Halbert Maugham faded from public attention—until a strange story emerged just five months later. On August 14, 1910, a bizarre headline on a back page of the *Washington Post* read "Gen. Custer's Brother-in-Law Found Clinging to a Rope."

In the wee hours of that morning, a policeman discovered a straw hat on the Hudson River pier at the end of West 39th Street in New York that bore the initials "JHM." As the story went, he "peeped through a hole in the planking, and saw a man in the water, clinging to the end of a rope. The man was pulled out. There were rats running in and out the timbers, and they made it uncomfortable for the man in the water, but he did not want to tell how he got overboard. He said that he had had $400 in his pockets earlier in the evening, and he thought somebody had taken it. The police sent him to Bellevue Hospital."

Earlier in the month, Ferguson Contracting had collapsed into bankruptcy under the weight of pending litigation and criminal investigations. It is hard to know exactly what was going through Maugham's mind that night.

In 1918, the seventy-four-year old married his third wife, thirty-one-year-old Margaret Jane Mahaffy, in Edgewater, New Jersey. It was a short marriage. Maugham died in April 1919.

As the Little Bighorn had left Nevin Johnson Custer the last of the Custer boys, Maggie's death now left him as the last of his generation.

Late in the spring of 1910, after Maggie's passing, an unnamed journalist came to Monroe to call on Nevin. It was something that should have happened sooner—much sooner. More than three decades had passed since he had become the last Custer boy, but no one had visited him for an in-depth interview.

Perhaps it was because the media interest was in his brother and in the tragically celebrated Custer *Clan*. Nevin was merely part of the Custer *family*. He had never ridden against the Confederates or the Lakota. He had never been to the Little Bighorn. He had never even been in the West.

Perhaps it was because he was not considered to be a good interview. By his own admission, "I can't remember things in order. They just come piecemeal, sort of by scattering."

Likely, it was because Nevin was a mild-mannered man, the archetype of the soft-spoken Midwest farmer who lets deeds speak more loudly than words, and whose deeds are confined to a slim slice of the world. His most conspicuous public profile had been his post as the superintendent of the Evangelical Church Sunday School in Ida Township.

The interview seems to have first appeared in the *News Tribune* of Detroit on May 10. It was then picked up by the Chicago *Inter Ocean*, and spilled across the top of the page in the Sunday edition on May 22. Through June, it was syndicated in many papers across the country.

The journalist found Nevin, clad in his black satin shirt and overalls "in a big white farm house fronting the historic River Raisin where he is up at daybreak to rattle down the hard coal burner and do the chores at the barn and of evenings he sits beside the kerosene lamp in the rag carpeted sitting room and reads the *Monroe Democrat* and the poultry journals to his wife and son."

His eldest son, George Armstrong Custer II, now forty-five and never married, had stayed on to help manage the place on River Road that would always be known as the Custer Farm.

Parenthetically, Marvin Samuel "Marvy" Custer, the son of Nevin's estranged half-brother, Brice William Custer, also had a son who was named George Armstrong Custer. He was born in 1882, eighteen years after Nevin's son, and lived to the age of seventy.

Acknowledging Nevin's solitude, it was written, "Not in years has the even flow of his life been interrupted. He lives today as he has lived since boyhood—quietly, unpretentiously, avoiding prominence, shunning public honors."

Pulling the ends of "his scraggy mustache," the old man told of the early days of the Custer boys in the Dining Fork, and of his brothers going off to the Civil War, recollections that are quoted earlier in this book.

"Things are pretty much jumbled in my mind after that . . . we didn't see much of each other, George and I," Nevin remembered of the years after the war, mentioning his brother, but steering the conversation toward his own overshadowed life. "He was away making a name for himself, taking an active part in things. And I stayed home and tended the farm. George liked the soldiering and the public honors; I never could have been satisfied that way. Why, pap wanted me to be a preacher and named me Johnson after a Presbyterian man who said he'd educate me into the clergy, but *pshaw*, I couldn't do it. Too conspicuous for me."

When pressed, as the reporter could have been expected to do, about the events of 1876, Nevin spilled his guts about something that had been eating at him for thirty-four years.

"I didn't intend to say it, an' I won't say much," he said, clinching his fists as his "little blue eyes flashed unconsciously like the gleam of steel."

"I'll tell yuh this, if it hadn't been for U.S. Grant, George Custer woulda been alive today. I won't tell you all about what Grant did to George. You can find out easy enough. It was the Belknap investigation, you know. Oh, I won't say any more. It makes my blood boil, and I'm liable to say something that I hadn't ought. But we don't like Grant around here."

As his eyes "fixed themselves sternly on the distant winding river . . . slowly the fires within their depths died away; the contracted brow relaxed."

Nevin's anger toward Grant is understandable given the rude and antagonistic way that he had treated George Armstrong Custer in the spring of 1876, though it must be recalled that Custer's Congressional testimony was equally harsh—albeit true—toward the Grant administration. Nevin's assertion that Grant was responsible for his brother's death, however, is contrary to the facts. If Grant would have had his way, and had not given in to Autie's pleas, then he would not have gone on the campaign that summer and he would have survived.

Waxing philosophically, Nevin continued, adding, "We've had some pretty rough times, we Custers. Name sort of stands for fight. And this old river has seen its bloody times too [in battles with the Potawatomi during the War of 1812], though you never would guess it today. I'm the only one left of the brothers now, and though it's nice, of course, to give George honors as he deserved, still the war is over, and the Indians are gone, and now that times are peaceful again, I can't imagine George as a fighting man half so well as I see him hoeing corn down in Ohio. I guess that's because I'm a farmer . . . It's no use tellin' yuh about his Indian fights, is it? Yuh got all those in history. Things went on about as usual here at the farm. Don't seem as if anything much ever happened here."

What did happen was that a couple of weeks later, on June 4, 1910, President William Howard Taft came to Monroe to unveil a grand equestrian statue of George Armstrong Custer in Loranger Square on First Street near Washington Street. With the statue the product of many years of effort by Elizabeth Custer, the dedication was called "the biggest celebration the town has ever experienced." It may well have been that the great bronze sculpture was the catalyst for sending a writer to Monroe in search of a story that month. The statue still stands, though it was relocated to the corner of North Monroe and West Elm Streets in 1955.

In 1910, his interviewer wrote that "Nevin Custer is still robust, bearing his sixty-eight years as lightly as though little more than half their burden rested on his shoulders."

By 1915, the years now numbering seventy-two, wore more heavily. On February 25 of that year, he drove into downtown Monroe, made a stop at the store owned by his friend, William Steiner, joked with some friends, and went shopping. At about 10:15 a.m., he returned, looking peaked, sat down in a chair and said that he didn't feel well.

Nevin was taken by automobile to the home of his daughter Claribel Vivian, where he died at 2:55 p.m. The cause of death was reported as "apoplexy," at the time, a term was used for sudden death beginning with an abrupt loss of consciousness. Today, we'd call it a stroke. The physician who had been summoned, Dr. Lou Knapp, was the same man who had attended to Nevin's youngest son, Charles Kendall Custer, as he had bled out from a gunshot wound sixteen years earlier.

His obituary in the Monroe *Record-Commercial* on March 4 confirmed that his demise was sudden "and entirely unexpected by his relatives and friends as he had been in apparently good health that morning."

Ann North Custer, now a widow three years after celebrating her golden wedding anniversary in 1912, hand picked the choir for the funeral service and asked the organist for "Beautiful Isle of Somewhere," a hymn that had been composed by Jessie Brown Pounds, with music by John Sylvester Fearis, in 1897. It had achieved notoriety after being used at the funeral of President William McKinley in 1901.

"Somewhere the sun is shining," it went, "Somewhere the songbirds dwell . . . Somewhere the clouds are rifted"—but not that winter for Ann North Custer.

She passed away on June 10, 1921, after having been ill with what the *Monroe Evening News* related as "heart trouble." She was laid to rest beside her husband at Woodland Cemetery in Monroe, having lived the better part of her seventy-eight years on the edge of that city.

Of the generation of the Custer siblings and their spouses, only Elizabeth Bacon Custer now remained.

CHAPTER 27
DESCENDANTS

OF THE CHILDREN of Nevin and Ann Custer, all listed in Appendix 6, two had moved away from Monroe before their parents passed. May and her husband Charles Elmer were in New York City, while William Bacon Custer, the youngest surviving child, had married Jessie Evangeline Shellabarger in Pennsylvania in 1916 and they were now living in Albany, New York. In 1914, after attending Monroe Business College, William had gone to work with Penick & Ford, a Louisiana-based food products company with interests around the United States that was famous for such brands as Br'er Rabbit molasses products and Vermont Maid maple syrup.

The other children had remained near their parents. George was on the farm and James Calhoun Custer, with his wife Elizabeth Ann lived in Monroe. After high school, Lula had studied nursing at Harper Hospital in Detroit, and had worked there as a nurse for twenty-five years. She had retired and returned to live on the Custer Farm around the time of Nevin's death.

The eldest of the siblings, Claribel, had married Andrew Vivian, manager of the Lotus Dairy on Monroe's East Front Street, in January 1905. They lived on the north side of East Third Street near Washington Street, in the house where Nevin Custer passed away. It was a late marriage for both. She was forty-two and he was fifty-four. They never had children.

After his death in October 1916, Claribel moved in with George and Lula on the Custer Farm. In that same year, when River Road was paved, it was named General Custer Road. It was later renamed North Custer Road, and the old family farmhouse where Nevin had lived for more than four decades, and where Lula and George Armstrong Custer II now lived, was numbered as 3048 North Custer Road.

As an unexpected tragedy had taken the life of Charles Kendall Custer in 1899, another claimed his brother thirty years later. At 9:00 p.m. on December 19, 1929, Lula and Claribel discovered George Armstrong Custer II lying on the floor of the garage at the Custer Farm. The *Monroe Evening News* of the following day reported that he was unconscious, and "the motor of the automobile was running, and the door of the car was open. He was still alive when found and his sisters carried him to the house but he died before a doctor could be summoned."

The death certificate listed the cause of death as "carbon monoxide gas," tersely calling it "accidental," and noted that there had been no autopsy. If there was any talk of it having been a suicide, this was not pursued by the media. In those days, the privacy of those who were not public figures, even if they were relatives of people who had been public figures, was generally respected.

In New York, May Custer Elmer and her husband Charles had lived in Manhattan at 209 Dyckman, but they later moved to Brooklyn. May became part of the social orbit of her aunt, Elizabeth Bacon Custer, and visited her frequently.

This circle also included Marguerite Merington, who spent a great deal of time with Libbie at her apartment at 71 Park Avenue and who acted as a sort of social secretary while Libbie was alive, and later as her literary executor. She and May would later edit Libbie's papers for publication, Merington in the editorial sense, while May edited the family legacy, determining which letters should and should *not* be preserved for posterity. As Merington wrote in the foreword of her book *The Custer Story*, "By the wish of Mrs. Charles Elmer . . . who was next of kin, many of the letters I copied were burned."

In 1925, Libbie, now nearing eighty-four, received a letter from J.A. Shoemaker, the secretary of the National Custer Memorial Association, inviting her to be a guest of honor at the Fiftieth Anniversary Commemoration of the Battle of the Little Bighorn to be held at the battle site. She mentioned this to photographer David Barry, an old friend from the Fort Lincoln days. He advised her not to go. In a March 4, 1926, letter he told her, "You want me to be honest. I think it would be a great mental strain to be shown certain points on that Field that I am quite familiar with."

She took his advice, and told Shoemaker that she had asked Charles and May Elmer to go in her place so that the promoters of the event would "have a Custer for the great day." May became the first Custer, and the only member of her generation to set foot on the battle site since 1876. In an Associated Press report, May said that she did not resent that Lakota were present at the commemoration. "They were only defending their country as they saw right," she said diplomatically.

When it came time for the fifty-fifth anniversary in 1929, May was running interference for her aunt with the press, who clamored for a statement, explaining to the *New York Times* that despite "her declining years and occasional attacks of neuritis" and her abandoning her daily walks through Murray Hill, she was "in good health."

As Libbie's infirmity progressed, Lula Custer, a trained nurse, came to New York from Monroe to act as a live-in caregiver. When she suffered the heart attack that would hasten her death, Lula was at her side. When she passed away on April 4, 1933, both sisters were present.

Lula had remained in New York with May after Libbie's passing, but in the spring of 1938, she was taken ill and returned to Monroe, where she was confined to Mercy Hospital. It was here that she died on December 18, 1938, at the age of sixty-eight.

William Bacon Custer was still working as a district manager for Penick & Ford in Albany when he died of a sudden heart attack at the age of sixty-six on March 17, 1940. He was buried near his siblings at Woodland. His wife, Jessie Evangeline Custer, eventually moved back to Pennsylvania, where she had been born, and where she passed away in 1973.

In the meantime, May Custer Elmer had helped to inspire an astronomical institute. Her husband, who was an amateur astronomer, had started inviting like-minded friends to join him for weekend gatherings. By 1927, this had led to their decision to formalize their shared interest by establishing an astronomy organization and observatory—which still exists to this day. They decided to name it the "Custer Institute," after May. In the institute's official narrative, this was "to honor the many years she had been their gracious hostess at their weekly informal gatherings." The oldest public observatory on Long Island, the Custer Institute in Southold, New York, now boasts a three-meter satellite TVRO dish for radio astronomy experiments.

As he was establishing his observatory, Charles Elmer was transitioning out of his day job of running a court reporting firm. One of his occasional amateur lectures on astronomy and telescopes was attended by Richard Perkin, a young investment banker with a background in chemical engineering. The two decided to transform their shared hobby into a precision optics business.

The Perkin-Elmer firm, founded in 1937 and incorporated in 1939, became a leading producer of optical rangefinders, bombsights, and reconnaissance systems during World War II. Perkin-Elmer still remains prominent in the field of instruments for industry, health sciences, and astronomy. However, the company's reputation was greatly damaged in the 1990s by serious imperfections in the optical telescope assembly that it had supplied for the Hubble Space Telescope, which were corrected only through costly retrofits while the Hubble was in orbit.

May and Charles were living in Stamford, Connecticut, when May died on February 2, 1945, at the age of seventy-seven. As Lula had been seven years earlier, she was brought home to Monroe for interment at Woodland Cemetery. Charles passed on December 7, 1954, in Greenport, New York.

When Claribel Custer Vivian died on July 9, 1950, at the age of eighty-six, the *Monroe Evening News* reported that she "had been in poor health since last December and in a serious condition since April." The paper reported that she had been living at 223 Washington Street in Monroe, but that she passed away at her brother's home at 3029 North Custer Road.

James Calhoun Custer lived out his final years in this house. It was located across the street from the old farmhouse at 3048 North Custer where Nevin had lived from 1871 to 1915, a house which had been sold to a man named Charles Ferguson in 1938.

James, the last of his generation, suffered a stroke on January 8, 1954, and died two days later at the age of eighty-two. The cause was listed as cerebral thrombosis. Like their siblings, both Claribel and James were buried at Woodland Cemetery. Both James and Claribel had each lost their spouses three decades before they died. As Nevin had been the only member of his generation with children, his son, James Calhoun Custer had that distinction in the next generation.

James Custer and his wife, Elizabeth Ann Renner, had four children, which are listed in Appendix 7. Neither Margaret Elizabeth nor Miriam Irene, born in 1896 and 1897, respectively, ever married, and they spent much of their lives in the house at 3029 North Custer Road with their father and their aunt Claribel. Margaret died on January 14, 1957, three years after the passing of her father, but Miriam lived until June 14, 1971. After the family home at 3029 North Custer was sold in 1962, Miriam had lived on North Roessler Street in Monroe. Of Margaret, the *Monroe Evening News* said that "her death was unexpected, but she had been in poor health for a year." The paper reported that Miriam died of uremic poisoning after being hospitalized for four days. Both were buried at Woodland.

While the sisters never ventured far from Monroe County, the opposite was true for their two brothers, Nevin's last two grandchildren. Brice Calhoun William Custer, born on June 9, 1901, and Charles Armstrong Custer, born on January 14, 1910, both followed the footsteps of their great uncles—George Armstrong Custer and Tom Custer—into careers as officers in the US Army.

In the May 27, 1961, issue of Montana's *Billings Gazette*, Brice explained why the interest in striving in the Army skipped a generation.

"Naturally, news of three brothers, a bother-in-law and a nephew being killed at the Battle of the Little Bighorn within a few feet of each other was a terrible blow to the family," he recalled. "Mainly as a result of this loss, neither my father nor his brothers had any military service. As a further blow, my father's younger brother, Charles, was accidentally killed in his own bedroom while showing his revolver to a friend."

Brice broke this trend, although he began his military career with the US Navy, *not* with the US Army. Like Tom Custer, he enlisted when he was not yet eighteen. Mustered in as a seaman apprentice on August 6, 1918, he hoped to see action in World War I, just as Tom had anticipated a role for himself in the Civil War. Within a few weeks, he was a seaman first class and assigned to Naval Station Great Lakes north of Chicago while waiting for an assignment aboard the battleship USS *Connecticut*. The armistice came before Brice shipped out and he was sent to Naval Station Norfolk at Hampton Roads, Virginia, where he remained until he was put on inactive duty in April 1919.

Brice was back in Monroe working at the post office when his official discharge arrived in 1921. The following year, he joined the Monroe howitzer company of the 125th Infantry Battalion of the Michigan National Guard. By 1927, he had risen through the ranks, commissioned as an officer, promoted to captain, and assigned to the Infantry School at Fort Benning, Georgia.

In the meantime, Brice had married Vida Lenore McLachlin on June 11, 1922, in Monroe. Their two sons, George Armstrong Custer III and Brice Calhoun Custer, were born in 1923 and 1927, respectively.

Brice Calhoun William Custer's younger brother, Charles Armstrong Custer, joined the Michigan National Guard in 1926, four years after Brice, and received his lieutenant's bars in 1930. Charles married Minnie Ann Weiss on March 28, 1931, and they had three children, Richard James Custer, Dacia Mae Custer, and Elizabeth Lou Custer, between 1932 and 1937. Their fourth, Thomas Calhoun Custer, was born in 1949.

As World War II engulfed Europe and the United States prepared for war, Brice and Charles Custer were among the National Guardsmen called up for active duty. When it was activated in 1940, they were both assigned to the 32nd Infantry Division, which was composed of Michigan and Wisconsin National Guard units. However, they each transferred to other units before going overseas.

Major Charles Custer went ashore on Omaha Beach during the Normandy Invasion on June 6, 1944, as a battalion commander within the 29th Infantry Division. Lieutenant Colonel Brice Custer arrived in southern France with the 232nd Infantry Regiment of the 42nd Infantry Division in December 1944.

The 42nd Division progressed north, turning eastward into France's Alsace region toward Strasbourg on the Rhine River. On January 6, 1945, Brice Custer earned the Silver Star for heroism near the commune of Stadtmatten in easternmost part of France's Alsace region. According to his citation, when two platoons from the 232nd became surrounded by the Germans, he organized a small relief force, which he led personally "against a much superior enemy force and in the face of German automatic weapons, small arms and rocket launcher fire." His efforts were successful; the Germans were routed and Stadtmatten recaptured.

The 232nd, which had come to be known as "Custer's Red Raiders," crossed the Rhine near Worms on Easter Sunday 1945 and participated in the difficult battle to capture Würzburg in early April. On April 10, they ran a flanking maneuver that helped encircle the city of Schweinfurt. They were in Austria when the Third Reich collapsed in May and were tasked with processing tens of thousands of German prisoners that flooded into the region ahead of Soviet advances from the east. When he returned to the States, Brice was the most highly decorated member of his family since Tom Custer. In addition to his Silver Star, Brice was awarded the Bronze Star and the French Croix de Guerre, among other medals.

After the war, Brice Custer served in the occupation of Japan, where he was named executive officer of the 7th Cavalry Regiment in Tokyo, becoming the first Custer to serve with the 7th since his great-uncles died in 1876. Afterward, for sixteen months, he was the military governor of Japan's Yamagata Prefecture.

In March 1953, as the Korean War was winding down, Colonel Brice Custer began a seventeen-month tour of duty with the US Military Advisory Group to the Republic of South Korea. According to a US Army press release, General Chung Il Kwon, the chief of staff of the Korean Army had high praise for Custer, commenting that he had surmounted difficulties in customs, language, climate, and strange terrain to use his "professional knowledge and profound ability" to help advise and shape the Korean 22nd Division.

After Korea, he was posted to command the Kansas Military District at Fort Riley, where his great uncles had served nearly a century before. He remained here until May 1959, when he retired after four decades of service.

Beginning in 1950, Charles Armstrong Custer served four years as an intelligence officer with Headquarters, US Army Europe in Heidelberg, Germany, going on to a post as advisor to the US Army Reserve in Southwest New Mexico at Las Cruces until 1957. After assignments in South

Korea, and at Fort Ord in California, he and his wife retired to Las Cruces, where he surrounded himself with memorabilia related to the careers of his two great uncles who had served in the US Army—notably the two Medals of Honor awarded to Thomas Ward Custer in 1865.

Through the years, Brice Custer's path also often crossed that of the legacy of great-uncles made famous by their actions in the Civil War and at the Little Bighorn. In 1951, he even had a bit part in the Paramount Pictures dramatic film *Warpath*, a Western that was filmed near Billings, north of the Little Bighorn battlefield, and which contains scenes depicting the battle. As a member of both the Custer Battlefield Historical and Museum Association and the Little Bighorn Association, he spoke at various commemorative events from Montana to Monroe.

Brice and his wife, Lenore, moved to Del Rey Oaks, near Monterey, California, where he died on November 24, 1969. Four days later, he was interred at Arlington National Cemetery, the first of his lineage to be so honored.

Brice's two sons also served in the armed forces, with George Armstrong Custer III following the family's tradition into the US Army, and Brice Calhoun Custer, Jr. serving in the US Navy and the US Air Force. George was in the Pacific Theater as an enlisted man during World War II, and was an officer with the 1st Cavalry Division in Korea in the mid-1950s. In 1960, he received his master's degree in nuclear engineering from the University of Virginia in Charlottesville, the same city that Autie and Tom had helped to capture in 1865. After serving at the Pentagon, George went to Vietnam as commander of the 2nd Battalion, the "Wolfhounds," of the 27th Infantry Regiment. He is well remembered for coordinating air support from a command and control helicopter during the Battle of Renegade Woods in Tay Ninh Province in April 1970. Like his father, he was a recipient of the Silver Star.

The younger Brice Custer enlisted in the US Navy in January 1945 before his eighteenth birthday, following that other family tradition pursued by his father and his great uncle, Tom. Mustered out after World War II, he enlisted in the Air Force at the start of the Korean War, earned his wings, and flew several combat missions with the 8th Fighter Bomber Squadron in 1953. He later served on the faculty of the Physics Department at the Air Force Academy, and with the Air Force Space and Missile Systems Organization.

Retired Lieutenant Colonel Charles Armstrong Custer, brother of the elder Brice and uncle to the younger, lived out his final years at the Mountain Shadows Nursing Home in Las Cruces. It was here that he passed away on November 25, 1992, at the age of eighty-two. Like so many other Custers before him, he was buried at the Custer-Reed Plot in Woodland Cemetery in Monroe.

Charles was the last member of his generation, and the last of his lineage to have looked into the eyes of a man, grandfather Nevin, with direct personal memories of those happy, innocent days in the Dining Fork of Ohio so very long ago. He was the last grandson of the last of the Custer boys.

THE END

ABOUT THE AUTHOR

BILL YENNE IS the award-winning author of more than three dozen books on historical topics, including many on military history and Western history. He has contributed to encyclopedias of both world wars. General Wesley Clark called his biography of Alexander the Great, the "best yet," while *The New Yorker* wrote of *Sitting Bull*, his biography of the great Lakota leader, that it "excels as a study in leadership." This biography was named to number five for nonfiction on Amazon's "Best Books of the Year."

The *Wall Street Journal* called Yenne's *Indian Wars: The Campaign for the American West* "splendid" and went on to say that it "has the rare quality of being both an excellent reference work and a pleasure to read." The reviewer also said that Mr. Yenne writes with "cinematic vividness."

Mr. Yenne grew up in Western Montana where his father was a backcountry trail guide and trails supervisor in Glacier National Park. He graduated from the University of Montana and has traveled extensively in all of the western states. He is an avid backcountry hiker and has walked the Little Bighorn Battlefield many times.

He appeared in the Parthenon Entertainment Ltd film production, *Mystery Files: Sitting Bull*, which aired on both the Smithsonian Channel and the National Geographic Channel. He served as a consultant for the *Command Decision* program covering the Battle of the Little Bighorn, which was shown on the History Channel. He has appeared in other documentaries airing on the History Channel and the Smithsonian Channel, as well as programs on ARD German Television and NHK Japanese Television. His talks and book signings have been covered by C-SPAN.

His book, *On The Trail of Lewis and Clark, Yesterday and Today*, is critically acclaimed, and led to his being selected by Stephenie Ambrose Tubbs and the Lewis and Clark Bicentennial Commission as a featured guest at "Clark on the Yellowstone," the National Lewis and Clark Bicentennial Signature Event held at one of the expedition's most important campsites in Montana.

Surrounded by remarkable children and grandchildren, he and his wife live in San Francisco. Visit him on the web at www.BillYenne.com.

This detail of a 1645 map by the cartographer Willem Blaeu and his son Johan shows the town of Kalderich (on the left, south of Venlo), which was the birthplace of Paulus Van Haren Küster, the patriarch of the Custers in America, and the first ancestor to bring his family across the Atlantic. He was born in Kalderich, also called, Kaldenkirchen, one year before this map appeared in the book *Theater of the World,* or *A New Atlas of Maps and Representations of All Regions.* The town was then in the Herzogtum (Duchy) of Jülich, and is now located in the German state of Nordrhein-Westfalen (North Rhine-Westphalia). For geographic orientation, the German city of Dusseldorf on the Rhine River (written here as "Duffeldorp") is in the lower right corner, 30 miles east of Kalderich. (Public domain image from author's collection).

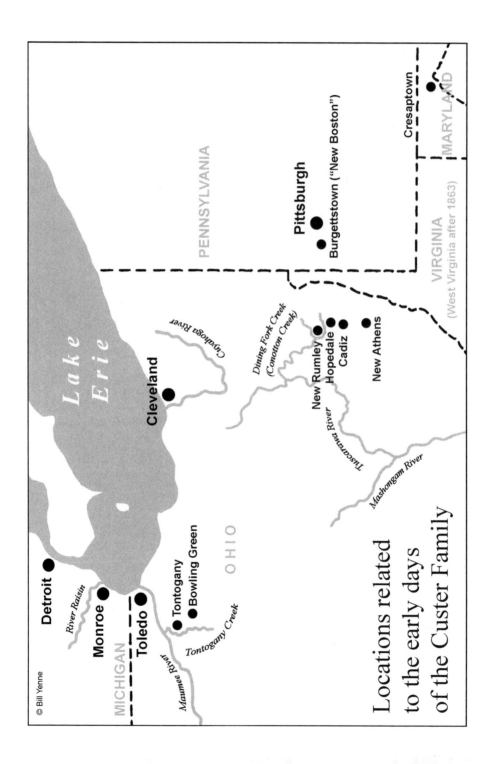

© Bill Yenne

Locations related
to the early days
of the Custer Family

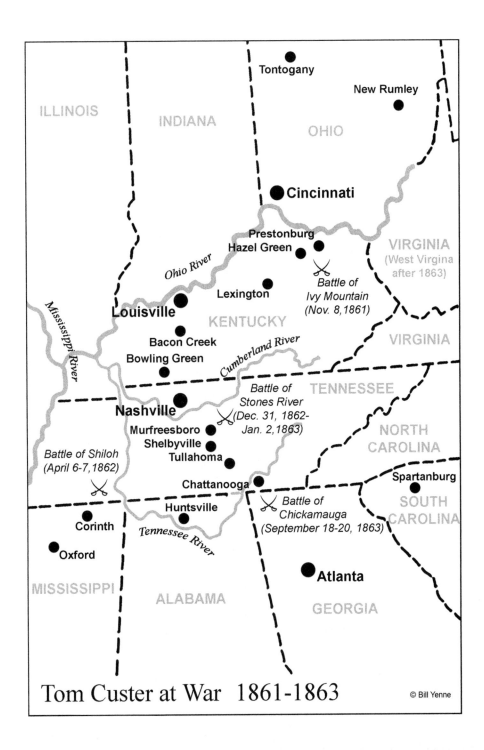

Tom Custer at War 1861-1863

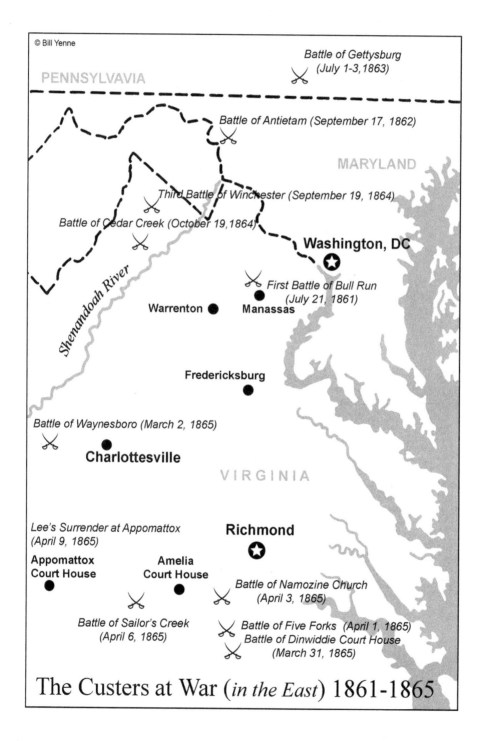

© Bill Yenne

PENNSYLVAVIA

Battle of Gettysburg
(July 1-3, 1863)

Battle of Antietam (September 17, 1862)

MARYLAND

Third Battle of Winchester (September 19, 1864)

Battle of Cedar Creek (October 19, 1864)

Washington, DC

Shenandoah River

First Battle of Bull Run
(July 21, 1861)

Warrenton   Manassas

Fredericksburg

Battle of Waynesboro (March 2, 1865)

Charlottesville

VIRGINIA

Lee's Surrender at Appomattox
(April 9, 1865)

Richmond

Appomattox
Court House

Amelia
Court House

Battle of Namozine Church
(April 3, 1865)

Battle of Sailor's Creek
(April 6, 1865)

Battle of Five Forks (April 1, 1865)
Battle of Dinwiddie Court House
(March 31, 1865)

The Custers at War (*in the East*) 1861-1865

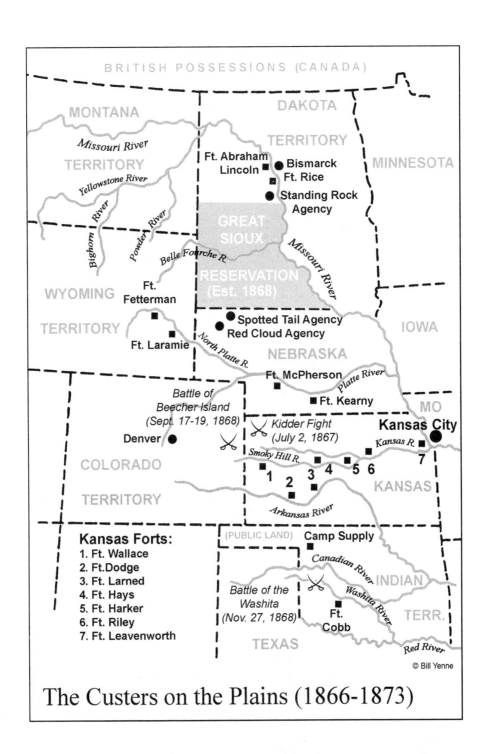

The Custers on the Plains (1866-1873)

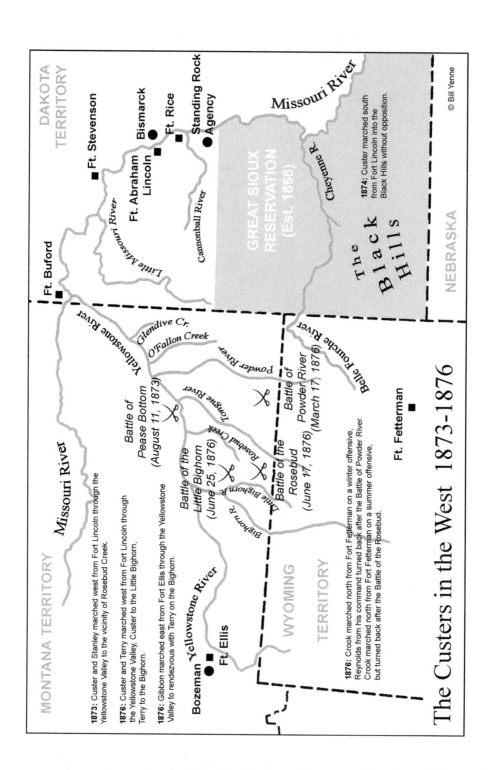

The Custers in the West 1873-1876

1873: Custer and Stanley marched west from Fort Lincoln through the Yellowstone Valley to the vicinity of Rosebud Creek.

1876: Custer and Terry marched west from Fort Lincoln through the Yellowstone Valley, Custer to the Little Bighorn, Terry to the Bighorn.

1876: Gibbon marched east from Fort Ellis through the Yellowstone Valley to rendezvous with Terry on the Bighorn.

1876: Crook marched north from Fort Fetterman on a winter offensive. Reynolds from his command turned back after the Battle of Powder River. Crook marched north from Fort Fetterman on a summer offensive, but turned back after the Battle of the Rosebud.

1874: Custer marched south from Fort Lincoln into the Black Hills without opposition.

© Bill Yenne

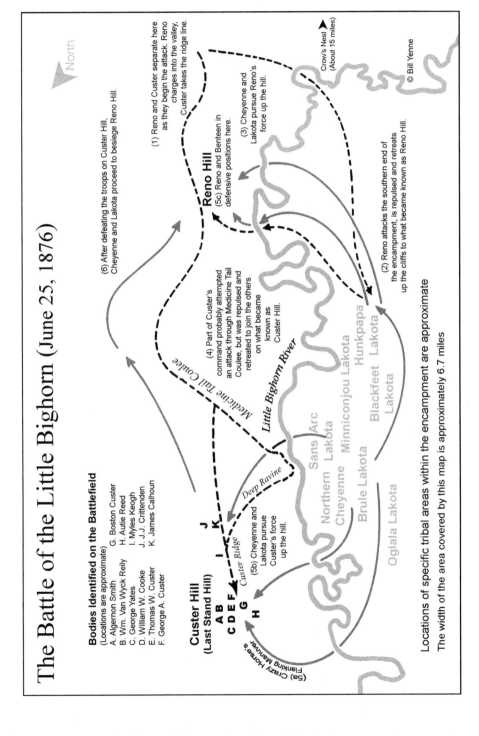

The Battle of the Little Bighorn (June 25, 1876)

Bodies Identified on the Battlefield
(Locations are approximate)
A. Algernon Smith   G. Boston Custer
B. Wm. Van Wyck Reily   H. Autie Reed
C. George Yates   I. Myles Keogh
D. William W. Cooke   J. J.J. Crittenden
E. Thomas W. Custer   K. James Calhoun
F. George A. Custer

Custer Hill
(Last Stand Hill)

Custer Ridge

(5a) Crazy Horse's Flanking Maneuver

Deep Ravine

(5b) Cheyenne and Lakota pursue Custer's force up the hill.

Medicine Tail Coulee

(4) Part of Custer's command probably attempted an attack through Medicine Tail Coulee, but was repulsed and retreated to join the others on what became known as Custer Hill.

Little Bighorn River

Oglala Lakota

Brule Lakota

Northern Cheyenne

Sans Arc Lakota

Minniconjou Lakota

Blackfeet Lakota

Hunkpapa Lakota

▲North

(6) After defeating the troops on Custer Hill, Cheyenne and Lakota proceed to besiege Reno Hill.

(1) Reno and Custer separate here as they begin the attack. Reno charges into the valley, Custer takes the ridge line.

Reno Hill

(5c) Reno and Benteen in defensive positions here.

(3) Cheyenne and Lakota pursue Reno's force up the hill.

(2) Reno attacks the southern end of the encampment, is repulsed and retreats up the cliffs to what became known as Reno Hill.

Crow's Nest (About 15 miles)

© Bill Yenne

Locations of specific tribal areas within the encampment are approximate
The width of the area covered by this map is approximately 6.7 miles

GENEALOGICAL APPENDICES

Appendix 1: The Direct Ancestors in America of the Custer Siblings

(On their father's side)

Paulus Van Haren Küster (1644–1707)
(Immigrated from the Duchy of Jülich)
Married
Gertrude Doors (?–?)

Arnold Doors Küster (1669–1739)
Married
Elizabeth Rebecca Sellen (?–?)

Nicholas Custer (1706–1784)
Married
Susannah Margaretta Hoppe (1714–1787)

Emanuel Custer (1754–1854)
Married
Anna Maria Fedele (1759–1799)

John Fedele Custer (1782–1830)
Married
Catherine Valentine Custer (1783–1877)

(Their son, Emanuel Henry Custer, was the father of the Custer siblings.
See Appendix 2.)

Appendix 2: The Direct Ancestors in America
of the Custer Siblings

(On their mother's side)

George Ward (1724–1811)
Immigrated from (Durhamshire, England)
Married
Mary Grier (1733–1819)

James Grier Ward (1765–1824)
Married
Catherine Rogers (1776–1829)

*(Their daughter, Maria Ward, was the mother of the Custer siblings.
See Appendix 3.)*

Appendix 3: The Father of the Custer Siblings
Emanuel Henry Custer (1806-1892)

First wife:
Matilda Viers (1804–1835)
Children:
   1. Hannah Custer (died in infancy)
   2. Brice William Custer (1831–1904)
      Married Maria Stockton (1834–1904)
   3. John Custer (1833–1836)
   4. Henry C. Custer (1833–1900)

Second wife:
Maria Ward Kirkpatrick (1807–1882)
Children: (See Appendix 5.)

Appendix 4: The Mother of the Custer Siblings:
Maria Ward Kirkpatrick (1807-1882)

First husband:
Israel Reed Kirkpatrick (1796–1835)

Children:
1. David Kirkpatrick (1823–1901)
   Married Cynthia Jane Patton (?–1907?)
   Married Nancy J. Grundy (1840–?)
2. Lydia Ann Kirkpatrick Reed (1825–1906)
   Married David Reed (1824–1913)
   Children:
   1. Marie E. Reed (1848–1931)
   2. Lilla Belle Reed (1854–1858)
   3. Emma Reed Calhoun (1856–1943)
      Married Frederic Sanxay Calhoun (1847–1904) (*No children*)
   4. Harry Armstrong "Autie" Reed (1858–1876)

Second husband:
Emanuel Henry Custer (1806–1892)
Children: (See Appendix 5)

Appendix 5: The Children of Emanuel Henry Custer and Maria Ward Custer

1. James Custer (1836–1837)
2. Samuel Custer (1838–1839)
3. George Armstrong Custer (1839–1876)
   Married Elizabeth ("Libbie") Clift Bacon (1842–1933) (*No children*)
4. Nevin Johnson Custer (1842–1915)
   Married Ann North (1843–1922) (*Seven children, see Appendix 6*)
5. Thomas Ward Custer (1845–1876)
6. Boston Custer (1848–1876)
7. Margaret Emma Custer (1852–1910)
   First husband: James Calhoun (1845–1876) (*No children*)
   Second husband: John Halbert Maugham (1844-1919) (*No children*)

Appendix 6: The Children of Nevin Johnson Custer

1. Claribel Custer (1863–1950)
   Married Andrew Vivian (1851–1916) (*No children*)
2. George Armstrong Custer (1864–1929)
3. May Reed Custer Elmer (1867–1945)
   Married Charles Wesley Elmer (1872–1954) (*No children*)
4. Lula B. Custer (1870–1938)

5. James Calhoun Custer (1871–1954)
    Married Elizabeth Ann Renner (1874–1924) (*Four children,*
    see Appendix 7)
6. William Bacon Custer (1874–1940)
    Married Jessie Evangeline Shellabarger (1875–1973) (*No children*)
7. Charles Kendall Custer (1879–1899)

Appendix 7: The Children of
James Calhoun Custer

Margaret Elizabeth Custer (1896–1957)
Miriam Irene Custer (1897–1971)
Brice Calhoun William Custer (1901–1969)
    Married Vida Lenore McLachlin (1903–1979)
Charles Armstrong Custer (1910–1992)
    Married Minnie Ann Weiss (1912–2000)

BIBLIOGRAPHY

Ambrose, Stephen E. *Crazy Horse and Custer: The Parallel Lives of Two American Warriors.* New York: Doubleday, 1975.

Barnett, Louise. *Touched by Fire: The Life, Death, and Mythic Afterlife of George Armstrong Custer.* New York: Henry Holt and Company, 1996.

Barnitz, Albert and Jennie. *Life in Custer's Cavalry: Diaries and Letters of Albert and Jennie Barnitz, 1867–1868.* New Haven: Yale University Press, 1977.

Bighead, Kate and Thomas B. Marquis. *She Watched Custer's Last Battle: Her Story, Interpreted in 1927.* Hardin, Montana: Custer Battle Museum, 1933.

Blaeu, Willem Janszoon and Johan Blaeu. *Theater of the World, or A New Atlas of Maps and Representations of All Regions.* Amsterdam: Self published, 1645.

Brady, Cyrus Townsend. *Indian Fights and Fighters.* New York: Philips & Company, 1904.

Brininstool, E.A. *Custer Massacre Controversy.* Columbus, Ohio: Hunter-Trader-Trapper Company, 1920.

Bryant, Arthur D. *On the Custer Mutilation.* Portland, Oregon: Pacific Monthly Publishing Company, 1908.

Bulkley, John McClelland. *History of Monroe County, Michigan: A Narrative Account of Its Historical Progress, Its People, and Its Principal Interests.* Chicago and New York: Lewis Publishing Company, 1913.

Butterfield & Butterfield. *Important Custer, Indian War & Western Memorabilia* (Auction catalog). San Francisco: Butterfield & Butterfield, 1995.

Calhoun, James. *With Custer in '74: James Calhoun's diary of the Black Hills Expedition* (Edited by Lawrence A. Frost). Provo, Utah: Brigham Young University Press, 1979.

Calkins, Chris M. *The Appomattox Campaign: March 29–April 9, 1865.* Conshohocken, Pennsylvania: Combined Publishing, 1997.

Canfield, Silas S. *History of the 21st Regiment Ohio Volunteer Infantry in the War of the Rebellion.* Toledo, Ohio: Vrooman Anderson and Bateman Printers, 1893.

Carroll, John M. (In collaboration with Nancy Allan). *Custer and His Times* (Three volumes). Fort Worth, Texas: Little Big Horn Associates, 1984–1987.

Carroll, John M. *Custer in Periodicals: A Bibliographic Checklist.* Fort Collins, Colorado: Old Army Press, 1975.

Carroll, John M. *The Benteen-Golden Letters on Custer and His Last Battle.* Lincoln: University of Nebraska Press, 1974.

Chapman Brothers: *Portrait and Biographical Album of Ingham and Livingston counties, Michigan, Containing Biographical Sketches of Prominent and Representative Citizens of the Counties, The Governors of the State and of All The Presidents of the United States.* Chicago: Chapman Brothers, 1891.

Clarksburg Telegram. *History of Clarksburg and Harrison County from its Earliest Settlement to the Present Time.* Clarksburg, West Virginia: Clarksburg Telegram, 1876.

Cole, A.D. and Jacqueline Hencken. *New Rumley, Harrison County, Ohio: Birthplace of General Custer.* Strasburg, Ohio: Spidell Printing Company, 1947.

Coleman, Thomas W. *I Buried Custer: The Diary of Pvt. Thomas W. Coleman* (Edited by Bruce R. Liddic; Introduction by John M. Carroll. College Station, Texas: Creative Publishing Company, 1979.

Commissioner of Indian Affairs. Annual Report of the Commissioner of Indian Affairs to the Secretary of the Interior. Washington, DC, 1874, 1875, 1876.

Connell, Evan S. *Son of the Morning Star.* San Francisco: North Point Press, 1984.

Cox, Kurt Hamilton. *Custer and His Commands: From West Point to Little Bighorn.* East Finchley, London, UK: Greenhill Books, 1999.

Cozzens, Peter. *No Better Place to Die: The Battle of Stones River.* Champaign: University of Illinois Press, 1990.

Custer, Boston, and Tom O'Neil (editor). *Letters from Boston Custer.* Brooklyn: Arrow and Trooper Publishing, 1993.

Custer, Elizabeth B., and Arlene Reynolds. *The Civil War Memories of Elizabeth Bacon Custer.* Austin: University of Texas Press, 1994.

Custer, Elizabeth B. *Boots and Saddles.* New York: Harper and Brothers, 1885.

Custer, Elizabeth B. *Boots and Saddles.* Norman: University of Oklahoma Press (reprint), 1961.

Custer, Elizabeth B. *Following the Guidon.* New York: Harper and Brothers, 1890.

Custer, Elizabeth B. *Following the Guidon.* Norman: University of Oklahoma Press (reprint), 1994.

Custer, Elizabeth B. *Tenting on the Plains.* New York: Harper and Brothers, 1893.

Custer, Elizabeth B. *Tenting on the Plains.* Norman: University of Oklahoma Press (reprint), 1994.

Custer, Elizabeth. "A Beau Sabreur." (In Theophilus Rodenbough's *The Bravest Five Hundred of '61*). New York: G.W. Dillingham 1891.

Custer, George Armstrong. *My Life On The Plains; Or, Personal Experiences With Indians.* New York: Sheldon and Company, 1874.

Custer, Milo. *The Custer Families.* Bloomington, Illinois: Privately published, 1912.

Day, Carl. *Tom Custer: Ride to Glory.* Spokane: Arthur H. Clarke and Company, 2002.

Donahue, Michael. *Drawing Battle Lines: Map Testimony of Custer's Last Fight.* El Segundo, California: Upton and Sons, 2009.

Dyer, Frederick H. *A Compendium of the War of the Rebellion*. Des Moines, Iowa: The Dyer Publishing Company, 1908.

Esgerly, Winfield Scott with George Clark. Scalp Dance: The Winfield Scott Edgerly Papers on the Battle of the Little Bighorn. Oswego, New York: Heritage Press, 1985.

Eicher, John H. Eicher, David J. *Civil War High Commands*. Stanford, California: Stanford University Press, 2001.

Fougera, Katherine Gibson. With Custer's Cavalry. Lincoln: University of Nebraska Press, 1986.

Fox, William F. *Regimental Losses in The American Civil War 1861-1865*. Albany: Albany Publishing Company, 1889.

Freeman, Douglas Southall. *George Washington: A Biography*, Volume I. New York: Scribner's, 1948.

Frost, Lawrence A. *Court Martial of General George Armstrong Custer*. Norman: University of Oklahoma Press, 1968.

Frost, Lawrence A. *Custer Legends*. Bowling Green, Ohio: Bowling Green University Popular Press, 1981.

Frost, Lawrence A. *Custer Slept Here*. Monroe, Michigan: Garry Owen Publishers, 1974.

Frost, Lawrence A. *General Custer's Libbie*. Seattle: Superior Publishing Company, 1976.

Frost, Lawrence A. General George Armstrong Custer: A Bibliography of Cataloged Materials In Special Collections of the Billings Public Library and Monroe County Library System. Monroe, Michigan: Monroe County Library System, 1976.

Frost, Lawrence A. *Let's Have A Fair Fight! General George Armstrong Custer's Early Years*. From a paper read before the Chicago Westerners May 27, 1957. Monroe, Michigan: Monroe County Historical Museum, 1965.

Frost, Lawrence A. *The Custer Album: A Pictorial Biography of General George A. Custer*. Seattle: Superior Publishing Company, 1964.

Godfrey, Edward Settle. General George A. Custer and the Battle of the Little Big Horn. New York: Century Company, 1908.

Graham, W.A. *The Custer Myth: A Sourcebook of Custeriana*. New York: Bonanza Books, 1953.

Gray, John S. *Centennial Campaign: The Sioux War of 1876*. Norman: University of Oklahoma Press, 1988.

Gray, John S. *Custer's Last Campaign: Mitch Boyer and the Little Bighorn Remembered*. Lincoln: University of Nebraska Press, 1993.

Grinnell, George Bird. *The Fighting Cheyennes*. Norman: The University of Oklahoma Press, 1956.

Harper, Gordon. *The Fights on the Little Horn Companion*. Havertown, Pennsylvania: Casemate, 2014.

Harrison, Joseph T. *The Story of the Dining Fork*. Cincinnati, Ohio: C. J. Krehbiel Company, 1927.

Heck, Earl Leon Werley. *Colonel William Ball of Virginia, the great-grandfather of Washington*. London: S.M. Dutton, 1928.

Howe, Henry. *Historical Collections of Ohio: An Encyclopedia of the State*. Columbus: Henry Howe and Son, various editions 1847–1907.

Hunt, Frazier. *Custer, The Last of the Cavaliers*. New York: Cosmopolitan Book Corporation, 1928.

Hutchison, Craig, and Kimberly A. Hutchison. *Monroe, Michigan: The Early Years*. Mount Pleasant, SC: Arcadia Publishing, 2005.

Hutton, Paul. *The Custer Reader*. Lincoln: University of Nebraska Press, 1992.

Kidd, J.H. *Riding with Custer: Recollections of a Cavalryman in the Civil War*. St. Louis: A.R. Fleming Printing Company, 1909.

King, Charles. *Custer's Last Battle*. New York: Harper and Brothers, 1890.

King, W. Kent. *Tombstones for Bluecoats: New Insights into the Custer Mystery*. Self published, 1980.

Kinsey, Margaret B. *Ball Cousins: Descendants of John and Sarah Ball and of William and Elizabeth Richards of Colonial Philadelphia Co., Penna.* Baltimore: Gateway Press, 1981.

Korn, Jerry. *Pursuit to Appomattox: The Last Battles*. Alexandria, VA: Time Life Books, 1987.

Libby, Orin Grant. *The Arikara Narrative of the Campaign against the Hostile Dakotas, June 1876*. Bismarck: State Historical Society of North Dakota, 1920.

Longacre, Edward G. *Custer and His Wolverines: The Michigan Cavalry Brigade, 1861–1865*. Conshohocken, Pennsylvania: Combined Publishing, 1997.

Longacre, Edward G. *Lincoln's Cavalrymen: A History of the Mounted Forces of the Army of the Potomac*. Mechanicsburg, Pennsylvania: Stackpole Books, 2000.

Masters, Joseph G. *Shadows Fall Across The Little Horn, Custer's Last Stand*. Laramie: University of Wyoming Library, 1951.

McDonough, James Lee. *Stones River: Bloody Winter in Tennessee*. Knoxville: University of Tennessee Press, 1980.

Merington, Marguerite. *The Custer Story: The Life and Intimate Letters of General George A. Custer and His Wife Elizabeth*. New York: Devin-Adair, 1950.

Reedstrom, E. Lisle. *Custer's 7th Cavalry: From Fort Riley to the Little Big Horn*. New York: Sterling, 1992.

Robbins, James S. *The Real Custer: From Boy General to Tragic Hero*. Washington, DC: Regnery Publishing, 2014.

Rodenbough, Theophilus. *The Bravest Five Hundred of '61: Their Noble Deeds Described by Themselves, Together With an Account of Some Gallant Exploits of Our Soldiers in Indian Warfare. How the Medal of Honor Was Won*. New York: G.W. Dillingham, 1891.

Sabin, Edwin L. *On the Plains with Custer: Western Life and Deeds of the Chief With The Yellow Hair*. Philadelphia: J.B. Lippincott Company, 1913.

Stewart, Edgar I. *Custer's Luck*. Norman, University of Oklahoma Press, 1955.

The Custer Semi-Centennial Ceremonies, 1876–June 25–26, 1926. Casper, Wyoming: The Casper Printing and Stationary Company, 1926.

Urwin, Gregory J.W. *Custer Victorious: The Civil War Battles of General George Armstrong Custer*. Lincoln: University of Nebraska Press, 1983.

US War Department. *War of the Rebellion: Official Records of the Union and Confederate Armies.* Washington DC: US War Department, 1880–1901.

Utley, Robert M. *Cavalier in Buckskin: George Armstrong Custer and the Western Military.* Norman: University of Oklahoma Press, 1988.

Van de Water, Frederic Franklyn. *Glory-Hunter: A Life of General Custer.* Indianapolis: The Bobbs-Merrill Company, 1934.

Vestal, Stanley. *Warpath: The True Story of the Fighting Sioux Told in a Biography of Chief White Bull.* Lincoln: University of Nebraska Press, 1934.

Viola, Herman J. *It Is a Good Day to Die: Indian Eyewitnesses Tell The Story of the Battle of the Little Bighorn.* New York: Crown, 1998.

Wallace, Charles B. *Custer's Ohio Boyhood: A Brief Account of the Early Life of Major General George Armstrong Custer.* Freeport, Ohio: Freeport Press, 1978.

Warner, Liberty P. Personal papers located at Bowling Green State University in Bowling Green, Ohio; donated by Brad Quinlin of Suwanee, Georgia in 1996.

Weibert, Henry. *Sixty-six Years in Custer's Shadow.* Billings, Montana: Bannack Publishing Company, 1985.

Whittaker, Frederick. *A Complete Life of General George A. Custer, Major General of Volunteers, Brevet Major U.S. Army and Lieutenant-Colonel Seventh U.S. Cavalry.* New York: Sheldon and Company, 1876.

Wilson, James Grant. *Two Modern Knights Errant.* Rochester, New York: Schlicht and Field, 1891.

Windolph, Charles. *I Fought With Custer; The Story of Sergeant Windolph, Last Survivor of the Battle of the Little Big Horn.* New York: C. Scribner's Sons, 1947.

Wing, Talcott Enoch. *History of Monroe County, Michigan.* New York: Munsell and Company, 1890.

Yenne, Bill: *Indian Wars: The Campaign For The American West.* Yardley, Pennsylvania: Westholme, 2005.

Periodicals cited:

Army and Navy Journal (Washington, DC)

Billings Gazette (Billings, Montana)

Bismarck Tribune (Bismarck, Dakota Territory)

Bozeman Times (Bozeman, Montana)

Cadiz Republican (Cadiz, Ohio)

Cavalry Journal (Washington, DC)

Cleveland Daily Leader (Cleveland, Ohio)

Congressional Record, (Washington, DC)

Evening Chronicle (Charlotte, North Carolina)

Evening News (Detroit, Michigan)

Financier (New York, New York)

Frank Leslie's Illustrated Weekly (New York, New York)
Galaxy magazine (New York, New York)
Helena Herald (Helena, Montana)
Indiana Democrat (Indiana, Pennsylvania)
Inquirer Cleveland, Ohio)
Inter Ocean (Chicago, Illinois)
Isabella County Enterprise (Mount Pleasant, Michigan)
Lawrence Daily Journal (Lawrence, Kansas)
Magazine of Albemarle County History (Charlottesville, Virginia)
Monroe Commercial (Monroe, Michigan)
Monroe Democrat (Monroe, Michigan)
Monroe Evening News (Monroe, Michigan)
Monroe Monitor (Monroe, Michigan)
Monroe Record-Commercial (Monroe, Michigan)
New York Herald (New York, New York)
New York Times (New York, New York)
New York Tribune (New York, New York)
Nickell Magazine (Boston, Massachusetts)
Outdoor Life (Denver, Colorado)
Petersburg Sun (Petersburg, Ohio)
Pittsburgh Commercial (Pittsburgh, Pennsylvania)
Sacramento Union (Sacramento, California)
San Francisco Chronicle (San Francisco, California)
Sentinel Tribune (Bowling Green, Ohio)
Smithsonian magazine (Washington, DC)
Southern Literary Messenger (Richmond, Virginia)
Times (Philadelphia, Pennsylvania)
Toledo Journal (Toledo, Ohio)
Turf, Field and Farm (New York, New York)
Washington Post, (Washington, DC)
Wood County Sentinel (Bowling Green, Ohio)

INDEX